STATE ARCHIVES OF ASSYRIA STUDIES

VOLUME VII

STATE ARCHIVES OF ASSYRIA STUDIES

Published by the Neo-Assyrian Text Corpus Project
of the University of Helsinki
in co-operation with
the Finnish Oriental Society

Project Director
Simo Parpola

Managing Editor
Robert M. Whiting

VOLUME VII

Martti Nissinen

REFERENCES TO PROPHECY IN NEO-ASSYRIAN SOURCES

THE NEO-ASSYRIAN TEXT CORPUS PROJECT

State Archives of Assyria Studies is a series of monographic studies relating to and supplementing the text editions published in the SAA series. Manuscripts are accepted in English, French and German. The responsibility for the contents of the volumes rests entirely with the authors.

Set in Times
Typography and layout by Teemu Lipasti
The Assyrian Royal Seal emblem drawn by Dominique Collon from original Seventh Century B.C. impressions (BM 84672 and 84677) in the British Museum
Ventura Publisher format and custom fonts by Robert M. Whiting and Timo Kiippa
Electronic pasteup by Robert M. Whiting

Printed in Finland
by Vammalan Kirjapaino Oy

ISBN 951-45-8079-6 (Volume 7)
ISSN 1235-1032 (Series)

REFERENCES TO PROPHECY IN NEO-ASSYRIAN SOURCES

By

Martti Nissinen

THE NEO-ASSYRIAN TEXT CORPUS PROJECT
1998

PREFACE

The texts included in this volume are not representatives of a common literary genre, nor do they form a thematic whole. They were chosen as the subject of investigation because they contain Neo-Assyrian references to prophetic activity and quotations of prophetic oracles from the time of the kings Esarhaddon (681-669) and Assurbanipal (668-627). As such, they constitute a supplement to the corpus of the contemporary Neo-Assyrian prophecies published by Simo Parpola in SAA 9, to which this study can be considered a companion.

Originating from non-prophetical circles, the texts examined in this study show a view of prophecy from a different angle than the actual prophetic oracles. Even if they provide haphazard crumbs of information rather than a coherent overall picture, they add substantially to our knowledge of the use of prophecy and the regard Neo-Assyrian society had for prophets. Moreover, they have relevance to the study of ancient Near Eastern and biblical prophecy in general. This is not to say that anything like the final word has been spoken. Investigating these sources has been much like fitting together a jigsaw puzzle of a thousand pieces, of which only a hundred are extant, and imagining the remaining, invisible part of the scene with the help of other pictures and a good deal of intuition.

Constructing the lost picture would not have been possible without the contribution of my teachers, colleagues and friends, to whom I have the pleasure of expressing my gratitude. This study could never have been even started, let alone completed, without the encouragement and interest of Prof. Simo Parpola who not only granted me unrestricted access to his collations, transliterations and translations but also readily shared with me his immense knowledge of Neo-Assyrian in countless conversations. He is the source of many ideas in this study, more than the footnotes reveal. A great debt of thanks is owed to Professors Manfried Dietrich (Münster), Oswald Loretz (Münster), Karel van der Toorn (Leiden) and Manfred Weippert (Heidelberg) for reading the manuscript and improving my work by invaluable comments. Moreover, Prof. Dietrich kindly provided me with his new collations of SAA 10 111, and Prof. Weippert, Prof. van der Toorn, as well as Dr. Christoph Uehlinger (Fribourg), allowed me to use their articles before having the final publication at hand. The staff of the Neo-Assyrian Text Corpus Project, especially Raija Mattila, Robert M. Whiting and Karen Radner, were always available when I needed help. Special thanks are due to Margot Stout Whiting for proofreading and language editing and to Robert M Whiting for typesetting the text and correcting a multitude of errors. I was also fortunate enough to receive financial support from the Ella and Georg Ehrnrooth Foundation.

Finally, the people I love more than anyone else, my wife Leena and my daughters Elina and Kaisa: Thank you for being there!

The transliteration of the cuneiform and the English orthography of proper names follow the conventions of the SAA series. Unless otherwise indicated, the translations of texts, when available, are also those of the SAA publications. The abbreviations follow those of the *Theologische Realenzyklopädie*.

Helsinki, St. Valentine's Day 1998 Martti Nissinen

CONTENTS

CHAPTER ONE

INTRODUCTION

Ancient Near Eastern Prophecy — A Whim of Chance?

It is no wonder that up to the time well past the Second World War, prophecy was predominantly a biblical domain, the historical yardstick of which was constituted by the prophets of ancient Israel. This was not because the scholars would not have been aware of ancient or modern phenomena comparable to ancient Israelite prophecy or showed any interest in them.[1] It was rather that the standards of comparison hardly came up to each other. The notion of prophecy was an established and prominent part of the biblical tradition conveyed from the formative period of the writings of the Hebrew Bible to modern times and usually shared by the scholars themselves, whereas the extra-biblical point of comparison was composed of an exotic and elusive assemblage of ecstatic and visionary activities from a variety of times and places. Therefore, the discussion was mainly centered around the question to what extent the different characteristics of ecstatic behavior were applicable to the prophets of Israel, especially to the "writing" ones.[2] In particular, since no written documents that could have been set against the biblical prophetic writings had been found or identified, the state of documentation was drastically uneven. A further problem was provided by the fact that the "myth and ritual" approach represented by some scholars who pursued comparative studies was generally shunned by the mainstream of the scholarly community.

The change slowly began with the excavation of the 18th century BCE archives of Mari, that from the late 1940's onwards brought to light the first extra-biblical corpus of texts commonly recognized as containing prophetic words.[3] To be sure, divine messages to the Assyrian kings Esarhaddon and Assurbanipal from the 7th century BCE. had already been found in the middle of the 19th century and were even published, for the most part, before the First World War.[4] Nevertheless, even though referred to as "prophecy" by some contemporary scholars,[5] these texts virtually escaped scholarly attention until the 1970's when the first scholarly contributions, again recognizing them as "prophecy," were published by Manfred Weippert, Manfried Dietrich

---

[1] The significance of the comparative approach was demonstrated already by Gustav Hölscher (1914), and subsequently acknowledged by religio-historically oriented scholars, such as Alfred Jepsen (1934) and the Swedes Johannes Lindblom (1934/1962), Alfred Haldar (1945) and Geo Widengren (1948). While the comparative material in the earlier version of Lindblom's study mainly came from (pre)modern times (North Asian shamans, Muslim dervishes, Finnish sleeping preachers, St. Birgitta of Sweden), Haldar – as if predicting times to come – attempted to establish a connection between the Mesopotamian *bārû* and *mahhû* and the prophets of Israel (see also Lindblom 1962, 30-31).

[2] For this discussion in the pre-WW II period, see Wilson 1980, 5-8; for the more recent contributions to the question of ecstasy and prophecy, see Grabbe 1995, 108-112.

[3] For an introduction to the prophetic texts from Mari, see Durand 1988, 377-412 and 1997. An updated list of the texts can be found in Heintz 1997, 214.

[4] A full bibliography of the pre-WW I contributions can be found in Parpola 1997c, CIX-CX.

[5] E.g. Delattre 1889, 25, 27; Strong 1893, 627, 634.

and Herbert B. Huffmon.[6] Since then, over a couple of decades, the Neo-Assyrian texts have little by little won an established status as an integral part of what is today called "ancient Near Eastern prophecy."[7] The most important milestones in this development include the systematic presentation of the Neo-Assyrian prophetic texts by Weippert (1981) and, at long last, their standard edition by Simo Parpola (SAA 9), to be published contemporaneously with this volume.

The somewhat fragmentary history of research, in a way, reflects the nature of the source material. In fact, it is virtually a matter of chance that the category of "ancient Near Eastern prophecy" could ever emerge.[8] The documents that today bear this label have passed three decisive stages on their way to the modern scholars' desks. Primarily, they are written on a material that has not been totally spoiled by the ravages of time; secondly, they are no longer buried in the modern Near Eastern earth but have been dug out by serendipitous archaeologists; and finally, there have been scholars whose eyes have been sharp enough to recognize their relation to what may be called "prophecy." Only two major corpora of texts unearthed thus far have been considered deserving of this time-honored designation, the one from Old Babylonian Mari and the other from Neo-Assyrian Nineveh, supplemented by a few occasional finds of individual texts, such as the 8th century Aramaic Balaam text from Deir ʿAlla[9] and the 18th century Kititum oracles from Ešnunna.[10] The growing attention paid to these documents has, more clearly than before, made even the prophecy of ancient Israel appear as a part of a larger cultural background. Accordingly, the specificity of the biblical tradition is increasingly seen in the literary process that formed the prophetic books of the Hebrew Bible after the destruction of Jerusalem in 587 rather than in the uniqueness of the ancient Israelite prophecy as a phenomenon.[11]

The temporal and geographical distribution of the relevant sources suggests that the extant documents of ancient Near Eastern prophecy constitute little more than the tip of an iceberg. What we have at our disposal is a series of unconnected threads rather than a representative sample on the basis of which

---

[6] Weippert 1972; Dietrich 1973, 38-43; Huffmon 1976a, 175-176; 1976b, 699-700. The way for the renewed interest in these texts was paved by the preliminary work of Karlheinz Deller and Simo Parpola in the 1960's which, however, has left few traces in the published contributions.

[7] See, e.g., Ishida 1977, 90-92; 114-116; Wilson 1980, 111-119; Dijkstra 1980, 147-170; Weippert 1981; 1982; 1985; 1988; Millard 1985; van der Toorn 1987; Ellis 1989; Nissinen 1991; 1993; 1996; Huffmon 1992; Zenger 1995, 300-302; Grabbe 1995, 91-92; Laato 1996, 173-188, 271-279. For a more complete bibliography, see Parpola 1997c, CIX-CXII.

[8] The most recent introductions to what is included in this category are those of Huffmon 1992 and Weippert 1997b.

[9] See, e.g., Dijkstra 1995; Weippert 1997a, 131-188; Lemaire 1997, 188-193 and the contributions in Hoftijzer & van der Kooij (ed.) 1991.

[10] See Ellis 1987.

[11] See, e.g., Kaiser 1993, 213, 231-232; Pohlmann 1994.

a definitive history of prophecy could be written. Consequently, any addition to the documentation of ancient Near Eastern prophecy is valuable. With this end in view, this study attempts to call attention to some poorly known or overlooked Neo-Assyrian sources.

The documents of what is today called Neo-Assyrian prophecy entirely derive from the regnal years of the the kings Esarhaddon (680-669) and Assurbanipal (668-627). As far as can be judged from the preserved sources, these kings, perhaps more intensively than their predecessors, consulted all kinds of specialists in different methods of divination. Among them were not only astrologers and haruspices, but also prophets whose words Esarhaddon and Assurbanipal regarded as significant enough to be copied, compiled and put in the royal files. The remains of these documents constitute the corpus of Neo-Assyrian prophecy available to us and now published in SAA 9. However, the prophetic activity is not only documented in the messages transmitted by themselves, but also in letters, inscriptions and other documents written by others. The primary objective of this study is to gather together and analyse provisionally these scattered pieces of evidence in the hope that they would improve our knowledge of prophetic activities in Assyria. Up to the present, non-prophetical Neo-Assyrian sources with reference to prophecy have neither been systematically brought together nor examined comprehensively. Since they can be expected to complement the picture of prophetic activities in Neo-Assyrian society, they deserve a study of their own.

Before setting about the analysis, two definitions are necessary: what is meant with "prophecy" in this study, and by which criteria the sources may be determined as referring to the phenomenon thus defined.

What Is Prophecy?

The use of the word "prophecy" is open to at least three kinds of criticism. The first has to do with the set of values attached to this word. It may be claimed that the very concept of "prophecy" is all too dependent on the biblical tradition and its scholarly interpretation. Some scholars are, therefore, disinclined to apply this category to cuneiform studies, while there may be others who feel reluctant to see the prophets of Israel lumped together with a variety of ancient sibyls and soothsayers.

The second potential point of criticism is a linguistic one. It is true that no single equivalent of the words "prophet" and "prophecy," derived from the Greek *profētēs/profēteia*, can be found in the languages of the ancient Near East which offer a plethora of designations that may interpreted as denoting related activities. Hence, the word can be seen as an application of an anachronistic concept.

Finally, the word "prophecy" is liable to semantic confusion: while in colloquial speech it is generally equated with any kind of foretelling the future, the scholarly community uses it in a more sophisticated and specific way. However, even the scholarly understanding of what may be called prophecy is not uniform.

To overcome these difficulties, and to avoid terminological confusion, it is necessary to determine what is meant in this study with "prophet" and "prophecy." The most recent definition which also serves as a sufficient and appropriate starting point for this study, has been formulated by Weippert, according to whom prophecy is in question when

> A person (a) through a cognitive experience (a vision, an auditory experience, an audio-visual appearance, a dream or the like) becomes the subject of the revelation of a deity, or several deities and, in addition, (b) is conscious of being commissioned by the deity or deities in question to convey the revelation in a verbal form (as a "prophecy" or a "prophetic speech"), or through nonverbal communicative acts ("symbolic acts"), to a third party who constitutes the actual addressee of the message.[12]

This definition applies to a specific and concrete type of what is presented as divine-human communication. The definitions and modifications presented by, for instance, Huffmon,[13] Malamat[14] and myself[15] are, though not identical in detail, for the most part consistent with it.

---

[12] Weippert 1997b, 197: "Bei religiöser Offenbarungsrede ist dann von P[rophetie] zu sprechen, wenn eine Person (a) in einem kognitiven Erlebnis (Vision, Audition, audiovisuelle Erscheinung, Traum o. ä.) der Offenbarung einer Gottheit oder mehreren Gottheiten teilhaftig wird und ferner (b) sich durch die betreffende(n) Gottheit(en) beauftragt wei, das ihr Geoffenbarte in sprachlicher Fassung (als 'P[rophetie]', 'Prophetenspruch') oder in averbalen Kommunikationsakten ('symbolischen' oder 'Zeichenhandlungen') an einen Dritten (oder Dritte), den (die) eigentlichen Adressaten, weiterzuleiten." This is a revised version of an earlier definition in Weippert 1988, 289-290, an English translation of which can be found in Barstad 1993, 46.

[13] Huffmon 1976a, 172: "In terms of ancient Near Eastern religious circles a useful definition of 'prophet' seems to be that the prophet is a person who through non-technical means receives a clear and immediate message from a deity for transmission to a third party." Cf. 1976b, 697; 1992, 477. A minor deviation of this definition from that of Weippert can be seen in the word "clear" which seems to denote a greater intelligibility than may be required by the "metalinguistic" aspect of Weippert.

[14] Malamat 1987, 34-35: "1. The prophetic manifestations are spontaneous and result from inspiration or divine initiative in contrast to the mechanical, inductive divination that is usually initiated by the king's request to acquire signs from the deity. [...]

2. The prophets are imbued with a consciousness of mission and take their stand before the authorities to present their divinely inspired message.

3. A more problematic characteristic is the ecstatic element in prophecy, for the definition of ecstasy is not unambiguous. We would do well to lend this concept a broad and liberal definition, letting it apply to anything from autosuggestion to the divinely infused dream. [...]"

Malamat's definition is more detailed than Weippert's, including the notions of spontaneousness and ecstasy consciously avoided by the latter.

[15] Nissinen 1996, 173: "Das Wort Prophetie bedeutet eine Übermittlung einer sprachlichen oder metasprachlichen Botschaft, die eine Person (ein Prophet oder eine Prophetin) ohne induktive Techniken angeblich von einer Gottheit empfängt, um sie an einen individuellen oder kollektiven Adressaten zu übermitteln."

According to the above definition, then, prophecy is understood as a process of communication consisting of the following four components: i) the divine sender of the message, ii) the message (the "revelation"), iii) the transmitter of the message (the prophet), and iv) the recipient of the message.[16] In the broadest possible sense, this process would cover any divine message received and transmitted by a human mediator to a third party.[17] However, if the process is determined as a prophetic one in the above-determined meaning, a few qualifications are necessary.

— There is a growing tendency in the study of biblical and ancient Near Eastern prophecy to consider prophecy, rather than being in contrast with divination (i.e., consulting the divine world by various means), an integral part of it.[18] However, irrespective of to what extent this line of thought is in line with Neo-Assyrian circumstances – this will be determined after the examination of the relevant sources – it is necessary to distinguish between different methods of becoming informed of what is believed to be the divine will. There are many possible ways to classify the variety of divinatory practices;[19] for the purposes of this study, the often-made distinction between non-inductive ("intuitive"/"inspired"/"direct") and inductive ("technical"/ "mechanical"/ "wisdom") divination, inclusive of the respective classes of specialists,[20] still appears as appropriate. Keeping in mind the warnings in recent studies about the implied value judgments in this distinction,[21] it should be applicable without getting stuck in traditional prejudices about divination. If classified as a form of divination, prophecy, together with dreams and visions, clearly belongs to the non-inductive type, which does not require skills in interpreting omens, unlike astrology or extispicy, which presupposed exhaustive studies in the traditional omen literature and experience in observing material objects like celestial bodies and the entrails of animals. This is not to say that no learned techniques would have been required of a prophet or a dreamer, only that they were of a totally different kind than those employed by astrologers, haruspices or exorcists.

— The distinctiveness of prophecy from (other) divinatory methods is visible also when we compare the manner in which the outcome of a divinatory act is expressed. Prophecies are, literally, words of gods, spoken by the prophet as their mouthpiece, whereas, say, the result of the extispicy is not a verbose speech of a god but a simple positive or negative answer to a query

---

[16] See also Nissinen 1996, 173 and cf. the more sophisticated model of Overholt 1989, 21-25.

[17] According to Grabbe 1995, 107, the common denominator of the discussion thus far is that "the prophet is a mediator who claims to receive messages direct from a divinity, by various means, and communicates these messages to recipients."

[18] See Ellis 1989, 144-146; Overholt 1989, 140-147; Cryer 1991; Barstad 1993, 47-48; Grabbe 1995, 150-151; Laato 1996, 153-154.

[19] Cf. the classifications of Cryer 1994, 124-187 and Grabbe 1995, 136-149.

[20] For this distinction, see Bottéro 1992, 125-126; van der Toorn 1987, 67-73; Weippert 1988, 290-291.

[21] E.g., Overholt 1989, 141-142; Cryer 1991, 82-83; Barstad 1993, 47-48.

formulated accordingly.[22] Neither do the gods "speak" in the astrological reports which never quote a direct speech from the mouth of the deities.

— The distinction made by Maria deJong Ellis between (i) "oracular reports" and (ii) "literary predictive texts"[23] is certainly appropriate. The Mesopotamian sources include two distinguishable types of texts, both of which have been characterized as "prophecy": i) the verbal messages, allegedly sent by a deity and transmitted by a human intermediary to the addressee (SAA 9), and ii) the "Akkadian Prophecies," also called "apocalypses," which predict historical events, mostly *ex eventu*.[24] In the first case, the texts are called prophecies on the basis of the implied process of communication, while in the second, it is apparently the predictive nature of the texts that has generated the use of the word "prophecy" with regard to them. If intermediation is seen as the primary quality of prophecy, the eventual predictive aspect is subordinate to this quality. This means that prophecies may or may not include predictions but not every prediction is a prophecy. Consequently, texts which are predictive without showing any sign of the process of a divine-human communication with a human mediator as a part of it cannot be called prophecy in the above-defined meaning.

— The designation "prophet" not only refers to the position of a person in the process of communication but also connotes a specific role and function assumed consciously by him or her. In the study of the biblical prophecy, a distinction has traditionally been made between "free" prophets who act upon an individual divine vocation independent from social institutions and generally in opposition to them, and others (the "cultic prophets" or "court prophets") who work as a part of the system, dependent on the political and religious establishment and more often than not suspected of delivering "false" prophecies. This dichotomy, even though largely initiated by the presentation of the Hebrew Bible itself,[25] begs a lot of questions concerning the relationship between historical phenomena and their interpretation by the editors of the prophetic books of the Bible,[26] and should no longer be upheld

---

[22] Note, however, that the the result of extispicy may be accompanied by an "oracle of encouragement" (*šīr takilti*); see below, pp. 33-34.

[23] Ellis 1989. Cf. also Weippert 1981, 71-72 who made a similar distinction between "Prophetie" and "Prophezeiungen" (similarly Röllig 1987/90, 65); note that he has later abandoned the designation "Prophezeiung" without giving up the distinction of the text classes (1988, 294). Grayson 1975b, 13-14 made the same distinction using the labels "Akkadian prophecies" (= "literary predictive texts"/"Prophezeiungen") and "Akkadian oracles" (= "oracular reports"/"Prophetie").

[24] The relevant texts include: i) the "Marduk Prophecy" (Borger 1971, 5-13, 16-20), ii) the "Šulgi Prophecy" (Borger 1971, 14-15, 20-21), iii) the "Uruk Prophecy" (Hunger & Kaufman 1975), iv) the "Dynastic Prophecy" (Grayson 1975b, 24-37) and v) the "Prophecy A" (KAR 421; Grayson & Lambert 1964, 12-16). For these texts, see Grayson 1975b, 13-23; Lambert 1978; Weippert 1988, 291-294; Ellis 1989, 146-157; Longman 1991, 131-190; Grabbe 1995, 92-94.

[25] See, e.g., Kaiser 1993, 220-229; Zenger 1995, 295-296.

[26] For these problems in general, see Carroll 1989 and 1990 and, from a different angle, Kaiser 1993, 231-261 and Pohlmann 1994, 337-341. Cf. also below, n. 29.

as a fundamental, generally applicable distinction. What matters more is that the epithet "prophet" in any case implies a social role and function which distinguishes the person thus designated from other members of the society, no matter what kind of a vocation may be understood to lie behind this role. What makes a prophet different from others is that he or she is believed to have the capacity of acting as the mouthpiece of God.

— As primary means of experiencing a divine revelation, dreams and visions self-evidently belong to the media of prophetic intermediation. Since, nevertheless, a dream or a vision can basically be experienced and reported by any individual, all visionary and oneiromantic practices are not prophecy.[27] To be defined as such, the dreams or visions must be experienced by a person who is otherwise qualified as a prophet, and they must include a divine message to be transmitted. To which extent the activity of visionaries and dreamers can be equated with prophecy depends on whether or not they otherwise assume a social role and function similar to that of a prophet. In practical terms, this is often very difficult to determine.

— It is a matter of further definition whether a purely literary imitation, or *Fortschreibung*,[28] of prophetic messages may be called "prophecy." This is a burning question in biblical studies[29] but is not without relevance in the study of prophecy in general. In strictly phenomenological terms, the subsequent literary interpretation of prophecy, liable to alter or invent prophetic words and figures, can no longer bear this designation. Nevertheless, if we admit that the history of the very concept of prophecy is deeply rooted in the biblical ideas of what (Israelite) prophets were and said, and if we allow that these ideas, at least initially, have a concrete model in actual prophetic activity, we may consider the literary interpretation of prophecy a secondary prolongation of the prophetic communicational process.[30]

— Finally, since prophecy cannot be expected to be a timeless and uniform category, any broad definition needs to be specified according to the requirements of time and place. The possibility must be reckoned with that manifestations of prophecy, such as the behavior and role of the prophets, or their place within the social organization, vary from society to society. The sources

---

27 See Parpola 1997c, XLVII.

28 For this term, see Zimmerli 1980; cf. also Nissinen 1991, 33-38.

29 Cf. the "poets not prophets" problem constituted by the conviction that the biblical representations of the prophets are largely created by later authors who portray the prophets according to their own standards of what prophecy should have looked like rather than give accurate descriptions of what they actually were; see Auld 1983; 1984; Carroll 1983 and, from outside of this discussion, Pohlmann 1994. Over against the "poets not prophets" view, some scholars emphasize the "social reality" of prophecy (Overholt 1990) as well as the relevance of the comparative Near Eastern material (e.g., Barstad 1993; Heintz 1997).

30 For the motivation of this process in the overcoming of the experiences of destruction in 587, see Pohlmann 1994, 340-341. Cf. the notion of "prophetic interpretation of the prophets" as a part of biblical prophecy in Zenger 1995, 296-298. For the problem "prophecy vs. literary prophecies," see also Grabbe 1995, 94, 105-107.

examined in this study reflect the Neo-Assyrian circumstances, to which the following specifications apply.

How to Identify a Reference to Prophecy?

Recognizing a reference to prophecy in a non-prophetical text is not always easy. Some texts may contain direct quotations of the words of deities while others rely on prophetic oracles without quoting them word by word. Sometimes prophets are mentioned without referring to the contents of their sayings at all. On the other hand, not all of the texts do explicitly mention prophets as the intermediaries of the divine messages. All this makes it necessary to formulate criteria for a reliable identification of references to prophecy, corresponding to the definition of prophecy determined above.

It is conceivable that a reference to prophecy is at hand,

i) when the text explicitly mentions a prophet, or

ii) when there is a quotation or a paraphrase of divine words that otherwise can be characterized as prophetic ones.

These criteria are in need of some further qualifications.

i) In Neo-Assyrian, two words implying prophetic activity in the above-defined sense are attested.[31] The first is *mahhû*, derived from *mahû* "to go/be in a frenzy, to become crazy." Being one of the standard words for a prophet at Mari,[32] its use in the Neo-Assyrian texts is restricted to the fixed compound *šipir mahhê* "messages of prophets" in the inscriptions of Esarhaddon and Assurbanipal,[33] with the addition of four occurrences of *mahhû(tu)* in literary texts, in a treaty, and in a decree of expenditures.[34] The second is *raggimu*, fem. *raggintu*, derived from *ragāmu* "to shout, to proclaim." This exclusively Neo-Assyrian[35] word is used by the extant prophecies of their proclaimers,[36] and can also be found in

---

[31] See Parpola 1997c, XLV-XLVII.

[32] For *muhhû(tu)m* in Mari, see Durand 1988, 386-388; 1997, 123-124.

[33] Borger 1956 (§ 2) 2 ii 12; (§ 27) 45 ii 6; Borger 1996, 104 B v 95//C vi 127; 141 T ii 16//C i 61.

[34] SAA 3 23:5, SAA 3 34:28//35:31, and SAA 2 6 §10:117, where it appears together with *raggimu* and *šāʾilu*, and SAA 12 69:29. Provided that the MÍ.GUB.BA in the prophecy fragment SAA 9 10 s.2 is to be pronounced *raggintu*, as suggested by Parpola 1997c, XLVI, the feminine *mahhûtu* occurs only in SAA 12 69, a decree of expenditures from the time of Adad-nerari III.

[35] Only the letter SAA 10 109 is written in Neo-Babylonian by Bel-ušezib, an Assyrianized Babylonian scholar. The alleged Middle-Assyrian attestation of *raggintu* (TR 2031:6; see Saggs 1968, 161-162 and cf. Huffmon 1976a, 175; Wilson 1980, 112 n. 57; Nissinen 1996, 178 n. 14) is now deleted by Parpola 1997c, CIII n. 226 who reads *ra-qi i+na*! instead of *ra-kin-tu*.

[36] SAA 9 3.5 iv 31; SAA 9 6 r.11 (*raggimu*); SAA 9 7:1 (*raggintu*); SAA 9 10 s.2 (MÍ.GUB.BA; cf. the two preceding notes).

Neo-Assyrian letters[37] and other documents, including a treaty,[38] a lexical text[39] and a lodging list.[40] The distribution of occurrences suggests that the word *mahhû* belongs to the literary register of Neo-Assyrian, whereas the more commonly used *raggimu* has replaced the archaic *mahhû*, not only in the colloquial speech but also in the formal writing.[41]

Sometimes the prophets, *raggimu* and *mahhû*, are grouped together with people called *šabrû*[42] and *šā'ilu*,[43] which indicates both commonality and distinctiveness of the respective groups. While the *šabrû* and *šā'ilu* are mainly associated with visionary activities and dream interpretation, they are never attested as acting as the direct mouthpieces of gods. Nevertheless, their social role and function apparently comes close to that of the prophets, and also the contents of their visions may be well comparable to the prophetic messages.

ii) If there is no designation of a prophet, the existence of a reference to prophecy must be deduced from the context and the contents of the passage in question. It is feasible to conclude that we have to do with prophecy,

- when the reference is made to the "word" (*abutu/amātu* or *dibbu*) of a deity, or the deity "says" (*qabû* or *dabābu*) something; the supposition of a reference to prophecy gains credence when the speaking deity is Ištar or Mullissu, the goddess(es)[44] of prophecy *par excellence*;
- when there is no mention of any other methods of divination or their practitioners; and
- when the Neo-Assyrian prophetic corpus (SAA 9) provides reasonable parallels.

All three conditions can rarely be fulfilled at the same time since every possible aspect of prophecy is seldom represented in a single reference. This inevitably causes problems in deciding whether or not a text indeed contains a reference to prophecy. There are borderline cases, notably dreams (*šuttu*) and visions (*diglu*), the origin of which is difficult to determine if the text does not include a clear indication of the dreamer or visionary.

Following the aforementioned criteria, sixteen texts (or excerpts from larger texts) have been investigated in this study. Nine of them are Neo-Assyrian letters (SAA 10 109; 111; 284; 294; 352; LAS 317; ABL 1217+; CT 53 17+; CT 53 938), the rest consisting of five excerpts from the inscriptions

---

37 SAA 10 109:9; SAA 10 294 r.31 (*raggimu*); SAA 10 109:9; SAA 10 352:23, r.1; LAS 317:7 (*raggintu*).

38 SAA 2 6 § 10:116 (*raggimu*).

39 MSL 12 226:134 (*raggimu*).

40 SAA 7 9 ii 23 (*raggimu*).

41 Parpola 1997c, XLVI.

42 MSL 12 226:134: lú.šabra (PA.AL) = ŠU-*u* = *rag-gi-*[*mu*]; see also Parpola 1997c, XLVI, CIV n. 231 and below, pp. 56-57.

43 SAA 2 6 § 10:116-117: *ina pî raggimi mahhê mār šā'ili amat ili* "from the mouth of a prophet, an ecstatic, an inquirer of oracles"; see below, pp. 160-161.

44 On the merging of Ištar and Mullissu into one divine being, see, e.g., SAA 3 7:11-12; 9:14-15; SAA 9 2.4 ii 30; 5:1, 3; 7 r.6; 9:1-3, r.1 and cf. Weippert 1985, 64; Menzel 1981, 64-65; Nissinen 1993, 228.

of Esarhaddon (Nin. A i 84 – ii 11; Ass. A i 31 – ii 26) and Assurbanipal (A ii 126 – iii 26; B v 46-49, 77 – vi 16; T ii 7-24), a paragraph of the Succession Treaty of Esarhaddon (SAA 2 6 § 10) and, finally, a Neo-Assyrian lodging list (SAA 7 9).

The texts, except the very short ones, are quoted at the head of each chapter only to the extent that is required to give a reasonable context for the references to prophecy; as for the rest, the reader is advised to consult the respective publications. However, three texts that still lack an up-to-date edition (ABL 1217 + CT 53 118; CT 53 17+107; CT 53 938) are displayed in their entity; the transliterations and translations of these texts are those of Simo Parpola.

The two-step method employed in this study is a rather primitive one. The analysis of each reference begins with surveying the historical circumstances reflected by the source in question: Who writes and for what purpose? What recognizable historical events may lie behind the text? What kind of message are the implied reader(s) expected to get? The second phase of analysis concentrates on prophecy as looked upon or utilized in the text: Why do the writers refer to prophecy? How does the reference to prophecy serve their purposes? How do they themselves relate to the prophets? The contemporary Neo-Assyrian sources will be utilized rather extensively to illuminate the historical, social and literary environment of the sources.

The reader may find it somewhat peculiar that the work at hand, written by a biblical scholar rather than a cuneiformist, eschews the comparison of the Neo-Assyrian sources to pertinent biblical texts, prophetic and others. This is a conscious decision, based on the conviction that a reasonable comparison is possible only when we know what we are comparing. Hence, both the Assyrian and the biblical texts deserve first to be examined in their own right, especially when dealing with such an insufficiently investigated set of sources as the Neo-Assyrian prophecies and references to them still are. On the other hand, the comparative approach leads into a methodological battlefield which is clearly outside the scope of this study.[45] This is why I have generally resisted the temptation of a comparative analysis, and contented myself with occasional and unsystematic noticing of apparent similarities. However, being the last person to deny the relevance of viewing the Hebrew Bible against its cultural environment and cognate literature, I hope that my study will contribute to the improvement of the preconditions for such a comparative approach.

---

[45] Cf., for instance, the different approaches of Overholt 1990 and Carroll 1990.

CHAPTER TWO

PROPHECY IN THE INSCRIPTIONS OF ESARHADDON AND ASSURBANIPAL

2.1. Esarhaddon's Rise to Power

Texts

Nin. A i 84 – ii 11[46]

[84]*ak-šu-dam-ma ina* KAR ÍD.MAŠ.GÚ.QAR [85]*ina qí-bit* ^{d}30 *ù* ^{d}UTU DINGIR.MEŠ EN *ka-a-ri* [86]*gi-mir* ERIM.HÁ-*ia* ÍD.MAŠ.GÚ.QAR DAGAL-*tum a-tap-piš ú-šá-áš-hi-iṭ* [87]*ina* ITI.ŠE ITI *mit-ga-ri* UD.8.KÁM UD ÈŠ.ÈŠ *šá* ^{d}PA ii [1]*ina qé-reb* NINA.KI URU *be-lu-ti-ia ha-diš e-ru-um-ma* [2]*ina* GIŠ.GU.ZA AD-*ia ṭa-biš ú-ši-ib* [3]*i-zi-qam-ma* IM.U$_{18}$.LU *ma-nit* ^{d}É.A [4]*šá-a-ru ša a-na e-peš* LUGAL-*u-ti za-aq-šú ṭa-a-ba* [5]*uk-ki-ba-nim-ma i-da-at dum-qí ina šá-ma-me u qaq-qa-ri* [6]*ši-pir mah-he-e na-áš-par-ti* DINGIR.MEŠ *u* ^{d}*iš-tar* [7]*ka-a-a-an ú-sad-di-ru-ni ú-šar-hi-ṣu-u-ni* ŠÀ-*bu* [8]LÚ.ERIM.MEŠ EN *hi-iṭ-ṭi ša a-na e-peš* LUGAL-*u-ti* KUR–*aš-šur*.KI [9]*a-na* ŠEŠ.MEŠ-*ia ú-šak-pi-du le-mut-tu* [10]*pu-hur-šu-nu ki-ma iš-ten a-hi-iṭ-ma an-nu kab-tú e-mid-su-nu-ti-ma* [11]*ú-hal-li-qa* NUMUN-*šu-un*

[84]I reached the embankment of the Tigris and, upon the command of Sin and Šamaš, the lords of the harbor, I let all my troops jump across the broad river Tigris as if it were nothing but a ditch. [87]In the month of Adar (XII), a favorable month, on the 8th day, the day of the *eššēšu* festival of Nabû, I joyfully entered into Nineveh, the residence of my lordship, and happily ascended the throne of my father. [3]The Southwind, the breeze of Ea, was blowing – the wind whose blowing portends well for exercising the kingship. Favorable omens in the sky and on earth came to me. [6]Oracles of prophets, messages of the gods and the Goddess,[47] were constantly sent to me and they encouraged my heart. The transgressors who had induced my brothers to the evil plans for taking over the kingship of Assyria I searched out, each and every one of them, imposed a heavy punishment upon them, and destroyed their seed.

---

[46] Borger 1956 (§ 27) 45.

[47] Since the prophetic oracles are predominantly pronounced as words of Ištar, the phrase *ilāni u Ištār* is neither necessarily a scribal error for the common DINGIR.MEŠ *u* ^{d}IŠ.TAR.MEŠ (Bauer 1933, 171), nor does the singular ^{d}*iš-tar* need to be taken as a collective epithet for all goddesses (Borger 1956, 45 *ad loc.*). In any case, the very designation *ištārāti* underlines the position of Ištar as the archetype and incorporation of all goddesses. This is also evident from the remnants of the prophecy of [Nabû]-hussanni (SAA 9 2.1), in which Ištar speaks in her different manifestations, one of them being "the goddesses [... i]n Esaggil" (lines 8-9: *a-ni-nu* ^{d}IŠ.TAR.MEŠ [*x x x x i*]*na* É.SAG.ÍL).

Ass. A i 31 – ii 26[48]

31 d[30 dUT]U DINGIR.MEŠ *maš-šu-ú-te* 32 *áš-*[*šu d*]*e-en kit-te* 33 *ù mi-šá-ri* 34 *a-n*[*a* KUR] *u* UN.MEŠ *šá-ra-ku* 35 ITI-*š*[*a*]*m-ma har-ra-an kit-te* 36 *ù mi-šá-ri ṣab-tu-ma* 37 UD.[*x*].KÁM UD.14.KÁM 38 *ú-*[*s*]*a-di-ru ta-mar-tú* 39 MUL.*dil-bat na-bat* MUL.MEŠ 40 *ina* IM.MAR.TU ii 1 [*ina* KASKAL *šu-u*]*t* dÉ.A 2 *in-na-mir-ma ša kun-nu* 3 *ma-a-te* [*ša*] *su-lum* 4 DINGIR.MEŠ-*šá ni-ṣir-tu* 5 *ik-šu-dam-ma it-bal* 6 MUL.*ṣal-bat-a-nu pa-ri-is* 7 *pur-se-e* KUR–MAR.TU.KI 8 *ina* KASKAL *šu-ut* dÉ.A 9 *ib-il ṣi-in-da-šú* 10 [*š*]*á da-na-an mal-ki u* KUR-*šú* 11 *ú-kal-lim is-kim-bu-uš* 12 *ši-pir* LÚ.*mah-he-e* 13 *ka-a-a-an su-ud-du-ra* 14 *ša* SUHUŠ GIŠ.GU.ZA 15 *šá-an-gu-ti-ia* 16 *šur-*⸢*šu*⸣*-di a-na* UD-*me ṣa-a-te* 17 *iš-šak-na-nim-ma* 18 *i-da-at dum-qí* 19 *ina* MÁŠ.MI *u ger-re-e* 20 *ša šur-šu-di kar-ri* 21 *šul-bur* BAL-*ia* 22 *it-ta-nab-ša-a* UGU-*ia* 23 GISKIM.MEŠ *du-un-qí* 24 *šu-a-ti-na a-mur-ma* 25 *lib-bu ar-hu-uṣ-ma* 26 *iṭ-ṭib ka-bat-ti*

> 31 The twin gods [Sin and Šam]aš, in or[der] to bestow a righteous and just [ju]dgement up[on the land] and the people, maintained monthly a path of righteousness and justice, appearing regularly on the [xth] and 14th days. 39 The brightest of the stars, Venus, appeared in the west [in the path of] Ea, reached its hypsoma predicting the stabilization of the land and the reconciliation of its gods, and disappeared. Mars, who passes the decision for the Westland, shone brightly in the path of Ea, announcing by his sign his decree concerning the strengthening of the king and his land.12 Messages of prophets concerning the establishment of the foundation of my sacerdotal throne until far-off days were constantly and regularly conveyed to me. 18 Good omens kept occurring to me in dreams and oracles concerning the establishment of my seat and the extension of my reign. Seeing these signs of good portent, my heart turned confident and my mood became good.

Background

The first excerpt quoted above is part of Esarhaddon's long, retrospective Nin. A inscription (Borger 1956 § 27), the initial episodes of which deal with the circumstances preceding Esarhaddon's rise to power in Assyria in 681/680, especially with his investiture as the crown prince and the subsequent events which led to a civil war, the murder of Sennacherib and, ultimately, to the enthronement of Esarhaddon. The inscription was composed in the month of Adar (XII), 673/2,[49] probably for the purpose of justifying Esarhaddon's decision to appoint Assurbanipal as the crown prince of Assyria by making the potential adversaries remember how Esarhaddon himself became

48 Borger 1956 (§2) 2.

49 All manuscripts bear a date of the eponym year (673) of Atar-ili, governor of Lahiru (Borger 1956, 64).

the king of Assyria and what happened to those who did not acknowledge his kingship.[50]

The second excerpt belongs to the Ass. A inscription of Esarhaddon (Borger 1956 § 2), composed in the month of Sivan (III)/Tammuz (IV), 679,[51] soon after Esarhaddon's ascending the throne. The main concern of the inscription is the renovation of Ešarra, the great Aššur temple in Assur, which Esarhaddon boasts of having accomplished during his very first regnal year. Some crucial lines in the beginning of the inscription are unreadable (i 18-30); they probably contained a description of Esarhaddon's rise to power. This can be discerned from the fact that the celestial phenomena described by him as good portents of his kingship (lines i 31 – ii 11) are datable to the years 681 and 680.[52]

The explicit inscriptional references to prophetic activity are meager as such – the Nin. A (§ 27) and Ass. A (§ 2) inscriptions both include one – but there are numerous points of convergence between the extant prophecies and inscriptions of Esarhaddon. Therefore it is feasible to wade through the crucial events of the period covered by the inscriptions, looking for points where inscriptional and prophetic proclamation meet each other. This must, however, be done in full awareness that reconstucting a *histoire événementielle* on the basis of the available sources is impeded by their tendentious character and possible only to the extent the "scribal filter" has let pieces of factual information pass through.[53]

Ever since the Middle Assyrian period, it had been a literary and chronographical convention that the Assyrian king reported his military victories and building achievements at the very outset of his reign using formulaic, literary-ideological patterns.[54] This also holds true for Esarhaddon, only the unique conditions of the succession of Sennacherib giving characteristic features to the account of his rise to power. His first military achievement was not a victory over foreign enemies but over his own brothers. So it was necessary for Esarhaddon to start the inscription from his designation as the crown prince of Assyria as a younger brother, not only because his designation as the heir apparent led to the civil war but also because a similar, no less controversial procedure was being repeated in regard to Assurbanipal when the Nin. A inscription (§ 27) was composed.[55]

---

50 Cf. Tadmor 1983, 45 and Parpola 1997c, LXIX-LXX.

51 The date is preserved in two manuscripts, of which A^1c dates from the month of Tammuz (IV) and A^4 from the month of Sivan (III), both from the eponym year (679) of Issi-Adad-aninu, governor of Megiddo (Borger 1956, 6).

52 According to Parpola 1997c, LXXIV, Venus' appearing in the west dates to 681-X-29, its reaching the hypsoma to 680-III-15 and its disappearing to 680-VII-11; the shining of Mars "in the path of Ea" dates to 680-V/VII.

53 Cf. Brinkman 1983, 36; van der Spek 1993, 262-263.

54 See Tadmor 1981, 14-25.

55 Tadmor (1981, 29; 1983, 38-45) calls this inscription straightforwardly an "apology"; cf. also Pečírková 1993, 247.

The royal succession was undoubtedly one of the paramount problems of the Assyrian court in the Sargonid period. Even though the succession was arranged to be as indisputable as possible by designating the crown prince as the legitimate heir who lived in the Palace of Succession (*bēt rēdūti*) already exercising administrative duties,[56] in reality it was not always so irrevocable as it was meant to be. Besides the fact that the designated crown prince could die prematurely,[57] the king also could change his mind and maneuvre the already promoted crown prince from this status by replacing him with another son. This apparently happened to Arda-Mullissi[58] who, as it now seems likely, had been appointed crown prince by Sennacherib as early as in 698,[59] soon after his elder brother Aššur-nadin-šumi[60] was installed as the King of Babylon. This arrangement was, however, to be totally changed by Senna-

---

[56] For the procedure, see below, pp. 156-159180.

[57] This was apparently the fate of Sin-nadin-apli, the eldest son of Esarhaddon, whom we know only from the oracle query SAA 4 149 (cf. Lewy 1952, 280-281; Kwasman & Parpola 1991, XXIX). That he really was appointed crown prince is true if he is the person called *mār šarri* in two purchase documents from the year 676 (SAA 6 210 r.14 and 239 r.7).

[58] As to the name and person of Arda-Mullissi, see Parpola 1980; Kwasman & Parpola 1991, XXXII. There are only logographic readings of the first part of the name so that it is not sure whether it should be pronounced as /arda/ (Bab.) or as /urda/ (Ass.). Since the latter part of the name, Mullissi, is syllabically attested and thus clearly Assyrian (the Babylonian equivalent would be pronounced /mullilti/), the pronunciation /urda/ would suggest itself. See, however, Parpola 1980, 178 n. 25.

[59] This conclusion has been recently drawn by Parpola in Kwasman & Parpola 1991, XXXII on the basis of SAA 6 103, a purchase document of Aplaya who is called the 'third man' of Arda-Mullissi, the crown prince (*Aplāja tašlīšu ša Arda-Mullissi mār šarri*). This document dates from 694-VII-12, but since the dossier of the same person covers the period of time from 698 to 683 (the year of designating Esarhaddon as the crown prince, see below) and he apparently has held his wealthy position all these years, it is conceivable that this period relates to his occupation as a royal charioteer of the crown prince Arda-Mullissi. The title of Aplaya closely resembles the titles of other royal charioteers, whose high status is emphasized by these titles; e. g. *Rēmanni-Adad mukīl appāti dannu ša Aššūr-bāni-apli šar māt Aššūr* "Remanni-Adad, chief chariot driver of Assurbanipal, king of Assyria" (SAA 6 335:11-12).

That Arda-Mullissi indeed was crown prince before Esarhaddon and became displaced by the latter was already suggested by Schmidtke 1916, 104-105. This suggestion was, however, subsequently rejected by e.g. Landsberger & Bauer 1927, 71-72 and Lewy 1952, 271 who failed to recognize *mār šarri* as the appellation of the crown prince. This is surprising in the case of Lewy who later on (p. 281 n. 85), nevertheless, does identify *mār šarri* as the crown prince. On the other hand, Lewy concluded that the investiture of Esarhaddon took place in 694 when Aššur-nadin-šumi, the eldest son of Sennacherib, had perished at the hands of Elamites (p. 271 n. 39; 281). This conclusion, however, turns out to be impossible; cf. the following footnotes.

[60] Aššur-nadin-šumi ruled as the king of Babylonia until 694 when he was captured and delivered over to the king of Elam. This happened in Babylonia while Sennacherib was carrying out his ship expedition against Chaldeans in the southern swamp district. See Parpola 1972, 32-33; Brinkman 1973, 92.

cherib as fifteen years later he designated his youngest[61] son Esarhaddon as the crown prince.

The conditions of displacing Arda-Mullissi from the position of the crown prince are virtually unknown. We know nothing about his possible incompetence or other deficiencies as crown prince. Be that as it may, it cannot be doubted that the queen Naqija (Zakutu) had a considerable influence on the decision of Sennacherib to change the previous arrangements of his succession.[62] Naqija was the mother of Esarhaddon whose brothers were not her sons.[63] It is quite beyond doubt that she favored Esarhaddon at the expense of his brothers, working consistently in preference for her own son.[64] Naqija, who was of Aramean origin,[65] is well known as a competent and ambitious queen who exercised actual power during the reign of her husband and son. Naqija could certainly calculate that raising her son to the throne would make it possible for her to have power over significant political issues as the queen mother – an objective that later on turned out to be right on target.[66]

In the month Nisan (I) of the year 683 Esarhaddon was officially designated as the crown prince of Assyria.[67] According to the Nin. A inscription (§ 27),[68] Sennacherib, following the order of Aššur, Sin, Šamaš, Bel and Nabû, Ištar of Nineveh and Ištar of Arbela appointed him, even if he was younger than

---

[61] Cf. Lewy 1952, 271 n. 38.

[62] See the evidence in Schmidtke 1916 and cf. Lewy 1952, 271-272; Parpola 1980, 175 and, concerning Sennacherib's favorite wife Tašmetu-šarrat, Borger 1988 and Mayer 1995, 377 n. 1 who puts forward the question: "War die Absetzung Arda-Mulissis und die Ernennung Asarhaddons der Preis, den Sanherib für Tašmetu-šarrat an Naqiʾa/Zakûtu bezahlen mußte?"

[63] SAA 9 1.8.

[64] Her special affection for Esarhaddon is evident also from the inscription on a bead donated to an unknown god, published by Van De Mieroop 1993: *ana* [...] *Zakūtu sēgallu* (for this transcription, see Parpola 1988) *ša Sîn-ahhē-rība šar māt Aššūr ana balāṭi Aššūr-ahu-iddina šar māt Aššūr marʾīša u šâša ana balāṭīša iqīš* "To the god [...], Zakutu, the queen of Sennacherib, king of Assyria, for the life of Esarhaddon, king of Assyria, her son, and for her own life, has donated."

[65] For the discussion about her origins see e.g. Lewy 1952, 272-275; Becking 1992, 91-92.

[66] On Naqija, see also Seux 1980/83, 162; Reade 1987, 142-143; Grayson 1991, 138-139.

[67] The date of Esarhaddon's promotion – Nisan 683 – has been calculated by Parpola who extracts this result from two sources. First, the mentioning of the Akitu Chapel of Assur together with its gods in the succession treaty of Sennacherib (SAA 2 3) confirms that the investiture cannot have taken place before the year 683 when the chapel was completed (Parpola 1987b, 164). On the other hand, a purchase document of Se'-madi, "village manager of the crown prince" (*rab ālāni ša mār šarri*), written just a couple of days before Esarhaddon's accession, can only refer to him as the crown prince (SAA 6 110). In another document of Se'-madi (SAA 6 109) which dates from the year 683, he already has the same title, whereas a later document from the very same person (SAA 6 111) dating from the first year of Esarhaddon's reign (680) omits the qualification *ša mār šarri*. See Kwasman & Parpola 1991, XXXIII-XXXIV, 100-101.

[68] Borger 1956 (§ 27) 40-41:8-22.

his brothers,[69] as the crown prince saying: "This will be my heir."[70] The selection was confirmed by extispicy and, as soon as the firm positive answer (*annu kēnu*) of the gods Šamaš and Adad was received, the entire population of Assyria, together with the royal family, was made to swear a solemn oath of allegiance to him as the crown prince.[71] Finally he entered into the Succession Palace (*bēt rēdūti*). All this follows the normal procedure of the promotion of the crown prince, and the oath sworn by the people most probably corresponds with the treaty available to us now as SAA 2 3.[72]

Prophecies attaching directly to the investiture of Esarhaddon have not been preserved, but the prophetic support of his crownprincehood is evident from the prophecies uttered a couple of years later. The prophecy of Bayâ, for instance, asserts that Esarhaddon was chosen by the Great Gods from his very childhood to be the king of Assyria (SAA 9 1.4 ii 20-33):

> *kī ummaka tušabšukāni 60 ilāni rabûti issīja ittitissu ittaṣarūka Sîn ina imittīka Šamaš ina sumēlīka 60 ilāni rabûti ina battibattīka izzazzū qabalka irtaksū ina muhhi amēlūti lā tatakkil mutuh ēnēka ana ajjāši dugulanni anāku Issār ša Arbail Aššūr issīka usallim ṣeherāka attaṣakka lā tapallah na''idāni*
>
> When your mother gave birth to you, sixty great gods stood with me and protected you. Sin was at your right side, Šamaš at your left; sixty great gods were standing around you and girded your loins. Do not trust in man. Lift up your eyes, look to me! I am Ištar of Arbela, I reconciled Aššur with you. When you were small, I took you to me. Do not fear; praise me!

This fully agrees with the Nin. A inscription (§ 27), according to which Esarhaddon was "the beloved of the Great Gods whom Aššur, Šamaš, Bel, Nabû, Ištar of Nineveh and Ištar of Arbela called to the kingship of Assyria when he still was a child."[73]

The unexpected promotion of Esarhaddon aroused mixed feelings in Assyria. It is hardly surprising that the displaced crown prince Arda-Mullissi found himself suffering an outrageous injustice and there were many who shared this feeling with him. The poor health of Esarhaddon, as far as it was already a public issue,[74] may also have aroused doubts about his ability to

---

[69] Borger 1956 (§ 27) 40:8: *ša ahhēja rabûti ahūšunu ṣehru anāku...* "Even though I was younger than my big brothers..."

[70] Borger 1956 (§ 27) 40:12: *annû māru rēdūtīja.*

[71] Borger 1956 (§ 27) 40:18-19: *aššu naṣar rēdūtīja zikiršun kabtu ušazkiršunūti* "To protect my succession he made them swear a solemn oath."

[72] Cf. Parpola 1987b, 163-164, 178-180; Watanabe & Parpola 1988, XXVIII.

[73] Borger 1956 (§ 27) 39-40:4-7: *migir ilāni rabûti ša ultu ṣeherīšu Aššūr Šamaš Bēl u Nabû Issār ša Nīnua Issār ša Arbail ana šarrūti māt Aššūr ibbû zikiršu.*

[74] The sickliness of Esarhaddon during his reign is well known (see Parpola 1983, 230ff); whether he already had health problems as crown prince is difficult to know. Cf., anyhow, SAA 10 328:15-18 "When the king, my lord, was crown prince and went [to... N]abû'a, a fever lingered [in (his) e]yes..." A still earlier reference to Šemahu, "doctor"

exercise kingship. It is no wonder that Arda-Mullissi with his brother[75] and other supporters did not simply accept the investiture of Esarhaddon but began to scheme for his overthrow, "forsake the gods, trusted in their own arrogant deeds and made evil plans,"[76] obviously winning people over to their side.

The Nin. A inscription (§ 27) reports that the brothers of Esarhaddon even turned the kind heart of his father against him – even though only ostensibly, since Sennacherib secretly commiserated with Esarhaddon and supported his future kingship.[77] This secret sympathy might have been the reason why Sennacherib in Nisan (I) 681,[78] i.e., two years after the investiture, let Esarhaddon flee from Nineveh to the western provinces to a "secure place" (*ašar niṣirti*)[79] where he could abide without risk to his life. According to the inscription, it was the Great Gods who transferred him to this refuge, extending their "sweet shade" (*ṣulūlšunu ṭābu*) over him and protecting him for the kingship. This protection found its expression also in prophetic oracles, several of which – including the above quoted prophecy of Bayâ – are likely to have been uttered during the exile of Esarhaddon. The oracle of Sinqiša-amur, for example, implies that Esarhaddon, troubled by enemies, is still crown prince even if he is already called 'king' by the prophetess (SAA 9 1.2 i 30-37):

> *šar māt Aššūr lā tapallah nakru ša šar māt Aššūr ana ṭabahhi addana* [*ina*] *bēt rēdūtēka* [*utaq*]*qanka* [*urabb*]*aka* [*bēltu* (?) *ra*]*bītu anāku* [*anāku Issār š*]*a Arbail*
>
> King of Assyria, have no fear! I will deliver up the enemy of the king of Assyria for slaughter. [I will] keep you safe and [*make*] you [*great* in] your Palace of Succession. I am the Gr[eat *Lady*, I am Ištar o]f Arbela.

(*asû*) of Esarhaddon, is included in SAA 6 126:9, a document from the year 697, when Esarhaddon was still a mere prince.

[75] Esarhaddon always mentions broadly his "brothers" without naming and numbering them. The prophecy SAA 9 1.8 (see below), however, refers clearly to two brothers. The Biblical tradition (2 Kings 19:37 = Is 37:38) also knows about two sons of Sennacherib called Adrammelech (*ʾAdrammælæk*) and Sharezer (*Śarʾæṣær*). The first name obviously stands for Arda-Mullissi (Parpola 1980, 174), whereas the second name (*x*-šarru-uṣur) remains unknown from other sources.

[76] Borger 1956 (§ 27) 41:24-25.

[77] Borger 1956 (§ 27) 41-42:29-31: *pašru libbu abīja ša lā ilāni uzennū ittīja šaplānu libbašu rēmu rašišūma ana epēš šarrūtīja šitkunā ēnāšu* "The gentle heart of my father they made angry with me against the will of the gods, though in his heart he secretly commiserated with me and his eyes were set on my kingship."

[78] According to the observation of Larsen 1974, 22 Esarhaddon would have left Nineveh in Nisan (I) 681; this is conceivable from the *ša arki* eponym dating of SAA 6 197 which dates from 681-II-5.

[79] Borger 1956 (§ 27) 42:39; cf. the commentary *ad loc*. That the refuge of Esarhaddon is to be sought in the west becomes evident from the mentioning of "the land of Hanigalbat" in Borger 1956 (§ 27) 44:70.

Moving Esarhaddon to a place of refuge was doubtless a clever move, since the brothers now found themselves in a stalemate: the Palace of Succession was unoccupied while the crown prince was still alive. Seemingly the brothers had got the upper hand over Esarhaddon but, in reality, they had no legitimate chance to seize the throne. The situation grew desperate enough for the brothers to conclude a "treaty of rebellion" (*adê ša sīhi*) for the purpose of murdering Sennacherib and taking over the kingship by a surprise attack.[80] This plan was put into practice and Sennacherib was murdered on the 20th of Tebet (X), 681.[81]

From now on, the plot of Arda-Mullissi and his associates no longer worked out as it was planned. When Esarhaddon heard about the fate of his father he immediately left his refuge and, as he put it, without even hasty preparations for war and in defiance of the hard winter marched to the east to confront his brothers' troops.[82] Esarhaddon showed himself superior in the battle and finally crossed the river Tigris and arrived in Nineveh where he ascended his father's throne in the month Adar of the same year.[83]

Since Esarhaddon let all the credit for his victory go to Ištar and other gods[84] he does not tell how it was possible for him to get together enough forces for a massive military action. Presumably he was not sent to his refuge without a substantial lifeguard, so that a sufficient potential for starting the counterblow would have existed.[85] Furthermore, the murder of the king strengthened the opposition against the murderers. Esarhaddon reports that in the course of the battle his adversaries went over to his side acknowledging his kingship.[86] Considering the fact that the war was over in less than two

---

[80] The existence of this conspiracy is confirmed by the letter ABL 1091 written after the murder of Sennacherib in order to unmask two officials – Nabû-šumu-iškun and Ṣillâ – who had been involved in the conspiracy. This letter proves that the leader of the plot against Sennacherib was Arda-Mullissi who thus is to be considered his actual murderer; see Parpola 1980.

[81] For the date, see Grayson 1975a, 81:34-35. The murder of Sennacherib has been an event remarkable enough to be mentioned in several documents of a later period – not only in the Bible (2 Kings 19:37 = Is 37:38; 2 Chr 32:21) and by Berossus (Jacoby 1958, 386:25-28, 404:11-14) but also by Greek authors Ktesias of Knidos and Nicolaus of Damascus whose accounts of Semiramis are generally assumed to have their historical background in the circumstances surrounding the death of Sennacherib (see Zawadzki 1990 and cf. Lewy 1952, 264-271, 283-286). Curiously enough, Esarhaddon leaves the murder of his father unmentioned altogether in his inscriptions. As suspicious as this might seem, the possibility that Sennacherib might have been murdered by Esarhaddon himself (Landsberger & Bauer 1927, 69) is ruled out by the evidence presented above.

[82] Borger 1956 (§ 27) 43-44:63-71.

[83] Borger 1956 (§ 27) 44-45:72-86.

[84] Borger 1956 (§ 27) 43:59-60; 44:72-76; 45:85; cf. Weippert 1972, 468.

[85] With regard to the short time required by Esarhaddon to march to Nineveh, Mayer 1995, 383 assumes that he was already prepared for hearing the message of his father's death and his troops were ready for the battle from the very day this message reached him.

[86] Borger 1956 (§ 27) 44:77: *ina puhrīšunu iqbû umma annû šarrāni* "They said in their midst: This will be our king!"

months this may not be far from the truth. Arda-Mullissi lost so many of his adherents that he finally could do nothing but flee with his associates "to an unknown land"[87] where he vanished without leaving a trace.

The most influential support for Esarhaddon during his exile was without doubt given by his mother Naqija who never lost her hope of seeing her son as the king of Assyria even if this at times did not seem probable. This becomes evident from the prophecy of Ahat-abiša received by Naqija when Esarhaddon's brothers seemed to have got the upper hand (SAA 9 1.8 v 12-23):

> *anāku bēlet Arbail ana ummi šarri kī tahhurīninni mā ša imitti ša šumēli ina sūnīki tassakni mā ījû ṣīt libbīja ṣēru tussarpidi ūmâ šarru lā tapallah šarrūtu ikkû danānu ikkûma*
>
> I am the Lady of Arbela. To the king's mother: Because you implored me, saying: "You have placed the ones at the (king's) right and left side in your lap, but made my own offspring roam the steppe" – Now fear not, king! The kingdom is yours, yours is the power!

While "roaming the steppe," an idiom probably alluding to the Gilgameš Epic,[88] doubtless refers to Esarhaddon's hiding in his refuge, the position of his brothers at the king's right and left side[89] clearly presents them as successors and implies their predominance over him at the moment when Naqija has made her request of the oracle. Calling Esarhaddon 'king', thus, indicates the conviction that the succession arrangements of Sennacherib and Naqija had divine support. The prophetic attitude towards the brothers' aspiration for power, well in line with that of the inscription, according to which they "went mad and did everything that is not good before the gods

---

[87] Borger 1956 (§ 27) 45:84: *ana māt lā idû*. Cf. Borger's commentary *ad loc.* and SAA 9 3.3 ii 20 (see below, p. 27). According to the Biblical tradition the murderers of Sennacherib fled to "the land of Ararat" (2 Kings 19:37 = Is 37:38). If this were true it would mean that Arda-Mullissi and his brother did the same as did many other political fugitives and took refuge in the bordering countries in the north (cf. Lanfranchi & Parpola 1990, XXIV and SAA 5 32, 34, 35, 52, 54); or they could have sought shelter under the Cimmerians, the constant northern enemies of Assyria, who would have welcomed them as useful informers on the Assyrian state of affairs (on the Cimmerian problem see Lanfranchi & Parpola 1990, XX; Starr 1990, LXI-LXII; Mayer 1993). All this is, of course, mere speculation since the men are never heard of again after the victory of Esarhaddon.

[88] The expression *ṣēru rapādu* is attested also in the prophecy SAA 9 9:8, 25; the allusion to Gilgameš was already noted by Zimmern 1910, 170-171. Cf. Gilg. ix 2-5 (Parpola 1997a, 101): *Gilgāmeš ana Enkīdu ibrīšu ṣarpiš ibakkima irappud ṣēru anāku amâtma ul kî Enkīdu mā nissatum īterub ina karšīja mūta aplahma arappud ṣēru* "Gilgameš wept bitterly for Enkidu, his comrade, and roamed the steppe. 'Shall I not die, too, like Enkidu? Worry has entered my mind. I am afraid of death, (so) I roam the steppe.'"

[89] Cf. SAA 10 185:5-13 on the investiture of Assurbanipal and Šamaš-šumu-ukin as crown princes of Assyria and Babylonia: "What has not been done in heaven, the king, my lord, has done upon earth and shown us: you have girded a son of yours with headband and entrusted to him the kingship of Assyria; your eldest son you have set to the kingship in Babylon. You have placed the first on your right, the second on your left side!"

and mankind,"[90] is expressed also by the prophecy of Issar-beli-da''ini for Naqija[91] (SAA 9 1.7 v 3-9):

> *kakkišāti pušhāti ša idabbabūni ina pān šēpēšu ubattaqšunu atti attīma šarru šarrīma*
>
> I will cut the conspiring weasels[92] and shrews to pieces before his feet. You (f.) are you. The king is my king!

Yet another prophecy for Naqija is partially preserved on the tablet SAA 9 5 and dates back to the time of the battle. It implies that the queen mother has once again appealed to the goddess on behalf of her son who now finds himself at war. The momentous and warlike tone of the oracle leaves no doubt about the acuteness of the situation (SAA 9 5:1-10):

> *abat Issār ša Arbail* [*ana ummi šarri*] *kinṣāja kanṣā an*[*a...*] *Mullissu ana killi* [*ša mūrīša tasseme*] *qablīki ruksī* [...] *ša Aššūr-ahu-iddina šar māt Aššūr* [...] *Inurta imittu u sumēlu š*[*a...*] *ajjābīšu ina šapal šēpē*[*šu ukabbas*] *ina ekal ṣēri ū*[*ṣa...*] *tuqqun ana A*[*ššūr-ahu-iddina šar māt Aššūr a*]*ddan*
>
> The word of Ištar of Arbela [*to the king's mother*:[93]...]. My knees are bent fo[r ...] Mullissu [has heard[94]] the cry [of *her calf*]. Gird (f.) your loins! [...] of Esarhaddon, king of Assyria [...] Ninurta [*shall go*] at the right and left side *o*[*f... shall* put[95]] his enemies under [his] foot [...] I will g[o out] to the Palace of the Steppe [...] I will give security for [Esarhaddon, king of Assyria.]

Going to the "Palace of the Steppe" (É.GAL EDIN) possibly refers to the sojourning of Ištar of Arbela in her *akītu*-chapel in the nearby town Milqia[96] during the absence of Esarhaddon; cf. SAA 9 1.9 quoted below.

It becomes evident from all this evidence that Naqija kept in contact with prophets and watched over the interests of Esarhaddon during his exile. A further document of the support for Esarhaddon in Nineveh and the position of Naqija as his proxy is the letter SAA 10 109 which shows that not only

---

90 Borger 1956 (§ 27) 42:41-42: *arkānu ahhēja immahûma mimma ša eli ilāni u amēlūti lā ṭâba ēpušūma.*

91 That the queen mother is in question is evident from the words *at-ti at-ti-ma* LUGAL *šar-ri-ma* "You (f.) are you. The king is my king" (lines 8-9); note that the king is referred to in the 3rd person sing. and the next oracle (SAA 9 1.8) is addressed to Naqija as well.

92 As to the word *kakkišu*, cf. below, pp. 74-75.

93 Except for the fact that Esarhaddon is never addressed in the 2nd person in the preserved part of the text, the feminine form of the exhortation *qablīki ruksī* "Gird your loins!" makes Naqija the most probable addressee of this oracle.

94 Cf. SAA 9 3.3 ii 14.

95 Cf. SAA 9 2.1 i 12.

96 On Milqia, see Menzel 1981, 113, 111*-112*; Parpola 1970b, 248; 1983, 192-193; Röllig 1993/97; Pongratz-Leisten 1997, 249-250.

prophets but also scholars were consulted by Naqija during the absence of Esarhaddon. In this letter Bel-ušezib, a Babylonian scholar, claims to have reported to the exorcist Dadâ and the queen mother Naqija "the omen of the kingship of my lord Esarhaddon, the crown prince." This letter will be examined later in this study (pp. 89-95).

Even though some of the prophecies addressed to Esarhaddon during his exile were received by his mother who resided in Nineveh, the expressions of divine support were not limited to the core district of Assyria. Esarhaddon tells himself how he, having heard about the evil deeds of his brothers, burst into wailing (*epšētīšunu lemnēti urruhiš ašmēma ū'a aqbīma*), rent his garments and prayed to the Great Gods who heard him.[97] Consequently, Esarhaddon received from them repeatedly the "oracle of encouragement" (*šīr takilti*)[98] saying:

> *alik lā kalâta idāka nittallakma ninâra gārēka*
>
> Go ahead, do not hold back! We walk by your side, we annihilate your enemies.[99]

This finally gives Esarhaddon the courage to start the military action. Even if the *šīr takilti* is transmitted by a haruspex rather than a prophet,[100] there are prophecies recalling the very same situation with similar phraseology; for example SAA 9 1.6 iii 30 – iv 10:

> *lā tapallah šarru aqṭibak lā aslik[a] utakki[lka] lā ubāš[ka] nāru ina tuqunni ušēbar[ka] Aššūr-ahu-iddina aplu kēnu mār Mullissi ha-an-ga-ru ak-ku ina qātēja nakarūtēka uqatta*
>
> Have no fear, king! I have spoken to you, I have not lied to you; I have given you faith, I will not let you come to shame. I will take you safely across the River. Esarhaddon, rightful heir, son of Mullissu! With an angry dagger[101] in my hand I will finish off your enemies.

This oracle of Ištar, spoken by an unknown prophet, gives the impression of being received when the battle was still going on. This dating is supported also by the fact that Esarhaddon is addressed not only as the king[102] but also

---

97 Borger 1956 (§ 27) 43:53-60.

98 For this term, see below, pp. 33-34.

99 Borger 1956 (§ 27) 43:61-62.

100 See below, pp. 33-34.

101 For the interpretation of the etymological crux *ha-an-ga-ru ak-ku*, see Parpola 1997c, 7 (*ad loc.*); von Soden 1977, 184 (no. 174), 187 (no. 188). An equivalent expression is *šibirru ezzu* 'angry scepter' in Borger 1956 (§ 65) 98:32. As an alternative translation for *akku*, 'sharp-edged' (< *akāku/ekēku* 'scratch') would provide itself; cf. Nissinen 1993, 232.

102 The prophecy assures repeatedly that Ištar will give Esarhaddon "long days and everlasting years" (*ūmē arkūte šanāte dārāte*) as the king of Assyria (SAA 9 1.6 iii 8-14, 19-22, iv 14-17).

as the legitimate heir (*aplu kēnu*). This designation would not have made sense if the accession had already taken place. Even though Esarhaddon is regularly called king by the prophets before his accession he could not possibly be called *aplu kēnu* after it happened. Furthermore, the river mentioned in the oracle is likely to mean the Tigris which had to be crossed before the final conquest of Nineveh was possible. Esarhaddon himself boasts of having let his troops stride across the Tigris as though it were nothing more than a ditch.[103]

Yet another oracle reflects unambiguously the same circumstances as the inscription of Esarhaddon and the above-quoted prophecy. The reference to previous words of Ištar supports Esarhaddon's own account according to which he repeatedly received prophecies during his exile, whereas the "woe" (*ū'a*) recalls the distress expressed in the inscription with the same word (SAA 9 1.1 i 15-27):[104]

> *ajjūte dibbīja ša aqqabakanni ina muhhi lā tazzizūni anāku Issār ša Arbail nakarūtēka ukāṣa addanakka anāku Issār ša Arbail ina pānātūka ina kutallīka allāka lā tapallah atta ina libbi muggi anāku ina libbi ū'a atabbi uššab*
>
> What words have I spoken to you that you could not rely upon? I am Ištar of Arbela! I will flay your enemies and give them to you. I am Ištar of Arbela! I will go before you and behind you. Fear not! You were paralysed, but in the midst of woe I will rise and sit down (beside you).[105]

The inscription states that Ištar , "Lady of warfare and battle" who loved his priesthood (i.e. kingship[106]), fell in beside him, broke the bows of the enemies and disrupted their ranks.[107] Likewise the prophecies, most of which are presented as the words of Ištar, mostly let the credit for the victory go to her. One prophecy which makes an explicit reference to the same events is,

---

[103] Borger 1956 (§ 27) 45:84-86: *akšudamma ina kār Idiqlat ina qibit Sîn u Šamaš ilāni bēl kāri gimir ummānīja Idiqlat rapaštum atappiš ušašhiṭ* "I reached the embankment of the Tigris and, upon the command of Sin and Šamaš, the lords of the harbor, I let all my troops jump across the broad river Tigris as if it were nothing but a ditch."

[104] Borger 1956 (§ 27) 43:56; cf. above.

[105] The getting up and sitting down of Ištar probably means that the goddess takes the responsibility for the fighting from the very beginning ("getting up") until the end ("sitting down"). Weippert 1981, 81-82 interprets the words *anāku ina libbi ū'a* as referring to the distress of the goddess who is filled with compassion for Esarhaddon.

[106] That kingship also implies priesthood of the great gods is well known; "priest" could even be used as a title of the king (see Seux 1967, 287-288).

[107] Borger 1956 (§ 27) 44:74-76: *Issār bēlit qabli u tāhāzi rā'imat šangūtīja idāja tazzizma qašassunu tašbir tāhāzāšunu raksu tapṭurma* "Ištar, the Lady of warfare and battle who loves my priesthood, stood by my side, broke their bows and put their ranks in disorder." Cf. Borger 1956 (§ 65) 98:27-29: *Issār bēltum rā'imat šangūtīja qaštu dannatu šiltāhu gešru mušamqit lā māgiri tušatmeha rittūja* "Ištar, the Lady who loves my priesthood, let my hand seize a mighty bow, a powerful arrow, that fells the insubordinate ones."

however, presented as the word of Aššur. This text belongs to the collection of oracles probably connectd with the enthronement ceremonies of Esarhaddon.[108] It takes a retrospective look at the past turbulence (SAA 9 3.3 ii 10-32):

> *annûrig sarsarrāni annūti ussadbibūka ussēṣūnikka iltibûka atta pīka taptitia mā anina Aššūr anāku killaka asseme issu libbi abul šamê attaqallalla lakrur išātu lušākilšunu atta ina bīrtuššunu tazzaz issu pānīka attiši ana šadê ussēlīšunu abnāti aqqullu ina muhhīšunu azzunun nakarūtēka uhtattip dāmēšunu nāru umtalli lēmurū lūna''idūni akī Aššūr bēl ilāni anākūni annû šulmu ša ina pān ṣalme ṭuppi adê anniu ša Aššūr ina muhhi ha'ūti ina pān šarri errab šamnu ṭābu izarriqū niqiāti eppušū riqiāti illukū ina pān šarri isassiū*
>
> Now then, these traitors provoked you, had you banished, and surrounded you; but you opened your mouth (and cried): "Hear me, O Aššur!" I heard your cry. I issued forth as a fiery glow from the gate of heaven, to hurl down fire and have it devour them. You were standing in their midst, so I removed them from your presence. I drove them up the mountain and rained (hail)-stones and fire of heaven upon them. I slaughtered your enemies and filled the river with their blood. Let them see (it) and praise me, (knowing) that I am Aššur, lord of the gods!
> This is the well-being (placed) before the Image. This covenant tablet of Aššur enters the king's presence on a *cushion*. Fragrant oil is sprinkled, sacrifices are made, incense is burnt, and they read it out in the king's presence.

This prophecy[109] echoes well the chain of events portrayed by Esarhaddon and matches his inscription in many details.[110] The brothers, called by Esarhaddon conventionally "rebels who make conspiracy and insurrection" (*hammā'ē ēpiš sīhi u bārti*),[111] who had evil designs on him (*ikappudū lemuttu*) and talked about him spitefully behind his back (*arkīja iddanabbubū zērāti*)[112] are here characterized as traitors (*sarsarrāni*) who literally "made (others) talk against you" (*ussadbibūka*), that is, disseminated rumors about Esarhaddon.

At first sight, the prophecy explains the expatriation of Esarhaddon as a the work of the brothers (*ussēṣūnikka*), whereas Esarhaddon only says that

[108] For the date of the collection SAA 9 3, see tentatively Weippert 1981, 95; 1997c, 157; Nissinen 1993, 228-229; Parpola 1997c, LXX. I hope to be able to confirm this date by further study.

[109] For this prophecy, see also Weippert 1972, 481-482; 1981, 93-96; 1997c, 157-160; Dijkstra 1980, 157-159; Lewis 1996, 406-408.

[110] Cf. Weippert 1981, 93-95. Quite recently, Weippert has suggested that the description of the destruction of the rebels (lines ii 10-18) is quoted from an earlier prophecy proclaimed before his enthronement (1997c, 159-160).

[111] Borger 1956 (§ 27) 44:82; *sīhu u bārtu epēšu* belongs to the standard treaty terminology, cf. SAA 2 6 § 14:166, 169, § 26:303, § 57:498 and many other occurrences.

[112] Borger 1956 (§ 27) 41:25-28.

the gods let him abide in a secure place out of the reach of evil deeds (*lapān epšēt lemuttim*) without saying anything about how he actually ended up in his refuge.[113] As reasoned above, the reference to Sennacherib's kind heart and secret sympathy suggests that it was in practice his father who helped him escape. In fact, the prophecy is not opposed to this interpretation, since it is self-evident that the flight was caused by the brothers who "surrounded" (or: harrassed[114]) Esarhaddon (*iltibûka*) in order to overthrow him. It should be noted that the verbs *dabābu* (Š), *uṣû* (Š) and *labû* describe the action of the brothers as a whole and therefore need not be understood as a chronological continuum.

The appeal of Esarhaddon to Aššur in the prophecy recalls his prayers in his inscription to Aššur and Marduk[115] and to all the Great Gods[116] who "heard his words" and encouraged him to fight. Both texts are careful about attributing the whole warfare to the gods as the actual fighters. The prophecy does not mention a single action performed by Esarhaddon himself during the battle. According to the inscription it was the fear of the great gods that made his enemies fall down.[117]

The situation when Esarhaddon "stood in the midst" of his enemies but who were "removed from his presence" seems to have taken place in "the land of Hanigalbat" where the way of Esarhaddon was blocked by the enemies who all, thanks to Ištar, finally came over to his side.[118] Whatever the actual events behind this legendary assertion might have been, the engagement of Esarhaddon now took a decisive turn and the brothers had to take to their heels and flee the country. The "unknown land" of the inscription is matched by the equally undetermined "mountains" mentioned in the prophecy. Both texts let the flight of the brothers precede the crossing of the Tigris which finally brought the victorious march of Esarhaddon to a climax. Yet the prophecy, according to which the river was filled with the blood of the enemies, clearly presupposes that it was not crossed without a fight.

All in all, the prophecy SAA 9 3.3 presents itself as a short summary of Esarhaddon's own account of the events which, however, was written almost a decade later. Since the prophecy's literary dependence on the inscription is impossible, it can be claimed that the prophecy lends historical support to the inscription of Esarhaddon, all the more as it dates from the very days of the event itself. The tendentious character of the texts should, in any case, be kept

---

113 Borger 1956 (§ 27) 42:38-40.

114 So according to Weippert 1972, 481 who derives the word from *la'ābu/le'ēbu* instead of *labû*.

115 Borger 1956 (§ 27) 42:35-37

116 Borger 1956 (§ 27) 43:59-60.

117 Borger 1956 (§ 27) 44:72: *puluhti ilāni rabūti bēlēja ishupšunūtima*. cf. SAA 3 3 r.4-6. This corresponds to the biblical idea of the War of Yahweh where Israel has only a passive part to play (e.g. Ex 14:14; 2 Chr 20:20-24); cf. Weippert 1972, 468, 483-484 and see below, pp. 54-55.

118 Borger 1956 (§ 27) 44:70-79.

in mind. Both of them clearly represent the point of view of the victors, not that of the vanquished. The purpose of the prophecy, just like that of the inscription, is to present the victory of Esarhaddon as the realization of the will of Aššur and the Great Gods, and his kingship as a binding divine ordinance. This is why the prophecy, which may be called an "oracle of well-being" or a "Heilsorakel" (*šulmu*), itself constituted a document of treaty (*ṭuppi adê*) between the god and the king.[119]

The victory of Esarhaddon was, of course, welcomed joyously by his adherents, including the prophetic circles who had animated him during the battle. On the basis of the preserved documents it is above all the Ištar cult of Arbela that in the persons of its prophets shows itself as the firmest support for his rule (SAA 9 1.3):

> *rīšāk issi Aššūr-ahu-iddina šarrīja rīši Arbail*
> *ša pī Rēmutti-Allati ša Dāra-ahūja ša birti šaddāni*
>
> I rejoice with Esarhaddon, my king! Arbela rejoices!
> – By the mouth of the woman Remutti-allati of Dara-ahuya, a town in the mountains.[120]

Even though the actual speaker is not mentioned explicitly in this miniature oracle, it is not likely to be understood as a personal message of the prophetess but rather as an oracle of Ištar of Arbela. The sending place, Dara-ahuya, presents no problem in this respect since oracles of Ištar of Arbela were not necessarily sent from this town.[121] It is quite natural for the goddess to call Esarhaddon "my king" while it could not possibly be said by a subject of the king who would have said "the king, my lord." The nonexistence of this form of address in the prophetic oracles, on the other hand, is due to the fact that the prophecies were by no means believed to be the private correspondence of the prophets but the words of gods transmitted by them.

In his inscription Esarhaddon reports that he marched into Nineveh and ascended the throne of his father on the 8th of Adar, the day of the *eššēšu*-festival of Nabû.[122] Obviously, this is the date of his entering into Nineveh but not that of his accession to the throne which, according to the chronicles, took place on 18th or (more likely) 28th of Adar (XII), 681.[123] One of the prophetic oracles unmistakably derives from the intermediate period between these dates. The actual message of the goddess is broken away but the initial greeting has remained (SAA 9 1.9 v 26-29):

---

[119] Cf. Ellis 1989, 144; Lewis 1996, 407-408.

[120] The wording of this prophecy is in itself too general to be connected with any historical event. As a part of the collection SAA 9 1 its connection with the events of 681 is ascertained.

[121] Cf. SAA 9 2.4, an oracle of Ištar of Arbela spoken by the prophetess Urkittu-šarrat from Calah.

[122] Borger 1956 (§ 27) 45 i 87 – ii 2.

[123] Grayson 1975a, 82:38.

šulmu ana Aššūr-ahu-iddina šar māt Aššūr Issār ša Arbail ana ṣēri tattūṣi šulmu ana mūrīša ina birit āli tassapra

All is well with Esarhaddon, king of Assyria. Ištar of Arbela has gone out to the steppe and sent (an oracle of) well-being to her calf[124] in the city.

This oracle is closely connected with the above-quoted prophecy addressed to the queen mother after the murder of Sennacherib (SAA 9 5). In that oracle Ištar of Arbela said that she will move to the Palace of the Steppe in Milqia from where she is now sending greetings. Since Esarhaddon was already "in the city" (in Nineveh, or, possibly, in Arbela[125]) and, on the other hand, Ištar was certainly no longer in the Palace of Steppe when the enthronement of Esarhaddon was celebrated (cf. SAA 9 3.4), the oracle must have been received after the conquest of Nineveh but before his accession to the throne. That Esarhaddon is already called the king presents no problem – we have already seen that this title is constantly given to him in the prophecies right after his father was murdered.

In the Ass. A inscription (Borger 1956 § 2) Esarhaddon, after giving an account of the celestial portents following his rise to power, affirms that he has constantly (*kajjān*) received prophetic messages (*šipir mahhê*) concerning the establishment of his "sacerdotal throne until far-off days." That this indeed happened can be confirmed by extant sources including this very message, for example SAA 9 1.6 iii 19-22, iv 14-17:

ūmē arkūte šanāte dārāte kussīka ina šapal šamê rabûte uktīn...
ina Libbi āli ūmē arkūte šanāte dārāte addanakka

For long days and everlasting years I have established your throne under the great heavens...
I will give you long days and everlasting years in the Inner City.

Another two prophecies, both spoken by La-dagil-ili probably right after Esarhaddon's ascending the throne, extend his reign over generations (SAA 9 1.10 vi 19-30 and 2.3 ii 11-14):

[n]irriṭu [is]su libbi ekallīja ušēṣa aklu taqnu takkal mê taqnūti tašatti ina libbi ekallīka tataqqun mara'ka mār mar'īka šarrūtu ina burki ša Inurta uppaš

I will banish [t]rembling [fr]om my palace. You shall eat safe food and drink safe water, and you shall be safe in your palace. Your son and grandson shall rule as kings on the lap of Ninurta.

ina ekallīka utaqqanka nikittu nirriṭu ušanṣaka mara'ka mār mar'īka šarrūtu ina pān Inurta uppaš

---

[124] On the designation "calf" (*mūru* cf. SAA 9 7 r.11) see Weippert 1985, 63; Nissinen 1991, 290-292.

[125] For the latter alternative, cf. ABL 1164 and Parpola 1983, 159.

> I will keep you safe in your palace; I will make you overcome anxiety and trembling. Your son and grandson shall rule as kings before Ninurta.

While both oracles sound the all clear indicating that the war is over, they direct attention to the future. The establishment of the throne until distant days implies in itself a dynastic ideology which is expressed unambiguously, not only in the above-quoted prophecy,[126] but also in the Ass. A (§ 2) and Nin A. (§ 27) inscriptions concerning the preservation of the royal monuments:[127]

> *narê muššarê ēpušma epšēt eteppušu qerebšun alṭur ana šarrāni mārēja arkûte ēzib ṣâtiš ina šarrāni mārēja ša Aššūr u Ištār ana belūt māti u nīšī inabbû zikiršu narû līmurma šamnu li*[*pšu*]*š ni*[*qê liqqi*] *ana* [*ašrīšu*] *l*[*itīr*]
>
> I made stelae and inscriptions, I wrote on them the deeds I have done and left (them) to my royal descendants forever and ever. When (one of) my royal descendants, whom Aššur and Ištar call by name, will see this stela, he shall an[oin]t it with oil, [make] of[ferings] and r[eturn it] to [its place].
>
> *ana arkāt ūme ina šarrāni mārēja ša Aššūr u Ištār ana belūt māti u nīšī inabbū zikiršu enūma ekallu šâtu ilabbirūma innahu anhūssa luddiš*
>
> In days to come, when this palace becomes old and dilapidated, may (one of) my royal descendants, whom Aššur and Ištar call by name, restore it.

The dynastic notion is another example of conceptual and ideological affinities between the prophecies and the inscriptions. The parallel examination of these two genres of literature has generally shown this basic ideological agreement.

Prophecy

The fact that the extensive inscriptional accounts of the rule of Esarhaddon include only two brief references to prophetic activity could be interpreted as a sign of a limited appreciation of prophecy by those who compiled them. Nevertheless, given that the inscriptions of his royal predecessors do not mention prophecy at all, even these tiny remarks are significant, all the more so because the passages mentioning prophecy so often coincide with the extant prophecies. The affinities between the initial part of the Nin. A (§ 27) inscription and the extant prophetic oracles received by Esarhaddon during the described period turn out to be too many and too striking to be quite accidental.

---

[126] Cf. van der Toorn 1987, 87; Nissinen 1993, 232-233 *pace* Ellis 1989, 175.

[127] Borger 1956 (§ 2) 6 vii 35 – viii 3; (§ 27) 64:65-68. Cf. Borger 1956 (§ 65) r.16-18 where Esarhaddon calls himself "a descendant of the eternal dynasty of Bel-Bani, son of Adasi, the founder of the kingship in Assyria" (*zēr šarrūti dārû ša Bēl-Bāni mār Adasi mukin šarrūti māt Aššūr*). Cf. also Borger 1956 (§ 53) 81:48-49.

In view of the manifold convergence between the inscriptions and the prophecies, it is not excluded that the writers of the inscription had actual access to the collections of prophecies now being published as SAA 9 1, 2 and 3. It has been plausibly suggested by Parpola that the collection of ten prophecies (SAA 9 1) spoken at the time of the civil war and Esarhaddon's rise to power was compiled contemporaneously and for the same purpose as the Nin. A (§ 27) inscription.[128] There is a considerable degree of probability that the compilation of this collection was done by the same learned circles who created the inscription.[129] It may also be considered probable that the retrospective prophecy concerning the defeat of the rebelling brothers proclaimed after it happened (SAA 9 3.3) was available to the draftsmen of the Nin. A (§ 27) inscription. It deserves attention that the prophecies which date from the years 681-680 cannot be dependent on the inscriptions but, the other way round, the prophecies may have been (re)used when the inscriptions were drawn up. In general, the pronounced role attributed to Ištar in Esarhaddon's war against his brothers[130] may be due to the availability of the numerous messages of the goddess addressed to Esarhaddon during the battle.

It is noteworthy that the scholars (*ummânī*) responsible for the wording and contents of the inscriptions[131] not only looked at the events from a similar viewpoint as the prophets but also shared the constituents of their religious-political ideology with them.[132] Providing additional proof that Esarhaddon was the god-chosen king whose everlasting rule was established by the great gods, the prophetic messages (*šipir mahhê*) corroborated the inscriptional proclamation and contributed to invalidating every possible confrontation against the legitimacy of his rule.[133] On the other hand, by referring to

---

[128] Parpola 1997c, LXVIII-LXIX.

[129] According to Tadmor 1981, 32, the composer of the Nin. A inscription could have been Issar-šumu-ereš, the chief scribe of Esarhaddon and Assurbanipal. This man is known from his extensive correspondence with both kings (SAA 10 5-38), in which he shows his expertise in astrology, hemerology, omen interpretation, politics and temple affairs. Even though he never mentions prophecy in his letters, he would hardly have been ignorant, much less unaware, of its existence. It deserves attention that he was active in arranging the treaty ceremonies on the occasion of the investiture of Assurbanipal in 672 (SAA 10 5-7).

[130] Borger 1956 (§27) 44:74-76.

[131] For the *ummânī* as the literary craftsmen of the inscriptions, see Tadmor 1981, 31-33; 1997, 328; Brinkman 1983, 37. On the evidence that other scholars, too, have been involved in their composition, see Tadmor & Landsberger & Parpola 1989, 50-51. The names of *ummânī* have been preserved in the Synchronic King List (Grayson 1980/83, 119 iii 95 – iv 13) which is an indication of their high hierarchical position (cf. already Schroeder 1920). In the tree-shaped diagram of the "Assyrian Cabinet" designed by Parpola 1995, 389-390, the *ummânu* holds a supreme position.

[132] That is, those writers whose attitude towards divination was favorable in general. This seems not to be true in every single case; for instance, the recension E of the Bab. A (§ 11) inscription of Esarhaddon does not bother to mention divination at all (see Cogan 1983, 78-84).

[133] Cf. Fales & Lanfranchi 1997, 113.

prophecy among other forms of divinatory expertise, the king also demonstrated his obedience to the divine jurisdiction and strengthened his image as a "king who is knowledgeable and wise" – a specificly Sargonid modification of the traditional profile of the Assyrian king.[134]

While recognizing the attention paid to the prophecy in the inscriptions, divine messages of another kind should not be ignored. It is important to notice that in both inscriptions, prophecy is mentioned together with different forms of divination, of which lines i 31 – ii 26 of the Ass. A (§ 2) inscription give a full account. The passage starts with the celestial phenomena accompanying Esarhaddon's rise to power. The (simultaneous) appearing of sun and moon, the "twin gods," bestows "a righteous and just judgment up[on the land] and the people" (*dēn kitti u mīšari*[135] *a*[*na māti*] *u nīšī*). The movements of Venus predict the "stabilization of the land and reconciliation of its gods" (*kunnu māti sulum ilānīša*), whereas the sign provided by Mars concerns "the strengthening of the king and his land" (*danān malki u mātīšu*). After the astronomical observations, the prophecies (*šipir mahhê*) are mentioned, and they are said to concern "the establishment of the foundation of my sacerdotal throne until far-off days" (*ša išid kussī šangûtīja šuršudi ana ūmē ṣâti*). Furthermore, dreams (*šuttu*) and speech omens (*egerrû*)[136] are said to have rendered "good omens"[137] (*idāt dumqi*) concerning "the establishment of my seat[138] and the extension of my reign" (*ša šuršudi karri šulbur palêja*) which made the king's heart confident. The functions ascribed to the celestial phenomena as well as to the prophecy, dreams and speech omens are expressed with terms that are virtually interchangeable, all aiming at the same goal: the establishment of the rule of Esarhaddon as the king of Assyria. That only the astrological portents are reported in detail and the non-astrological ones only sketched in, may reflect "the top rank of astrology among predictive sciences at this period."[139]

Hence, from the point of view of the writer of the inscription, prophecy appears as one branch of divination among others, with a function similar to that of astrology and dream interpretation. At the same time it is notable that prophecy also appears as a domain of its own: prophecies are not called *ittu* ('omens') but *šipru*. This word is generally used of different kinds of professional skills and activities,[140] but when classified among methods aiming at

---

[134] See Fales & Lanfranchi 1997, 110-111.

[135] For the word-pair *kittu u mīšaru*, cf. AHw 659-660; CAD K 470-471.

[136] On *egerrû* omens, see Oppenheim 1954/56; Cryer 1994, 160-161; CAD E 44-45.

[137] The word *idāt* is understood as pl. st. cstr. of *ittu* 'sign'; also in Borger 1956 (§ 2) 2 ii 18; (§ 11) 16:D12; (§ 53) 81 r.2; SAA 10 13 r.12; cf. *idāt lemutti/lemnēti* 'bad omens' Borger 1956 (§ 11) 12:Á0; 14:B11.

[138] The word *karru*, which literally means a "knaufartige, im Boden eingelassene Thronstütze" (AHw 450; cf. CAD K 221), is clearly used as a synonym of *kussiu* ("throne," line ii 14).

[139] Fales & Lanfranchi 1997, 108.

[140] Cf. e.g. SAA 10 23 r.3; 218 r.15. Hence the usual translation "works of ecstatics" for *šipir mahhê*.

transmitting an intelligible interpretation of the divine will, it must be understood in its basic meaning of 'message'. An act of extispicy can also be called *šipru*[141] but in these cases the connection is made with *bārû*, not with *mahhû*.

In the Nin. A inscription (§ 27), the *šipir mahhê* which are explicitly defined as "messages from the gods and the Goddess" (*našparti ilāni u Ištār*)[142] are also preceded by "good omens" (*idāt dumqi*) in the sky and on earth, this time of unspecified nature. As mentioned above, this inscription also reports on the answer of the gods to Esarhaddon's lamentation and prayer as *šīr takilti*, an "oracle of encouragement" (lines i 60-62):[143]

> *ina annīšunu kēnim sīr takilti ištapparūnimma alik lā kalâta idāka nittallakma ninâra gārêka*
>
> Answering me with their firm positive 'yes' they constantly sent me this oracle of encouragement: "Go ahead, do not hold back! We go by your side, we annihilate your enemies."

As far as the very wording of this oracle is concerned, it could well be understood as a prophetic one. On closer examination, however, it is questionable that a prophecy would be quoted here.[144] The word *šīru*, the literal meaning of which is 'flesh', refers to the result of the observation of the exta of a sacrificial animal.[145] Furthermore the compound *šīr ta/ikilti* can be found in the Bab. A (§ 11) inscription of Esarhaddon where it is explicitly attached to the activity of haruspices (*bārû*):[146]

> In the *mākaltu* bowl[147] of the haruspices oracles of encouragement (*šīrē tukulti*) were set for me. Concerning the rebuilding of Babylon and the

---

[141] E.g. Borger 1956 (§53) 83:25.

[142] Cf. n. 47 above.

[143] In the Hebrew Bible, a similar case can be found in Judg 20:26-29: lamenting their defeat in the civil war against the Benjaminites, the allied troops of the Israelite tribes inquire of Yahweh who answers: "Go up! For tomorrow I will give them into your hand." In the Aramaic inscription of Zakkur, king of Hamath and Lu'aš (KAI 202 A 9-15), a similar prayer, classified by Zobel 1971 as a "Gebet um Abwendung der Not," is followed by prophetic oracles (*byd ḥzyn w byd ʿddn*). See also Weippert 1988, 300-301; Lemaire 1997, 172-175.

[144] Thus in contrast to my earlier statement about *šīr takilti*: "Obwohl dabei nicht explizite genannt wird, daß das Orakel gerade durch den Mund eines Propheten erteilt wird, ist dies doch sehr wahrscheinlich..." (1991, 145-146).

[145] See AHw 1249 (sub *šīru(m)* 7); CAD Š/3 121-122 (sub *šīru* A 4) and cf. the standard formula of the oracle queries "Be present in this ram, place in it a firm positive answer, favorable designs, favorable, propitious omens (UZU.MEŠ = *šīru* pl.) by the oracular command of your great divinity, and may I see them" (cf. Starr 1990, XXVIII; SAA 4 1 r.3-4 and passim).

[146] Borger 1956 (§ 11A) 19:12-17; cf. Borger 1956 (§ 53) 82-83:20-27, of which see below, p. 38. Other occurrences of this compound are Sg. 8, 319 (Thureau-Dangin 1912, 48) and Borger 1956 (§ 4) 7 iii 5 (see Weippert 1972, 467).

[147] For *mākaltu bārûti*, see CAD M 123 (sub *mākaltu* C 1 b).

> restoration of Esaggil I had a liver omen (*amūtu*) written out. I trusted in their firm positive answer (*ana annīšunu kēnu atkalma*).

Since *annu kē/īnu* is a haruspical *terminus technicus*, the standard expression for the "firm positive answer" required in the opening lines of the oracle queries[148] and mentioned also in the beginning of the Nin. A inscription itself,[149] there is no room for doubt that the inscription means extispicy when referring to the *šīr takilti*.[150]

Even though the "oracle of encouragement," thus, is to be understood as the outcome of haruspicial rather than prophetic mediation, it clearly fulfils the same function, i.e. encouraging the king in a critical situation, that is also ascribed to the "messages of the prophets." The war, according to the ideology of the inscriptions, is initiated by the gods whose command is its only and sufficient justification. This is why the gods must be consulted before starting the war.[151] Once the king has obeyed the will of the gods and gone off to war, the divine encouragement follows him all through the battle: it makes him take up arms, it supports him during the action and finally opens up promising vistas of the future. The divinatory apparatus is there to mediate this encouragement. For the purposes of the inscription it is obviously less important which kind of mediation the encouraging messages result from. Nevertheless, as we have seen, the functions ascribed to prophecy, encouragement (Nin. A § 27) and the promises of the establishment of the king's rule (Ass. A § 2), not only conform to the literary conventions but also agree with the substance of the extant prophetic messages. This indicates that the compilers of the inscriptions knew in quite concrete terms what they were talking about when referring to the *šipir mahhê*.[152]

---

[148] *Šamaš bēlu rabû ša ašallūka anna kīna apalanni* "Šamaš, great lord, answer me with a firm 'yes' to what I ask you." (cf. Aro 1966, 109-110; Starr 1990, XVI; SAA 4 1:1 and passim).

[149] Borger 1956 (§ 27) 40:13-14: "He (Sennacherib) consulted Šamaš and Adad by extispicy, and they gave him a firm positive answer (*annu kēnu*): 'He (Esarhaddon) will be your successor.'" Cf. Borger 1956 (§ 2) 3 iii 43 – iv 6; (§ 11) 18:A41-49, B7-9.

[150] Cf. also Dijkstra 1980, 144-145; van der Toorn 1987, 69-70. The Hebrew Bible includes similar oracular answers of Yahweh of a non-prophetic nature (Judg 18:6; 20:23,28; 1 Sam 23:9-12; 30:7-8; 2 Sam 2:1). For these and other comparable texts, cf. Cryer 1994, 298-305.

[151] On consulting Yahweh before military actions in the Hebrew Bible, see e.g. Judg 20:12-29; 1 Sam 23:1-13; 1 Kings 22:1-28.

[152] Note, however, that all inscriptionists were not equally in favor of divination: the recension E of the Bab. A (§ 11) inscription is careful in omitting any reference to divination when reporting on Esarhaddon's rebuilding of Babylon. See Cogan 1983, 78-85.

2.2. Assurbanipal's Pious Works

Text

Prism T ii 7-24[153]

[7]É.MAŠ.MAŠ É.GAŠAN.KALAM.MA KUG.UD KUG.GI [8]*ú-za-ʾi-in lu-le-e ú-mal-li* [9] ^{d}*šar-rat–kid-mu-ri ša ina ug-gat* ŠÀ-*bi-ša* [10]*at-man-šá e-zi-bu* [11]*ú-ši-bu a-šar la si-ma-a-ti-šá* [12]*ina* BALA-*ia dam-qí ša* AN.ŠÁR *iš-ru-ka* [13]*tar-šá-a sa-li-mu* [14]*a-na šuk-lul* DINGIR-*ti-šá ṣir-ti* [15]*šur-ru-hu mi-se-e-šá šu-qu-ru-u-ti* [16]*ina* MÁŠ.MI *ši-pir mah-he-e* [17]*iš-ta-nap-pa-ra ka-a-a-na* [18] ^{d}UTU ^{d}IM *áš-al-ma* [19]*e-pu-lu-in-ni an-nu ke-e-nu* [20]*si-mat* DINGIR-*ti-šá* GAL-*ti ú-šar-rih* [21]*ú-še-šib-ši ina* BÁRA.MAH-*hi* [22]*šu-bat da-ra-a-ti* [23]*par-ṣe-e-šá šu-qu-ru-ti ú-kin-ma* [24]*ú-šal-li-ma mi-se-e-šá*

> [7] Emašmaš and Egašankalamma I covered with silver and gold, filled it with splendor. The Lady of Kidmuri, who in her anger had left her cella and taken residence in a place unworthy of her, relented during my good reign which Aššur had presented and, to make perfect her majestic divinity and glorify her precious rites, constantly sent me (orders) through dreams and prophetic messages. [18] I asked Šamaš and Adad and they gave me a firm positive answer. I made the insignia of her great godhead magnificent, I made her live forever and ever in the inner sanctum (?). I confirmed her precious rites and carried out her rituals properly.

Background

The first reference to prophecy in the inscriptions of Assurbanipal is to be found within the introduction of Assurbanipal's Prisms C and T, concerning his restoration works on Assyrian temples. The quoted section deals with the temples of Ištar, of which Emašmaš, the temple of Ištar in Nineveh,[154] and Egašankalamma, her temple in Arbela,[155] are passed by with only a brief mention about their decoration, presumably because these major temples already housed an established cult and were without doubt in good repair at the beginning of Assurbanipal's reign and actively supported by him.[156]

---

[153] Borger 1996, 140-141. Cf. Thompson 1931, pl. 14.

[154] See Menzel 1981, 116-117.

[155] See Menzel 1981, 6-7.

[156] Assurbanipal's preference for these temples is suggested in the dialogue between him and the god Nabû (SAA 3 13:15-17): "Your figure, which I created, prays incessantly to me in Emašmaš. Your fate, which I devised, incessantly prays to me thus: 'Bring safety into Egašankalamma!'" Interestingly enough, the speaker is Nabû, not Ištar. Nabû, the god of scribes, was specially favored by Assurbanipal who boasted of his own scribal

The temple of the Lady of Kidmuri, however, is described as deserted or at least severely undervalued, and Assurbanipal introduces himself as the one who had rescued the temple from oblivion. To what extent this can be regarded as mirroring historical fact must be considered with regard to the fact that the objective of the inscription is to present the king as an enthusiastic supporter of pious works and, hence, its primary concern is religious explanation rather that historical narrative.[157] Therefore, before the claim of Assurbanipal that he had re-established the cult of the Lady of Kidmuri can be evaluated historically, a brief look at the remaining records of this goddess and her sanctuary in Neo-Assyrian times is necessary.

The Lady of Kidmuri (*Šarrat Kidmuri*) is originally the designation of Ištar of Calah whose temple Bet Kidmuri[158] was restored by Assurnasirpal II in the 9th century. In Nineveh there was a temple dedicated to the Lady of Kidmuri as well.[159] Both of them existed in the Neo-Assyrian period,[160] which makes it virtually impossible to know which of the two is referred to in the inscription of Assurbanipal.

There is no mention of the Lady of Kidmuri or her sanctuary in the inscriptions of Esarhaddon, from which it could be deduced that the worship of the Lady of Kidmuri actually suffered from a neglected status in the time before Assurbanipal. Nevertheless, there exists a letter from Dadî, a priest of Bet Kidmuri, to the crown prince, presumably Assurbanipal (ABL 152). Furthermore, the correspondence of the "secretary of the New Palace" (*ṭupšar bēt ešši*), Ubru-Nabû, which also is partly addressed to the crown prince (ABL 187 and 189), presupposes the existence of the cult of the Lady of

---

abilities (cf. SAA 3 47 r.4-10). Karel van der Toorn refers to the possibility that Nabû acts here as an intercessory god (private communication).

[157] Brinkman 1983, 41.

[158] See Postgate & Reade 1976/80, 308-309; Menzel 1981, 102-103.

[159] This temple is the the recipient of votive gifts of Adad-nerari III from the years 797 and 793(?) in SAA 12 76:10, 12, 26, 29 (cf. Postgate 1969, 101-105), and Sennacherib mentions it in his annals (Luckenbill 1924, 99:44). For other sources, see Menzel 1981, 121-122, 118*-119*.

[160] The Bet Kidmuri and/or the Lady of Kidmuri are frequently mentioned in Neo-Assyrian sources, but many of them are undatable and it is seldom clear which one of the two temples is referred to. Issar-duri, the priest of Bet Kidmuri in the time of Sargon and the writer of the letters ABL 707-711 is probably affiliated with temple of Calah (Menzel 1981, 103), and the same temple seems to be in question in SAA 6 11 r.10 (from the year 717, with *x*-iddina, steward of Bet Kidmuri, as witness) and SAA 12 94 r.13 (late reign of Assurbanipal, with Urad-Issar, priest of Bet Kidmuri, as witness). The undatable list of assemblages of precious goods assigned to different deities, SAA 7 62, includes Bet Kidmuri on lines ii 2-6. In SAA 4 309, a query concerning a priest of the Lady of Kidmuri, the eponym year is unfortunately broken away; the "report" format (for the difference between "queries" and "reports," see Aro 1966, 109-111; Starr 1990, XIV) suggests a date not too early in Assurbanipal's reign. The mythological texts SAA 3 34 (Bet Kidmuri: line 73), 35 (Bet Kidmuri: line 70) and 36 (Lady of Kidmuri: line 6) are undatable.

Kidmuri (ABL 186 and 187).[161] SAA 10 197, a letter of the king's exorcist Adad-šumu-uṣur which dates from Esarhaddon's rather than from Assurbanipal's reign,[162] also includes the Lady of Kidmuri between the Ištars of Nineveh and Arbela in its greeting.[163] All this indicates that the cult of the Lady of Kidmuri was not abandoned altogether in the last years of Esarhaddon. However, judging from the high relative frequency of references to this goddess and her temple(s) in the time of Assurbanipal, either as the crown prince or as the king, it may be true that reviving her cult and restoring her sanctuary was actually promoted by him, perhaps beginning when he was crown prince.

In Assurbanipal's time there is no doubt about an active worship of the Lady of Kidmuri. His inscriptions, especially Prism A, regularly repeat the triad Ištar of Nineveh – Lady of Kidmuri – Ištar of Arbela.[164] Urad-Gula, the "forlorn scholar" whose petition to Assurbanipal will be examined later in this study (pp. 84-88), claims to have arranged a *qarītu* banquet in Bet Kidmuri (SAA 10 294 r.23).

Prophecy

The function of prophecy in the restoration of Bet Kidmuri is pronounced with clear words: "To make perfect her majestic divinity and glorify her precious rites he (Aššur) constantly sent me (orders) through dreams and prophetic messages" (*ana šuklul ilūtīša ṣirti šurruhu mēsēša šūqurūti ina šutti šipir mahhê ištanappara kajjāna*). The prophetic encouragement and exhortation, already familiar to us from military contexts, is now attached to the other principal task of an Assyrian king: temple restoration.

Again, just as in the previously discussed building inscription of Esarhaddon concerning the restoration of Ešarra (Ass. A § 2), the prophetic messages appear side by side with dreams, here concerning the concrete works in the sanctuary. The dreams and the prophecies belong to the preparatory stage of the restoration, encouraging Assurbanipal to himself undertake the rebuilding of Bet Kidmuri, or even telling him to do so. However, at least in this particular case, the dreams and prophecies are not sufficient to make the king

---

[161] The Lady of Kidmuri is included in the greetings of ABL 186 (line 5) and 187 (line 6), and the former deals with *kidinnu* (cf. CAD K 342-344) left in the protection of Mullissu and the Lady of Kidmuri. ABL 187 and 189 are addressed to the crown prince.

[162] Parpola dates it to May, 670 (1983, 109).

[163] It is interesting that within the extensive correspondence of Adad-šumu-uṣur this is the only time when he uses this triad, typical of Assurbanipal's Prism A, in a greeting of a letter written by him. Another person whose greetings include the triad Ištar of Nineveh – Lady of Kidmuri – Ištar of Arbela is Itti-Šamaš-balaṭu, the writer of the letters ABL 992 and 1110 to Assurbanipal.

[164] Almost all attestations of this triad belong to Prism A; cf. Borger 1996, 15 (A i 16), 33 (A ii 128), 36 (A iii 13), 38 (A iii 30), 43 (A iv 47), 58 (A vi 127), 62-64 (A viii 21, 54, 75), 67-68 (A ix 63, 99), 71-72 (A x 35, 61) 75 (A x 119), 115 (C x 53) 194 (J 18-19).

start the work: only the "firm positive answer" (*annu kēnu*) of the gods gave Assurbanipal the green light to begin to accomplish the task; in other words, the dreams and prophecies had to be confirmed by an extispicy. Here the king evidently follows the example of his royal father who, as we have seen, consulted the gods before starting constructing or restoring temples by means of extispicy in order to obtain a "oracle of encouragement" (*šīr tikilti*):[165]

> Before the judgment of Šamaš and Adad I prostrated myself with reverence. Upon their firm decision I commissioned haruspices (*mar'ē bārâni*[166]) (to inquire) about entering the *bēt mummi*. I performed an extispicy concerning Assur, Babylon and Nineveh, as well as the masters (*mar'ē ummânī*) who should perform the task (*epiš šipri*) and get to know the secret lore (*šūrub pirišti*). I shared the task (between the haruspices) one by one (*qātāte ahennâ ukīnma*).[167] The oracles were unanimous (*kī pî ištēn*) and (the gods) gave me a firm positive answer (*annu kēnu*). In Assur, the city of the government, the residence of the father of the gods of Assur, they told me to enter the *bēt mummi* and determined the names of the masters who should perform the task. Upon oracle(s) of encouragement and well-being (*šīr tikilti šalmūte*) they ordered the performing of this task, saying: "Bring quickly the ...[168] of the storehouse, do not give up and do not incline your ear to anything else!" I trusted in their firm positive and unchanging answer (*annāšun kēnu lā mušpēlu attakilma*) and my heart was confident (*artahuṣ libbu*).

All this makes clear that the Assyrian king could not just go and build temples without the proper authorization of the deities who were supposed to dwell in them. Once again prophecy appears as one piece of the divinatory apparatus needed by the king to base his decisions on divine orders.

The abandonment of Bet Kidmuri finds a theological explanation: the Lady of Kidmuri had "in her anger" (*ina uggat libbīša*) left her cella, moved to a place where she does not belong (*ašar lā simātīša*), and stayed there until Assurbanipal "confirmed her precious rites" and "carried out her rituals properly" (*parṣēša šūqurūti ukīnma ušallima mēsēša*). The dwelling of the angry goddess in a place unworthy of her and her subsequent return to her proper sanctuary appears like a concise presentation of an idea, according to which the absence of a deity is a sign of her/his anger and alienation from the worshippers, whereas her/his return manifests the reconciliation between the human and divine spheres. This "divine alienation – divine reconciliation"

---

165 Borger 1956 (§ 53) 82-83:20-27; cf. Borger 1956 (§ 11A) 19:12-17 concerning the rebuilding of Esaggil (see above, pp. 33-34). For dividing the diviners into groups, cf. SAA 3 33:13-24; 1 Kings 22:13 (cf. also Weinfeld 1977, 184-185). For the role of the *ummânī* in this text as the specialists in the secret tradition, see van der Toorn 1997a, 235-236.

166 DUMU.MEŠ LÚ.HAL.MEŠ; cf. SAA 3 33:21.

167 A free translation of the phrase which literally means 'establishing the parts/portions one by one'.

168 The signs ID ID cannot be translated.

pattern is demonstrated in large scale by the Babylon inscription (§ 11) of Esarhaddon:[169] infuriated with the Babylonians' cultic negligence and lack of honesty, Marduk, together with other gods, abandons Babylon in his anger[170] and stays away until Esarhaddon restores Esaggil for the gods to return.[171] In an inscription of Nabonidus, also concerning the goddess of Uruk, the pattern is even closer to Assurbanipal's prism:[172]

> Ištar ([d]INNIN) of Uruk... whose cult the Urukeans changed during the reign of Eriba-Marduk... left in her anger Eanna (*ina uzzi ištu qereb Eanna tūṣuma*) and dwelt in a residence not hers. In her shrine they made dwell a goddess (*lamassu*) who did not belong in Eanna (*lā simat Eanna*). He (Nebuchadnezzar II?[173]) conciliated Ištar ([d]15) and re-established her cella (*ušallim atmanšu ukīn*)... He removed from Eanna the inappropriate Ištar ([d]15 *lā simātu*) and returned Ištar ([d]*in-nin-na*) to Eanna, her sanctuary.

Further examples of divine abandonment of similar kind (not always accompanied by divine reconciliation) are abundantly represented in ancient Near Eastern sources from the Tukulti-Ninurta Epic[174] to the Hebrew Bible in which the destruction of Jerusalem is the demonstration of the anger of Yahweh who abandons his temple because of the sins of his people (2 Kings 24:20, Lam 2:6-8, Ez 21:7-10, Zech 7:7-14 etc.) but, once the period of punishment is over, returns to dwell there again (Ez 20:40, 43:1-9, Zech 8 etc.).

The same concern is also represented in a specific group of sources, namely in the "literary predictive texts," which must not be equated with prophecy as such,[175] but which at this point clearly share similar purposes. The "Marduk Prophecy"[176] and the Late Babylonian "Uruk Prophecy"[177] both predict (*ex eventu*!) that "a king will arise" and renew abandoned and neglected cults and sanctuaries.[178] Two passages of the "Uruk Prophecy" are especially interesting in our context:[179]

---

[169] See Brinkman 1983, 40-42; Cogan 1974, 12-13; 1983, 78-79.

[170] Borger 1956 (§ 11) 13-14.

[171] Borger 1956 (§ 11) 21-24.

[172] Langdon 1912, 274-276 iii 11-34. This passage is strikingly paralleled by the so-called Uruk Prophecy (cf. below).

[173] See below, n. 182.

[174] See Machinist 1976, 458.

[175] See above, p. 7.

[176] See Borger 1971, 16-20 and Longman 1991, 138-141 who date the text to the reign of Nebuchadnezzar I (1125-1104); cf. also Mayer 1988, 157; 1995, 230 who opts for a Neo-Assyrian date.

[177] See Hunger & Kaufman 1975; Longman 1991, 146-149; Beaulieu 1993.

[178] Cf. also the "Šulgi Prophecy" (Borger 1971, 20-21; Longman 1991, 142-146) in which the deified King Šulgi presents himself as a renewer and constructor of sanctuaries.

[179] Hunger & Kaufman 1975, 371-372 r.3-5, 11-14.

> [Aft]er him a king (# 2) will arise... The old protective goddess (*lamassu*) of Uruk he will take away from Uruk and make her dwell in Babylon. He will make dwell in her sanctuary a protective goddess not belonging to Uruk and dedicate to her people not belonging to her...
>
> After him a king (# 10) will arise in Uruk... He will establish the rites of the cult of Anu in Uruk. The old protective goddess of Uruk he will take away from Babylon and make dwell in Uruk, in her sanctuary. He will dedicate to her people belonging to her. He will rebuild the temples of Uruk. He will restore the sanctuaries.

Without exactly representing the "divine alienation – divine reconciliation" pattern (it is not the anger of the gods that makes them leave their proper sanctuaries), these passages clearly reflect similar thinking. The "Uruk Prophecy" not only strikingly resembles the above-quoted inscription of Nabonidus, but is even historically connected with it:[180] the king (# 2) who takes the *lamassu* of Uruk away probably refers to Eriba-Marduk[181] while the king (# 10) who brings it back is Nebuchadnezzar II (605-562).[182]

The "Uruk Prophecy" is closely paralleled also with a passage in the almost century older inscriptions of Assurbanipal concerning the returning of the goddess Nanaya to Uruk (A vi 107-124; cf. F v 72 – vi 11; T v 9-32):[183]

> Nanaya, who 1365 years (ago) became angry (*tasbušu*), went away and settled down in Elam in a place unworthy of her (*ašar lā simātīša*) – in those days (already) she and the gods, her fathers, appointed me to the kingship of the lands. She entrusted me with the returning of her godhead (saying): "Assurbanipal will take me away from the evil Elam and bring me back to Eanna." (This) word, their divine command (*amat qibīt ilūtīšun*[184]), that they had spoken (*iqbû*) since distant days, they now revealed (*ukallimū*) to the coming generation. I grasped the hands of her great divinity, and she, heart full of joy, took the shortest way to Eanna. In the month of Kislimu (IX), on the first day, I made her enter Uruk and settled her in an eternal sanctuary in her beloved Ehilianna.

---

[180] For the relationship between the Nabonidus inscription, the Uruk Prophecy and history, see Beaulieu 1993, 44-47.

[181] The exact regnal years of this king of Babylonia are unknown; his reign ended at some point before 760; see Frame 1995, 114.

[182] Thus already Hunger & Kaufman 1975, 373-374 and, again, Longman 1991, 148-149 and Beaulieu 1993, 45-47 contra the reservations of Lambert 1978, 10-12. Cf. Nebuchadnezzar's own account (Langdon 1912, 92 ii 50-54): "I reinstated the original cult features and the former rites of Ištar of Uruk, the Holy Lady of Uruk. I returned to Uruk her protective genius (*šēdūšu*) and to Eanna its beneficent protective goddess (*lamassa ša damiqti*)."

[183] Borger 1996, 57-58.

[184] Thus A vi 116; T v 24 (*-šunu*); other manuscripts have "her" (*-ša*). Respectively, A and T employ 3. plur. forms of the following verbs while other manuscripts have 3. fem. sing.; see Borger 1996, 58 *ad loc.*

The statue of Nanaya which had been transported to Elam in the distant past was recovered from Susa on the occasion of Assurbanipal's second campaign against the Elamite king Humban-haltaš III (c. 646[185]) who had refused to return it to Babylonia.[186] Assurbanipal takes the opportunity to get the credit for escorting it back to Uruk, representing himself as the one who has been predestined to accomplish this religious duty. According to the inscription, the gods had now revealed (*kullumu*) something that had been in force from time immemorial, though concealed from the earlier generations: "Assurbanipal will take me away from the evil Elam and bring me back to Eanna." The "word" (*amātu*) and "command" (*qibītu*) of the gods, or the goddess, is formulated as direct speech, the wording of which may well be a creation of the writer of the inscription. The close affinity of the passage to the "Uruk Prophecy" and other representatives of literary predictive texts strongly suggests that the writer, instead of prophecy,[187] had something similar to that genre in mind. The inscription follows, in a way, the "king-will-arise" pattern, that is, a variant of an idea of an age-old divine ordinance revealed as a *vaticinum ex eventu* to those for whom it is of current interest. This pattern is typical of the literary predictive texts (and may have influenced later apocalypticism[188]), but is not represented in the extant Neo-Assyrian prophecies.

In any case, the royal initiative in establishing cults and sanctuaries is an emphatically prophetic concern. Even though the role of prophecy in proclaiming divine alienation and reconciliation may be less decisive in Assyrian sources than it is in the Hebrew Bible, colleagues of Haggai and Zechariah, prophetic advocates of temple restoring, evidently existed in Assyria. This becomes probable from a prophetic exhortation from the time of Esarhaddon (SAA 9 2.3 ii 22-27):

> *dibbīja annūti issu libbi Arbail ina bētānukka esip*
> *ilāni ša Esaggil ina ṣēri lemni balli šarbubū arhiš šitta maqaluāti ina pānīšunu lušēṣiū lillikū šulamka liqbiū*
> *issu pī ša Lā-dāgil-ili arbailāja*
>
> Gather into your innards these words of mine from Arbela:
> The gods of Esaggil languish in the 'steppe' of stirred-up evil. Quickly let two burnt offerings be sent out to their presence, and let them go and announce your well-being!
> – From the mouth of La-dagil-ili from Arbela.

---

[185] On the date, see Frame 1992, 293-295.

[186] Streck 1916, 174-176 r.6-8 (cf. Borger 1996, 126); cf. Cogan 1974, 13-15.

[187] Laato 1996, 180 counts it among references to prophecy. Tadmor 1983, 50 also speaks here of "old prophecy" and its fulfillment and refers to a similar case in which Assurbanipal is predestined to restore Ehulhul, the temple of Sin in Harran (Borger 1996, 142 T ii 29-35); cf. also Gerardi 1987, 201-207.

[188] See Lambert 1978.

This passage belongs to the collection of prophecies from Esarhaddon's first regnal year[189] when the gods of Babylon were still in exile, and it lends support to the contention of Assurbanipal's inscription that the kings received prophetic orders concerning the re-establishment of the cult of deities who are "languishing" in a place where they do not belong. The solidarity of the prophet from Arbela with the cult of the gods of Esaggil is noteworthy: it shows that the rebuilding of Babylon, which Sennacherib had destroyed, was regarded by the prophets as such an important sign of divine reconciliation that it was imposed on Esarhaddon from the very beginning of his rule as a prerequisite for his "well-being" (*šulmu*).[190]

---

[189] For the date of SAA 9 2, see Parpola 1997c, LXIX.

[190] Cf. below, pp. 100-101. On Esarhaddon's problems in fulfilling this task, see, e.g., Brinkman 1984, 70-77.

2.3. Assurbanipal's Mannean and Elamite Wars

Texts

Prism A ii 126 – iii 26[191]

ii ^{126}*ina* 4-*e gir-ri-ia ad-ke* ERIM.HI-*ia* UGU ^{m}*ah-še-e-ri* ^{127}MAN KUR–*man-na-a-a uš-te-še-ra har-ra-nu ina qí-bit* AN.ŠÁR ^{d}30 ^{d}UTU ^{128} ^{d}IM $^{d+}$EN ^{d}AG ^{d}15 *šá* NINA.KI ^{d}GAŠAN–*kid-mu-ri* ^{d}15 *šá arba-ìl* ^{129} ^{d}MAŠ ^{d}U.GUR ^{d}PA.TÚG *qé-reb* KUR–*man-na-a-a e-ru-ub it-ta-lak šal-ṭiš* ^{130}URU.MEŠ-*šú dan-nu-ti a-di* TUR.MEŠ *šá ni-i-ba la i-šu-u* ^{131}*a-di qé-reb* URU.*i-zir-ti* KUR-*ud ap-pul aq-qur ina* ^{d}GIŠ.BAR *aq-mu* ^{132}UN.MEŠ ANŠE.KUR.RA.MEŠ ANŠE.MEŠ GU_4.MEŠ *u ṣe-e-ni* TA* *qé-reb* URU.MEŠ *šá-a-tú-nu* ^{133}*ú-še-ṣa-am-ma šal-la-tiš am-nu* ^{m}*ah-še-e-ri a-lak gir-ri-ia* ^{134}*iš-me-ma ú-maš-šir* URU.*i-zir-tu* URU LUGAL-*ti-šu* iii ^{1}*a-na* URU.*iš-ta-at-ti* URU KU-*ti-šú in-na-bit-ma e-hu-uz* ^{2}*mar-qí-tú na-gu-u šu-a-tú ak-šu-ud ma-lak* 10 UD-*me* 5 UD-*me* ^{3}*ú-šah-rib-ma šá-qu-um-ma-tú at-bu-uk* ^{4} ^{m}*ah-še-e-ri la pa-lih* EN-*ti-ia i-na a-mat* ^{d}15 ^{5}*a-ši-bat* URU.*arba-ìl ša* TA* *re-e-ši taq-bu-ú* ^{6}*um-ma a-na-ku mi-tu-tu* ^{m}*ah-še-e-ri* MAN KUR–*man-na-a-a* ^{7}*ki-i šá aq-bu-u ep-pu-uš ina* ŠU.2 ARAD.MEŠ-*šú tam-nu-šu-u-ma* ^{8}UN.MEŠ KUR-*šú si-hu* UGU-*šú ú-šab-šú ina* SILA URU-*šú* LÚ.*šá-lam-ta-šú* ^{9}*id-du-u in-da-áš-šá-ru pa-gar-šú* ^{10}ŠEŠ.MEŠ-*šú qin-nu-šú* NUMUN É AD-*šú ú-šam-qí-tú ina* GIŠ.TUKUL.MEŠ ^{11}EGIR-*nu* ^{m}*ú-al-li-i* DUMU-*šú ú-šib ina* GIŠ.GU.ZA-*šú* ^{12}*da-na-an* AN.ŠÁR ^{d}30 ^{d}UTU ^{d}IM $^{d+}$EN $^{d+}$AG ^{13} ^{d}15 *šá* NINA.KI ^{d}*šar-rat–kid-mu-ri* ^{14} ^{d}15 *šá arba-ìl*.KI ^{d}MAŠ ^{d}U.GUR ^{d}PA.TÚG ^{15}DINGIR.MEŠ GAL.MEŠ EN.MEŠ-*ia e-mur-ma* ^{16}*ik-nu-šá a-na* GIŠ.ŠUDUN-*ia* ^{17}*áš-šú ba-laṭ* ZI-*tim-šú up-na-a-šú ip-ta-a ú-ṣal-la-a* EN-*u-ti* ^{18} ^{m}*e-ri-si-in-ni* DUMU *ri-du-ti-šú* ^{19}*a-na* NINA.KI *iš-pur-am-ma ú-na-áš-ši-qa* GÌR.2-*ia* ^{20}*re-e-mu ar-ši-šu-u-ma* ^{21}LÚ.A–KIN-*ia šá šul-me ú-ma-'i-ir* EDIN-*uš-šú* ^{22}DUMU.MÍ *ṣi-it* ŠÀ-*bi-šú ú-še-bi-la a-na e-peš* MÍ.AGRIG-*u-ti* ^{23}*ma-da-at-ta-šú mah-ri-tú šá ina tir-ṣi* LUGAL.MEŠ AD.MEŠ-*ia* ^{24}*ú-šab-ṭi-lu iš-šu-u-ni a-di mah-ri-ia* ^{25}30 ANŠE.KUR.RA.MEŠ *e-li ma-da-ti-šú mah-ri-ti* ^{26}*ú-rad-di-i-ma e-mì-is-su*

^{126}In my fourth campaign I mobilized my troops and took the straightest way against Ahšeri, the king of Mannea. Upon the command of Aššur, Sin, Šamaš, Adad, Bel, Nabû, Ištar of Nineveh, the Lady of Kidmuri, Ištar of Arbela, Ninurta, Nergal and Nusku I entered in the midst of Mannea and triumphantly marched (through it). ^{130}I conquered, devastated, destroyed and burned with fire its fortified cities and its numberless small (towns) up to Izirtu. The people, horses, rams, bulls and sheep I removed from these cities and counted them among the booty.

^{133}Ahšeri fled when he heard my troops (coming) and left Izirtu, his royal residence. He fled to Ištatti, his stronghold, and sought shelter

---

[191] Borger 1996, 32-36. Cf. Streck 1916, 22-27.

there. I conquered this area, devastated a stretch of 15 days and brought about a complete silence.

^{4}Ištar, who dwells in Arbela, delivered Ahšeri, who did not fear my lordship, up to his servants, according to the word that she had said in the very beginning: "I will, as I have said, take care of the execution of Ahšeri, the king of Mannea." ^{8}The people of his country rose in rebellion against him, threw his corpse on the street of his city and hauled his corpse to and fro.[192] With weapons they beat his brothers, his family and his kinsmen down.

^{11}Afterwards his son Ualli ascended his throne. He acknowledged the authority of Aššur, Sin, Šamaš, Adad, Bel, Nabû, Ištar of Nineveh, the Lady of Kidmuri, Ištar of Arbela, Ninurta, Nergal, Nusku, the Great Gods, my lords, and submitted to my yoke. ^{17}For the sake of his life he opened his hands and implored my lordship. His crown prince Erisinni he sent to Nineveh (where) he kissed my feet. I was merciful to him and sent to him an envoy of peace. ^{22}He let bring me a daughter of his own offspring to be my housekeeper. His former tribute that he had interrupted in the time of the kings, my fathers, was brought to me (again). I added thirty horses to his former tribute and imposed (them) on him.

Prism B v 46-49, 77 – vi 16[193]

^{46}*in-he-ia šu-nu-hu-u-ti* ^{d}15 *iš-me-e-ma* ^{47}*la ta-pal-làh iq-ba-a ú-šar-hi-ṣa-an-ni* ŠÀ-*bu* ^{48}*a-na ni-iš* ŠU.2-*ka ša taš-šá-a* IGI.2-*ka im-la-a di-im-tú* ^{49}*ar-ta-ši re-e-mu*

> ^{46}Ištar heard my desperate sighs and said to me: "Have no fear!" She made my heart confident (saying): ^{48}"Because of the 'hand-lifting' prayer you said, your eyes being filled with tears, I have mercy upon you."

^{77}*ina* ITI.KIN *ši-pir* $^{d+}$INNIN.MEŠ *i-sin-ni* AN.ŠÁR MAH-*i-ri* ^{78}ITI ^{d}30 *na-an-nàr* AN-*e u* KI-*tim at-kil a-na* EŠ.BAR ^{79} ^{d}ŠEŠ.KI-*ri nam-ri u ši-pir* ^{d}15 GAŠAN-*ia ša la in-nen-nu-u* ^{80}*ad-ke* ERIM.MEŠ MÈ-*ia mun-dah-ṣe ša ina qí-bit* AN.ŠÁR ^{81} ^{d}30 *u* ^{d}15 *it-ta-na-áš-rab-bi-ṭu ina* MURUB$_4$ *tam-ha-ri* ^{82}*e-li* ^{m}*te-um-man* LUGAL KUR.NIM.MA.KI *ur-hu aṣ-bat-ma* ^{83}*uš-te-eš-še-ra har-ra-nu el-la-mu-u-a* ^{m}*te-um-man* LUGAL KUR.NIM.MA ^{84}*ina* URU.É–^{m}*im-bi-i na-di ma-dak-tu e-reb* LUGAL-*ti-ia* ^{85}*šá qé-reb* URU.BÀD.AN.KI *iš-me-e-ma iṣ-bat-su hat-tu* ^{86} ^{m}*te-um-man ip-làh-ma* EGIR-*šu i-tur e-ru-ub qé-reb* URU.*šu-šá-an* ^{87}KUG.UD KUG.GI *a-na šu-zu-ub* zi-*tim-šú* ^{88}*ú-za-ʾi-iz a-na* UN.MEŠ KUR-*šu* ^{89}*re-ṣe-e-šu a-lik* Á.2-*šu pa-nu-uš-šú ú-tir-ram-ma* ^{90}*ug-dáp-pi-šá a-na mah-ri-ia* ^{91}ÍD.*ú-la-a-a a-na dan-nu-ti-šú iš-kun* ^{92}*iṣ-bat pa-an maš-qé-e* ^{93}*ina qí-bit* AN.ŠÁR

---

[192] The verb *indaššarū* is understood as Gt of *mašāru* "to drag around" (CAD M 360 sub *mašāru* 5).

[193] Borger 1996, 100, 103-104. Cf. Streck 1916, 120-121.

^{d}AMAR.UTU DINGIR.MEŠ GAL.MEŠ EN.MEŠ-*ia* ^{94}*šá ú-tak-kil-ú-in-ni* ^{95}*ina* GISKIM.MEŠ SIG$_{5}$.MEŠ MÁŠ.GI$_{6}$ INIM.GAR *ši-pir mah-he-e* ^{96}*ina qé-reb* DU$_{6}$ URU.*tu-ba* IGI.IGI-*šú-nu aš-kun* ^{97}*ina* ADDA.MEŠ-*šú-nu* ÍD.*ú-la-a-a as-ki-ir* ^{98}*šal-ma-a-ti-šu-nu ki-ma* GIŠ.DÌH *u* GIŠ.KIŠI$_{16}$ ^{99}*ú-ma-al-la-a ta-mir-ti* URU.*šu-šá-an* $^{vi\ 1}$SAG.DU ^{m}*te-um-man* LUGAL KUR.NIM.MA.KI ^{2}*ina qí-bit* ^{d}AN.ŠÁR ^{d}AMAR.UTU DINGIR.MEŠ GAL.MEŠ EN.MEŠ-*ia* ^{3}KUD-*is ina* UKKIN ERIM.HI.A-*šú* ^{4}*mi-lam-me* ^{d}AN.ŠÁR *u* ^{d}15 KUR.NIM.MA.KI ^{5}*is-hu-up-ma ik-nu-šú a-na ni-ri-ia* ^{6} ^{m}*um-man-i-gaš ša in-nab-tu* ^{7}*iṣ-ba-tu* GÌR.2-*ia ina* GIŠ.GU.ZA-*šú ú-še-šib* ^{8} ^{m}*tam-ma-ri-tu* ŠEŠ-*šu šal-šá-a-a* ^{9}*ina* URU.*hi-da-a-lu ana* LUGAL-*u-ti áš-kun* ^{10}GIŠ.GIGIR.MEŠ GIŠ.*ṣu-um-bi* ANŠE.KUR.RA.MEŠ ANŠE. KUNGA.MEŠ ^{11}*ṣi-mit-ti ni-i-ri* GIŠ.*til-le si-mat* MÈ ^{12}*ša ina tu-kul-ti* AN.ŠÁR ^{d}15 DINGIR.MEŠ GAL.MEŠ EN.MEŠ-*ia* ^{13}*bi-rit* URU.*šu-šá-an u* ÍD.*ú-la-a-a ik-šu-da* ŠU.2-*a-a* ^{14}*ina qí-bit* AN.ŠÁR ^{d}AMAR.UTU DINGIR.MEŠ GAL.MEŠ EN.MEŠ-*ia* ^{15}*ul-tu qé-reb* KUR.NIM.MA.KI *ha-diš ú-ṣa-am-ma* ^{16}*a-na gi-mir* ERIM.HI.A-*ia ša-lim-tu šak-na-at*

^{77} In the month of Elul, (the month of) the messages of the goddesses (and) the feast of the exalted Aššur, the month of Sin, the light of heaven and earth, I trusted in the decision of the bright Luminary and in the unchanging message of Ištar, my lady. ^{80} I mobilized my combat forces, the fighters, who upon the command of Aššur, Sin and Ištar dashed into the heat of the fight. Against Teumman, the king of Elam, I made my way, taking the straightest route.

^{83} Teumman, the king of Elam, had encamped against me in Bit Imbi. When he heard of my royal entry into Der, he became horror-stricken. Teumman was afraid, turned around and withdrew to Susa. ^{87} To save his life he dispensed silver and gold to the people of his country. The henchmen who came to his rescue he returned (to the front?) and convened in front of me. (By) the river Ulaya he set up his stronghold and blocked off (the way to) the watering place.

^{93} Upon the command of Aššur and Marduk, the Great Gods, my lords, who encouraged me with good omens, dreams, speech omens and prophetic messages, I defeated him in Tell Tuba. With their corpses I stuffed up Ulaya. With their corpses, as if with thorn and thistle, I filled the outskirts of Susa. $^{vi\ 1}$ Upon the command of Aššur and Marduk, the Great Gods, my lords, I cut off the head of Teumman, the king of Elam, before his assembled troops. The splendor of Aššur and Ištar beat (the people of) Elam down and they submitted to my yoke.

^{6} Humban-nikaš, who had fled and grasped my feet, I seated upon his throne. Tammaritu, the third among his brothers, I placed in the kingship of Hidalu. Chariots, wagons, horses, mules, draft animals, weapons carriers(?) and (other) matériel which my hands, trusting in Aššur and Ištar, the Great Gods, my lords, captured between Susa and Ulaya – upon the command of Aššur, Marduk and the Great Gods I joyfully left Elam (carrying off this booty). My entire army was well.

Background

The first of the above-quoted excerpts belongs to a passage of Prism A reporting on Assurbanipal's successful campaign against the Manneans, a people living in the northwestern Iran, south of Lake Urmia. His war against Ahšeri, the king of Mannea, is also recorded in Prisms B, C, D, F and H,[194] of which the accounts of B and C are the most extensive and more detailed than others. However, Prism A is the only one containing a reference to prophecy.

The historical records of Mannea span from the 9th century, when Mannea was from time to time invaded by Urartian and Assyrian kings (Shalmaneser III, Tiglath-Pileser III), down to the Median conquests in the 7th century when the Manneans disappear from history.[195] During the reigns of Sargon and Sennacherib Mannea was not incorporated into Assyrian territory. Esarhaddon, in his inscriptions, makes a laconic note about "scattering" (*sapāhu* D) the Manneans.[196] His military actions against them are indeed the subject of a series of oracle queries (SAA 4 28-34),[197] and his correspondence with Bel-ušezib shows that he, though vacillating about undertaking the campaign because he was uncertain about the intentions of the Cimmerians in that quarter (SAA 10 111),[198] captured fortresses and plundered cities of the Manneans in the year 675 (SAA 10 112).[199]

It remains uncertain to what extent Esarhaddon succeeded in exercising control over Mannea. The victory over the Manneans cannot have been a total one, since there were several districts and cities claimed by the Assyrians which, according to Assurbanipal's Prisms B and C, were taken by the Manneans in the time of his predecessors.[200] These cities include Šarru-iqbi,[201] the subject of one of Esarhaddon's queries concerning his Mannean expedition (SAA 4 29). Obviously the reltionship of Assyria with the Manneans was not yet settled when Assurbanipal became king.

Even though Assurbanipal conventionally presents the disloyalty of Ahšeri, the king of Mannea, as the basic reason for the war,[202] the territorial claims may have given the impetus to undertake the campaign. This can be

---

[194] B: Piepkorn 1933, 50-57 iii 16 - iv 2; C: Bauer 1933, 15 iv 31-62; D: Piepkorn 1933, 97; F: Aynard 1957, 36-39 ii 21-52; H: Nassouhi 1924/25, 102-103.

[195] See Postgate 1987/90, 340-341.

[196] Borger 1956 (§ 21) 34:30; (§ 27) 52 A iii 59; cf. (§ 66) 100:21.

[197] See Starr 1990, LIX-LX.

[198] See Fales & Lanfranchi 1981 and cf. below, pp. 96-99.

[199] Cf. below, pp. 96-97, 146.

[200] Borger 1996, 34-35 B iii 52-81//C iv 65-90; see also Mayer 1995, 387, 402.

[201] Borger 1996, 35 B iii 71//C iv 82.

[202] Borger 1996, 34 B iii 17-19: *Ahšēri šar māt Mannāja... ša ana šarrāni abīja lā kitnušu itappalu dāṣāti* "Ahšeri, the king of Mannea,... who was not loyal to the kings, my fathers, and was constantly looking for trouble." A "moral judgment" of this kind is part and parcel of the Assyrian "ideology of *nakrūtu*"; cf. Fales 1982, 428-430.

confirmed by one of Assurbanipal's three extant queries concerning the Mannean war (SAA 4 267-269) in which the territorial motivation is expressed with unambiguous words (SAA 4 267 r.7-11 [cf. lines 2-7]):

> I ask you, Šamaš, great lord, whether Nabû-šarru-uṣur, chief eunuch, and the men, horses, and army of Assurbanipal, king of Assyria at his disposal, should go to recover the Assyrian fortresses which the Manneans conquered, and whether he, be it by waging war, or through friendliness and peaceful negotiations, or by whatever tricks, will recover those fortresses.

The answer of Šamaš must have been a firm positive one, since the troops of Assurbanipal, presumably under the command of his chief eunuch Nabû-šarru-uṣur,[203] invaded Mannea and forced their way as far as Izirtu, the Mannean royal capital. According to Grayson's chronological sketch this happened in the year 660 approximately; a more precise dating is impossible.[204]

Prisms B and C, probably correctly, present Assurbanipal as successful in reannexing the lost areas to Assyria. All relevant inscriptions are unanimous about the fate of Ahšeri, the king of Mannea – he was killed in a revolt by his own people and his dead body was desecrated[205] – but only Prism A mentions the (prophetic) word of Ištar of Arbela as the ultimate reason for Ahšeri's death.[206] The inscriptions also agree in reporting that Ahšeri's throne was ascended by his son Ualli who demonstrated his pacific intentions by starting to pay again the tribute to Assyria which had been withheld by his predecessor(s) and to which now 30 horses were added, and sending his son Erisinni, the crown prince, and one of his daughters to the Assyrian court.[207] So, an alliance based on the vassalage of Ualli was established according to the best rules of the game. There are no records of further problems between Assyria and Mannea.

The second reference to prophecy belongs to a lengthy account in Prisms B and C[208] of Assurbanipal's campaign against Teumman, king of Elam, of which only two excerpts are cited above.

---

[203] For him, see also below, pp. 148-149, nn. 554-555. Nabû-šarru-uṣur was to be in charge of Assurbanipal's intended actions against Gambulu as well (cf. SAA 4 270-271).

[204] Grayson 1980, 230, 233; cf. Starr 1990, LXXV, n. 267. The year ±660 suggests itself because 1) the Mannean war must have taken place between Assurbanipal's first Egyptian campaign (667) and the Šamaš-šumu-ukin revolt (652-648), 2) it is preceded by half a dozen other campaigns, provided that the chronological order of the inscriptions is correct, and 3) it is not included in the so-called Harran Tablet (Streck 1916, 158-175) which was composed in 664/3 at the earliest (see Cogan & Tadmor 1977, 81).

[205] Borger 1996, 35 B iii 82-85//C iv 91-94//F ii 38-40.

[206] Borger 1996, 35 A iii 4-10.

[207] Borger 1996, 35-37 A iii 11-26//B iii 86 – iv 2//C iv 95-129//F ii 41-52; cf. J 4; H iii 1-9; see also Mayer 1995, 402-403.

[208] Borger 1996, 97-105 B iv 87 – vi 16//C v 93-114 – vii 9. A shorter version of the episode can be found in Prisms A, F and H (Borger 1996, 37-39 A iii 27-49//F ii 53-71; 190 H3 iii 1-5). Also, SAA 3 31 (cf. Bauer 1933, 70) gives a short account of the events.

Esarhaddon had established peaceful relations with the Elamites by concluding a treaty with Urtaku, the king of Elam, in the year 674.[209] Assurbanipal's troubles with the Elamites began when Urtaku, in the year 664 at the latest,[210] invaded Babylonia with the support of Bel-iqiša, ruler of the Gambulu tribe, Nabû-šumu-ereš, the governor of Nippur,[211] and Marduk-šumu-ibni, a Babylonian general of Urtaku. Even if the invasion of Urtaku to Babylonia came as a total surprise to Assurbanipal which, together with false messages of goodwill by Urtaku's ambassador in Assyria, caused some delay in mobilizing his troops, the attack was beaten off.[212] Urtaku and his three allies all died in that year. Assurbanipal took Nippur under his direct control.[213] The Elamite throne was seized by Teumman (Tepti-Humban-Inšušinak) whom Assurbanipal calls "image of a demon" (*gallu*).[214] He was not the legitimate heir, and the inscription of Assurbanipal suggests that his usurpation was not a bloodless one: three sons of Urtaku, Humban-nikaš, Ummanappa[215] and Tammaritu, together with two sons of the former king Humban-haltaš II, 60 further members of the royal family and other Elamite aristocracy, had to take flight to Assyria escaping "the murders of Teumman."[216]

---

[209] Borger 1956 (§ 27) 58-59:26-33. The subject of the query SAA 4 74 is the honesty of the peace initiative of Urtaku, and the peace negotiations are referred to in ABL 328:9-15. In ABL 918 Esarhaddon calls Urtaku his "brother" (see Parpola & Watanabe 1988, XVII). On the relations of Esarhaddon with the Elamites, see Brinkman 1984, 78-79; Carter & Stolper 1984, 49; Gerardi 1987, 249-250; Grayson 1991, 130-132; Mayer 1995, 385-386.

[210] The year 664 suggests itself, if the deposition of Urtaku and the flight of the members of the Elamite royal family, datable to 664 on the basis of a chronicle entry concerning the flight of an Elamite prince, probably Humban-nikaš, to Assyria (see below n. 216), belong to the consequences of Urtaku's invasion; see Brinkman 1984, 87 (n. 423), 91. Dietrich 1970, 66 and Carter & Stolper 1984, 50 suggest that the campaign was undertaken a year before (665). On the other hand, Grayson (1980, 230; 1991, 147), on the basis of an inscriptional fragment (Rm 281; see Borger 1996, 26-27) which indicates that Urtaku attacked while Assurbanipal was in Egypt, dates the campaign to 667 when Assurbanipal's first Egyptian campaign took place. However, another inscriptional passage claims that Assurbanipal was in Assyria when Urtaku attacked (Borger 1996, 95 B iv 35-38). See the discussion in Gerardi 1987, 127-130; Frame 1992, 119 n. 93.

Recently, Mayer 1995, 410-411 has suggested a date as late as 655, assuming that Urtaku's Babylonian invasion took place only after Assurbanipal's Mannean war and contemporaneously with the revolt of Psammetich in Egypt, which, according to him, happened in 656/5.

[211] For Nabû-šumu-ereš, see Cole 1996, 54.

[212] Borger 1996, 94-96 B iv 18-53//C v 24-61. For this battle, see also Brinkman 1984, 91-92; Gerardi 1987, 122-134; Grayson 1991, 147; Frame 1992, 119-121; Mayer 1995, 404-405.

[213] See Cole 1996, 74.

[214] Borger 1996, 97 B iv 74//C v 80.

[215] No Elamite equivalent of this name is attested.

[216] Borger 1996, 96-97 B iv 54-86//C v 62-92. The flight of an Elamite prince on the 12th of Tishri (VII), 664 is also recorded in the Šamaš-šumu-ukin chronicle (Grayson 1975a, 128:2-3), generally understood as referring to Humban-nikaš, the son of Urtaku.

The presence of the Elamite establishment under the protection of Assurbanipal, including the legitimate crown prince and his brothers, certainly did not promise well for Teumman's attitudes towards Assyria.[217] That the loyalty of the Gambulu tribe, who lived in the buffer zone between Elam and Babylonia and was allied with Urtaku, also was questionable, is demonstrated by a series of oracle queries of Assurbanipal from the years 658 and 657 in which he asks whether he should send the chief eunuch Nabû-šarru-uṣur to teach the Gambuleans a lesson (SAA 4 270-273).[218] There are no records confirming that this campaign actually took place; nevertheless, Dunanu, the leader of the Gambuleans and the son of Bel-iqiša, was without doubt allied with Teumman.[219]

According to the inscription, the hostilities finally broke out because Assurbanipal rejected the repeated demands of Teumman to extradite the Elamite princes to whom he had granted asylum.[220] In fact, it is not quite clear when Teumman delivered his ultimatums; for the purposes of the inscription they constitute a suitable *casus belli*, showing the arrogance of the enemy. It is possible that the war against Teumman was at least partly initiated by the exiled princes of Elam; a letter of Assurbanipal to the Elamite elders states explicitly that Humban-nikaš himself took part in the war.[221] Presumably it was also Assurbanipal's intention to install Elamite protégés in the kingship of Elam and in this way eliminate the political threat from that direction.[222]

Although, according to the inscription, Teumman was struck by severe physical symptoms well recognizable as unfavorable portents, he assembled his troops against Assyria. Whether or not he actually invaded Assyrian territory is not clear;[223] in any case, his manoeuvers turned out to be a total

217 According to Gerardi 1987, 134, Assurbanipal's acceptance of the members of Urtaku's family under his protection suggests an "immediate antipathy toward Te-Umman."

218 The name of the eponym has been preserved in SAA 4 271 (Ša-Nabû-šû = 658) and 272 (Labasi = 657). SAA 4 270 and 273 are likely to belong to the same period (Aro 1966, 117). For the evidence concerning the Assyrian dominion at that time over Nippur, the governor of which was also allied with Urtaku, see Brinkman 1984, 92 n. 455; Frame 1992, 121; Cole 1996, 74-78.

219 Borger 1996, 105-106 B vi 17-20, 39-42//C vii 10-14, 36-39.

220 Borger 1996, 97-98 B iv 87 – v 3//C v 93-114; cf. also SAA 3 31:4-9.

221 BM 132980:8ff (quoted from Parpola & Watanabe 1988, xx): "When Humban-nikaš came and grasped my feet, and I sent my troops with him, and they fought with Teumman, did we set out [sic!] feet in the temples, cities, or anywhere? Did we take plunder? Did we not pour oil upon blood and become your benefactors?" With regard to the inscriptional account on the bloodshed during the battle and the substantial amount of booty carried off from Elam, these rhetorical quetions of Assurbanipal have a rather propagandistic sound.

222 See Gerardi 1987, 149-150.

223 SAA 3 31:11-13 indicates that his final goal was Nineveh, but this is to be interpreted as a description of his arrogance rather than a historical evidence of his military strategy. Gerardi 1987, 146-147 points out that there is no mention of an Elamite attack in the Assyrian or Babylonian territory.

disaster. When the Assyrian forces reached Der, a city on the Elamite-Babylonian border, Teumman retreated to Susa, his capital, and tried to block off the way of the Assyrians at the river Ulaya (modern Karkheh or Karun[224]). The Elamite troops were crushed in a massacre at Tell Tuba.[225] Teumman's head was cut and later put on display in Nineveh,[226] and the royal dynasty of Elam was rehabilitated by Assurbanipal who let the exiled prince Humban-nikaš (II) seize the throne of his father and gave his brother Tammaritu the kingship of Hidalu, east of Susa.[227] In practical terms, this campaign which most probably took place in 653,[228] led to the virtual annexation of Elam to Assyria.[229] Humban-nikaš and Tammaritu were nothing but puppet kings obliged to pay tax and tribute to Assyria[230] and to swear loyalty to Assurbanipal.[231] The victorious campaign against Elam was followed by another against Gambulu with very similar results: Dunanu, the ally of Teumman, surrendered, was taken captive, and the freshly cut head of Teumman was hung around his neck; the Gambulean capital Ša-pi-bel was totally destroyed and a large amount of booty, including the inhabitants of the country, was taken to Assyria.[232]

The defeat of Elam and Gambulu did not stabilize the political situation. The revolt of Assurbanipal's brother Šamaš-šumu-ukin broke out the very next year and won immediately the support of Humban-nikaš II whose loyalty

---

[224] See Parpola 1970b, 406.

[225] See Parpola 1970b, 355.

[226] Borger 1996, 107 B vi 66-69/C vii 63-66. Cf. also SAA 3 31 r.8-9 and the illustration in Livingstone 1989, 68 showing Teumman's head hanging from a tree (BM 124920).

[227] For the location, see the literature in Frame 1992, 122 n. 111.

[228] The lunar eclipse preceding the war and referred to in Prism B v 5-6 is dated by Mayr to July 13, 653 (see Piepkorn 1933, 105-109 and cf. Parpola 1983, 383, 403). An earlier date, August 663, is suggested by F. R. Stephenson in Reade & Walker 1981/82, 122. However, according to Prism B, the eclipse in question took place in the fourth month of the Babylonian year as it actually did in the year 653, whereas the eclipse of 663 took place in the fifth month; see Gerardi 1987, 144-145; Frame 1992, 123-124, n. 112.

[229] See Carter & Stolper 1984, 51, 53; Parpola & Watanabe 1988, XX-XXI. In SAA 4 274:2 Assurbanipal is called "the king of Elam." The political status of Elam after the year 653 is also lucidly reflected by the letter ABL 839, the writer of which, Nabû-bel-šumati, suggests that the king "should place one of the princes among his servants to the governorship (*pāhatūtu*) of Elam." See Mattila 1987.

[230] SAA 3 31 r.12-17: "[By] the might of my gods and their [*righteous*] command, [I established] a [cre]ation of my own hands to kingship over them ([*ši*]*kin qātēja ana šarrūti ina muhhīšunu* [*assakan*]). [By the command] of Aššur, Bel, Nabû, Nergal, Ištar of [Nineveh], and the Lady of Arbela I unified (the whole) of Elam; I settled Assyrians [there], and imposed tax and tribute upon them."

[231] Assurbanipal, in his letter to Tammaritu, writes: "What (even) a father does not do for a son, I have [done] and given to you! As for you, remember [this], strive to return to me in full these favours [that I have done to you], and keep the [treaty] that I have made you swear before the gods of heaven and earth!" (ABL 1022 r. 19-23.)

[232] Borger 1996, 105-106 B vi 17-56//C vii 10-54; cf. Gerardi 1987, 154-147.

to Assurbanipal, hence, turned out to be of a less than durable nature.[233] The revolt was also supported by the Gambuleans.[234]

The account of the defeat of Teumman follows roughly the same pattern as that of Ahšeri, the king of Mannea: the horrified enemy tries to reach safety in a stronghold but cannot escape his destiny determined by the Great Gods of Assyria who use the king Assurbanipal as a tool of their unchanging will, according to which the enemy is executed and his throne is given to a loyal puppet. Only the general tone of the Elam account is more verbose and excited, and special attention is paid to divine messages of different kinds that encouraged Assurbanipal to undertake the campaign. This may be at least partly due to the fact that Prism B was written in the year 649,[235] i.e., only four years after the described events happened. At that time the Šamaš-šumu-ukin revolt was in full swing, and the Elamites were deeply involved in it. The situation in Elam, however, was changing constantly. In the meantime Tammaritu (II?[236]) had rebelled, killed Humban-nikaš II and replaced him on the throne of Elam. Tammaritu, too, supported Šamaš-šumu-ukin, but when he, in turn, was replaced in a rebellion by Indabibi he, surprisingly enough, sought shelter in Assyria.[237] This happened during the year 649, and in the same year Assurbanipal wrote to Indabibi calling him his "brother" (ABL 1151) which indicates that a treaty between the two had been concluded.[238] The reign of Indabibi lasted only until he was overthrown by Humban-haltaš III some time before or after the fall of Babylon in 648.[239] Since Prism B mentions Indabibi but not Humban-haltaš III, its editing obviously took place earlier than the latter staged his coup. It can be concluded for certain that the relations between Assyria and Elam were anything but stable at that time. In the course of the following years, Assurbanipal would launch two further offensives against Humban-haltaš III.[240]

---

[233] On the involvement of the Elamites in the Šamaš-šumu-ukin revolt, see Frame 1992, 182-186.

[234] On the Gambuleans, see Frame 1992, 169-170.

[235] The manuscript is dated by eponym; see Grayson 1980, 245; Gerardi 1987, 57-58.

[236] This person is not necessarily identical with the Tammaritu (I) who was installed by Assurbanipal at Hidalu; see Dietrich 1970, 78 n. 3.

[237] Borger 1996, 41-42 A iv 1-10, 110-112; B vii 43-76.

[238] For the events of that year, see Dietrich 1970, 104-107; Carter & Stolper 1984, 51; Gerardi 1987, 179; Grayson 1991, 151-152; Frame 1992, 184-186.

[239] Grayson 1991, 152 considers it possible that Indabibi was overthrown already in 649; Frame 1992, 186, however, finds no clear evidence that Humban-haltaš III might have been on the throne of Elam already during the Šamaš-šumu-ukin revolt.

[240] See Carter & Stolper 1984, 51-53; Brinkman 1984, 101-103; Gerardi 1987, 181-194; Frame 1992, 204-205 and (concerning the date) 293-295.

Prophecy

That prophecy is referred to in the inscriptional passages concerning Assurbanipal's second Elamite war is ascertained by the expression *šipir mahhê* (B v 95). In the case of the Mannean war, again, there is a quotation of a "word of Ištar, who dwells in Arbela, which she had said from the very beginning: 'I will, as I have said, take care of the execution of Ahšeri, the king of Mannea.'" (*amat Ištār āšibat Arbail ša issu rēši taqbû umma anāku mītūtu Ahšēri šar māt Mannāja kî ša aqbû eppuš*) (A iii 4-7). In theory, other kinds of divination cannot be excluded as the source of this oracle;[241] since, however, *ab/mat* DN is one of the standard opening formulae of Neo-Assyrian prophetic speeches, Ištar of Arbela being their sender *par excellence*,[242] prophecy remains the most probable alternative.

In the report on the defeat of Ahšeri the quotation of the prophecy is embedded in a grammatically complicated sentence concerning the death of the Mannean king and the desecration of his corpse. The quotation is a double flashback to the words of Ištar, who "right from the beginning" (*issu rēši*) – i.e., probably, the beginning of the warfare – had promised to take care of the death of Ahšeri, referring to a similar, still earlier word (*kî ša aqbû*). This is not so much an example of a prediction-fulfillment pattern – which is indeed attested in the case of the returning of the statue of Nanaya to Uruk[243] – than a reminder of a divine promise that has now been carried out.[244] The quotation of the word of Ištar is the only reference to any kind of divination in the account of the Mannean war, save the general statement about the command of the Great Gods who, according to B iii 32, "encouraged" (*utakkilūni*) the king.

If the Ahšeri episode is rather sparing with references to divination, the Teumman episode overflows with them. This, together with the intense tone of the report in general, may be due to the turbulence of the time when Prism B was composed.[245]

---

[241] Weippert 1981, 98: "Freilich kann der hier zitierte Spruch eventuell auch Auslegung eines technischen Orakels sein."

[242] SAA 9 2.4 ii 30 (Ištar of Arbela & Mullissu), ii 38 (Ištar of [Arbela]); 3.4 ii 33 (Ištar of Arbela); 3.5 iii 16 (Ištar of Arbela); 5:1 (Ištar of Arbela); 7:2 (Mullissu). For the formula, see Weippert 1981, 76-77; Parpola 1997c, LXV.

[243] A vi 107-124; see above, pp. 40-41 and cf. Laato 1996, 181, 188.

[244] Cf. SAA 9 1.1 i 15-17: *ajjūte dibbīja ša aqabakanni ina muhhi lā tazzizūni* "What words have I spoken to you that you could not rely upon?"; 9 1.10 vi 7-12: *dabābu pāniu ša aqabakanni ina muhhi lā tazzīzi ūmâ ina muhhi urkī'i tazzazma* "Could you not rely on the previous utterance which I spoke to you? Now you can rely on this later one too." Comparable assurances of past and future divine support are common in the corpus of the Neo-Assyrian prophecies; see Parpola 1997c, LXVI.

[245] Gerardi 1987, 149 thinks that the recounting of the celestial omens and theophanies served the purpose of justifying Assurbanipal's replacing of Teumman by the Elamite princes that were under his protection.

The passage reporting on the battle against Teumman (B v 77 – vi 16) is preceded by a thorough account of the events leading to the war (B v 3-76).[246] Here the divine messages play a decisive role. The gods send evil portents – celestial phenomena and physical injuries – to Teumman who does not take heed of them (B v 3-14). Assurbanipal, for his part, takes part in an Ištar festival in Arbela, "her beloved city" (*āl narām libbīša*) in the month of Ab (V). Shedding tears the king implores the goddess, "the lady of the ladies, the goddess of warfare, the lady of battle" (*bēlet bēlēti ilat qabli bēlet tāhāzi*) to nullify Teumman's schemes (B v 15-46).[247] His nightly[248] prayer does not remain unanswered (B v 46-49):

> *inhēja šūnuhūti Ištār išmēma lā tapallah iqbâ ušarhiṣanni libbu*
> *ana nīš qātēka ša taššâ ēnāka imlâ dimtu artaši rēmu*
>
> Ištar heard my desperate sighs and said to me: "Have no fear!" She made my heart confident (saying): "Because of the 'hand-lifting' prayer you said, your eyes being filled with tears, I have mercy upon you."

This "Erhörungsorakel,"[249] possibly paraphrased in SAA 3 31:18 as well,[250] shares many features with the extant prophecies.[251] Not only the "fear not" formula is without doubt the best known distinguishing mark of Neo-Assyrian prophecies,[252] but the verb *qabû* also generally introduces prophecies, and "giving confidence" (usually, though, expressed with *takālu* D) belongs to their standard phraseology. Furthermore, the reference to the king's prayer has a parallel in the oracle of Ištar of Arbela to the queen mother Naqija (SAA 9 1.8): *kî tahhurīninni mā* "Because you implored me, saying..." All this gives good reason to define this speech as a prophetic one.

Still in the same night (*ina šāt mūši šuātu*), the answer of Ištar is followed by a divine message of another kind. A person called *šabrû* has a dream (*šuttu*), a theophany of Ištar of Arbela who promises to undertake the warfare (B v 49-76).[253] This verbosely reported dream explains and reinforces the

---

[246] Cf. C v 115 – vi 78. The lines B v 15-76 are also paralleled by K 2652 and a few other manuscripts; see Borger 1996, 101-103.

[247] Cf. SAA 3 31:13-17: "When I heard [this piece of insolence], I opened my hands (in supplication) to [Ištar, the lady of Arbela], saying: 'I am Assurbanipal, whom [your] own father, [Aššur, engende]red. I have [come] to worship you; why is [Teu]mman fa[lling] upon me?'"

[248] Cf. B v 49: "in that same night..."

[249] Thus Weippert 1981, 97. The prayer, paralleled by the lamentation of Esarhaddon during the civil war (Borger 1956 [§ 27] 43:53-62; cf. above, pp. 24, 25) provides itself as a further representative of a "Gebet um Abwendung der Not" for which see Zobel 1971.

[250] *[Issār taqṭib]anni mā anāku ana qab[si x x x x]* "[Ištar sa]id to me: 'I myself [...] in the centre of [...].'"

[251] This has been noted by Fales & Lanfranchi 1997, 109.

[252] See, e.g., Nissinen 1993, 247-248; Parpola 1997c, LXVI.

[253] For this passage, see Oppenheim 1956, 249; cf. also Wilson 1980, 113; Weippert 1981, 97-98; Millard 1985, 130; Gerardi 1987, 145-147.

foregoing prophecy. Noteworthy in the dream is the idea that it is the goddess who goes to war, while the king plays only an insignificant part, if any at all (B v 61-68):

> You said to her: "Wherever you go, I will go with you!" But the Lady of Ladies answered you: "You stay here in your place! Eat food, drink beer, make merry and praise my godhead, until I go to accomplish that task, making you attain your heart's desire." She sheltered you in her sweet embrace, she protected your entire body.

While the maternal characteristics of the protection of Ištar are common in the prophecies,[254] the idea of the king's inactivity is to be found in them as well (SAA 9 2.4 iii 11 and SAA 9 11 r.4-5):[255]

> *atta lū qālāka Aššūr-ahu-iddina*
>
> As for you, keep silent, Esarhaddon!
>
> *nakru akaššad ša Aššūr-bāni-apli [x x x x x x]*
> *mā šībi mātāti utaqq[an x x x x x]*
>
> I will vanquish the enemy of Assurbanipal [...]
> Sit down! I will put the lands in orde[r!...]

We have already seen that the idea of the gods as the primary warlords is part and parcel of the line of thought of the inscriptions and the prophecies alike.[256] The total passivity of the king turns this idea into a hyperbole, the purpose of which is to make the essential point of the ideology of Holy War crystal clear: every justified war is a divine war in which the human armies are nothing but tools in the hands of the gods and can act only upon their command.[257]

That the king is not really intended to remain idle is obvious from what follows: in the next month of Elul (VI) Assurbanipal goes off to the war. However, he does not start it on his own initiative but upon the command (*ina qibīt*) of Aššur, Sin and Ištar (B v 80-81) delivered to him by means of astrology (*nannari namri*) and prophecy (*šipir Ištār bēltīja*).[258] The same

---

[254] See Nissinen 1993, 242-247. In this context, the motherly attitude of Ištar has been noted by Fales & Lanfranchi 1997, 110.

[255] This idea is represented in the Hebrew Bible as well (Ex 14:14): "Yahweh will fight for you, you keep silent!" Cf. also SAA 9 1.1 i 24-27: *lā tapallah atta ina libbi muggi anāku ina libbi ū'a atabbi uššab* "Fear not! You are paralyzed, but in the midst of woe I will rise and sit down." This assertion, however, has a different nuance, since it refers to the situation when Esarhaddon was expatriated and really incapable of acting (see above, pp. 25-27).

[256] See above, pp. 25-28 and cf. Weippert 1972, 466-468.

[257] For this ideology in general, see e.g. Weippert 1972 and van der Spek 1993.

[258] On the expression *ina qibīt* as a reference to any means by which divine order and support was obtained, see Fales & Lanfranchi 1997, 104-105.

idea is expressed in the response of Aššur to Assurbanipal's report on the Šamaš-šumu-ukin revolt (SAA 3 44 r.22):

> [*ina*] *amat ilūtīja aqbīkama atta ēpuš*
>
> I spoke to you [with] my divine word and you acted.

The correct timing of the divine messages is also hemerologically ascertained: they have been obtained in the month of the "messages of the goddesses" (*šipir ištarāti*) – an expression that in all likelihood refers to prophetic activity. Under such circumstances the war could only be expected to be victorious, thus the result comes up to all expectations:

> *ina qibīt Aššūr Marduk ilāni rabûti bēlānīja ša utakkilūni ina ittāti damqāti šutti egerrê šipir mahhê ina qereb Til-Tuba abiktašunu aškun*
>
> Upon the command of Aššur and Marduk, the Great Gods, my lords, who encouraged me with good omens, dreams, speech omens and prophetic messages, I defeated him in Tell Tuba.

While this statement strikes one like a nutshell manifesto of the Assyrian ideology of Holy War, it also presents prophecy in a customary way: as an integral part of divination, yet classified as a category in its own right. The list of the forms of divination should not be taken as a random sample of synonyms for fortune-telling – on the contrary, it indicates that the inscriptionists really knew the difference between them. Admittedly, though, there are cases where the borderline between prophecy and visionary experiences remains vague. In the Teumman episode, as we have briefly seen, a piece of divine speech which for good reasons can be defined as a prophetic one is immediately followed by a dream which is a theophany experienced by a *šabrû* rather than direct divine speech.[259] A dream of a *šabrû* – provided that the sign LÚ.KAL actually stands for *šabrû*[260] – is also reported in the inscriptions of Assurbanipal in connection with the Šamaš-šumu-ukin revolt (A iii 118-127):[261]

> At that time a *šabrû* (LÚ.KAL) was sleeping in the middle of the night (*ina šāt mūši*) and had a dream: It stood written on the pedestal of Sin: "Whoever has evil plans against Assurbanipal and picks a quarrel (with him) – these people I will finish off with an evil death. I will make an end of their life with a swift sword, a rain of fire, famine and pestilence." I heard (this) and trusted in the word (*amat*) of Sin.

---

259 Cf. Parpola 1997c, XLVII.

260 See Wilson 1980, 113-114; Huffmon 1992, 480. Borger 1996, 40 (cf. Oppenheim 1956, 249) transcribes LÚ.GURUŠ (*eṭlu*) and translates "ein Mann" (p. 233).

261 Borger 1996, 40-41; cf. Weippert 1972, 471-472, and Dijkstra 1980, 150-151 who points out the similarity of this dream and the response of Aššur to Assurbanipal (SAA 3 44).

This dream, like the one in the Teumman episode, is a report of an audio-visual experience, even though it is difficult to make a distinction between its visual and acoustic aspect; apparently the message is thought to have been seen and heard simultaneously.

The title *šabrû*, probably derived from *barû*,[262] can be defined as a visionary, designating a person who, to quote CAD, "acts as a seer beside *raggimu, maḫḫû*, etc."[263] The interpretative connotation is suggested by a text in which a *šabrû* is told to repeat the words of a *zabbu* ("ecstatic").[264] A Neo-Assyrian lexical text equates *raggimu* and *šabrû*,[265] while *mahhû* and *šabrû* appear close to each other in the omen series Šumma alu.[266] It is discernible from this evidence that the *šabrû* constitutes a distinctive class, closely comparable to the prophets without being identical with them.[267] The realm of the *šabrû* apparently consists of visionary dreams and their interpretation, while the prophets act as mouthpieces of the gods delivering their words in the form of direct speech. That this distinction was actually made is evident from the fact that dreams and prophecies are classified as separate categories, not only in the above-quoted passage but elsewhere, too.[268] This is not to say that prophets would not have seen visions (*diglu*) and dreams (*šuttu*) – prophets certainly appear as visionaries and dreamers[269] but every visionary and dreamer is not a prophet.[270]

For the scholars who composed the inscriptions of Assurbanipal, the functional difference between prophets and dreamers seems not to have been decisive; while acknowledging the distinction, they utilize the divine messages of prophets and dreamers side by side for equal purposes. Dreams play

---

[262] According to CAD Š/1 15, the word may either "have been secondarily etymologized as derived from the verb *barû*, or may have been a true derivative of *barû*" (see also Wilson 1980, 112-113).

[263] CAD Š/1 15.

[264] LKA 29d ii 2 (Ebeling 1953, 39): *zabbu liqbâkkima šabrû lišannakki* "Let the *zabbu* tell you, the *šabrû* repeat it to you."

[265] MSL 12 226:134: lú.šabra (PA.AL) = ŠU-*u* = *rag-gi-*[*mu*]; see also Parpola 1997c, XLVI, CIV n. 231.

[266] CT 38 4 81-82: "If there appear many prophets (LÚ.GUB.BA.MEŠ) in a city... If there appear many prophetesses (LÚ.MÍ.GUB.BA.MEŠ) in a city"; CT 38 4 87-88: "If there appear many *šabrû*s in a city... If there appear many female *šabrû*s in a city."

[267] Huffmon 1992, 480 actually notes the difference even if he lists *šabrû* among the prophetic titles.

[268] Cf. also Borger 1956 (§ 2) 2 ii 12-22.

[269] SAA 9 11 combines a prophetic oracle with a *diglu* (lines 6ff), and the reluctant prophet consulted by Urad-Gula is said to have lacked a *diglu* (SAA 10 294 r.32). In the Hebrew Bible, the visions are inseparable from the prophetic activity; cf. e.g. Is 6; Jer 1:11-19; Ez 1:1 – 3:15; 8-11; 37:1-14; Am 7:1-9; 8:1-3. There are no unambiguous Assyrian records of prophets as dreamers, while in the Hebrew Bible this is taken for granted (cf. Jer 23:25-28 etc.).

[270] Cf. Parpola 1997c, XLVII and CIV nn. 235, 236, 243. The non-prophetic dreamers and visionaries include, for instance, Mar-Issar (cf. SAA 10 316 and 365) and Nabû-rehtu-uṣur (CT 53 17:10 and 938:10) whose letters will be dealt with later in this study.

an important role in the inscriptions even without any reference to their transmitters, for instance in a passage referring to Assurbanipal's second campaign against Humban-haltaš III (A v 95-103) which claims that the whole army had simultaneously the same dream:[271]

> My troops saw Idide, the violent flood, and were afraid to cross it. But Ištar who dwells in Arbela let my troops have a dream (*šuttu*) in the night (*ina šāt mūši*). She spoke to them as follows: "I will go before Assurbanipal, the king whom my hands created." My troops trusted in this dream and crossed safely the river Idide.

The words of Ištar are explicitly said to have been spoken in a collective dream, by whatever means this is thought of to happen; otherwise they could well be characterized as a prophecy – not only because of their encouraging function but also because they have a close parallel in SAA 9 9, a prophecy to Assurbanipal from the year 650.[272] Another dream, the content of which is related to prophecy, is the one reported in the narrative concerning Gyges, king of Lydia, and his voluntary submission to Assurbanipal. The narrative is recorded in various prisms, the redactional history of which is examined by Cogan and Tadmor (1977); according to their composite version, the dream is introduced as follows:[273]

> Gyges, king of Lydia, a district by the passes of the sea, a distant place, whose name the kings, my ancestors, had not heard – Aššur, my begetter, revealed a word of my kingship to him in a dream: "Assurbanipal, king of Assyria, the beloved of Aššur, king of the gods, lord of all – lay hold of his princely feet! Revere his sovereignty, implore his rule. As obeisance and tribute-bearing, let your prayers come before him. By invoking his name (*ina zikir šumīšu*), conquer your enemies!" On the (very) day he had this dream, he dispatched his rider (*rakbû*) to inquire my well-being. Through his messenger (*mār šipri*) he sent to relate to me the dream that he had. From that day he laid hold of my royal feet.

Nothing suggests that this dream would be of prophetic provenance, even though the message itself is reminiscent of prophecies proclaiming victory

---

[271] Borger 1996, 50. For the historical circumstances, see Carter & Stolper 1984, 52

[272] SAA 9 9:3-6, r.1-3: [*šinām*]*a ina ilāni dannā* [*ira*]*ʾʾamā u raʾāmšina* [*ana*] *Aššūr-bāni-apli binūt qātīšina iltanapparā*... [*Mul*]*lissu u Bēlet Arbail* [*ana*] *Aššūr-bāni-apli binūt qātīšina luballiṭā ana dāri* "[They] are the strongest among the gods; they [lov]e and keep sending their love [to] Assurbanipal, the creation of their hands... May Mullissu and the Lady of Arbela keep Assurbanipal, the creation of their hands, alive for ever!" Note, however, that calling Assurbanipal the creation of the hands of the gods is not typical of prophetic sources alone but familiar from literary texts as well, e.g., SAA 3 3:8, 10, 23, r.16: "I am Assurbanipal... product (*binūt*) of Emašmaš and Egašankalamma... I am Assurbanipal, the creation of the hands of the great gods (*binūt qātī ilāni rabûti*)... the Lady of Arbela, my creator (*bā*[*nī*]*tīja*), ordered everlasting life (for me)"; SAA 3 11:15: "Assurbanipal is the [...] of Aššur, the creation of his hands (*binūt qātīšu*)."

[273] Translation from Cogan & Tadmor 1977, 75-76; cf. Borger 1996, 30-31 A ii 95-110//F ii 10-20//B ii 93 – iii 4//C iv 1-12, 181-183 (E-prisms).

for the Assyrian king over his enemies who bring their tribute before him.[274] However, there are no prophecies in which the victory of the Assyrian king was announced to a foreign king; in this respect, the biblical story of Balaam (Num 22-24) would provide the nearest (but not an exact!) parallel.[275] It deserves attention that Assurbanipal relates to Gyges like the gods to Assurbanipal: it is *his* name, by the invoking of which Gyges is supposed to conquer his enemies.[276] Hence, Assurbanipal, begotten by the god Aššur, actually represents the Assyrian gods in relation to Gyges.

In the later editions of the Gyges narrative, the dream is said to have reached Assurbanipal's ears by means of a messenger (*mār šipri*) of Gyges who repeats it to Assurbanipal in intelligible words; in the earliest edition E_1, however, it is the foreign rider (*rakbû*) who brings the message of Gyges speaking a language that nobody can understand. Since the edition E_1 was composed soon after the narrated episode,[277] it may be closer to the historical reality than the other versions; this makes the impression even stronger that the dream reported by the *mār šipri* is a propagandistic invention of later writers who put orthodox words in the mouth of the messenger of Gyges.[278] This, finally, raises the question, to what extent the prophecies and other divine messages included in the inscriptions of Assurbanipal in general are literary creations rather than being quotations of actual oracles.[279]

It deserves attention that references to prophecy are included in some inscriptions while others reporting on the same events leave them unmentioned. The Ahšeri episode includes a quotation of the words of Ištar only in the Prism A version, whereas only B and C concentrate on divination on the occasion of the Teumman campaign. Some references to dreams and visions are included only on Prism A which is comparatively late (c. 643/2[280]), ideologically refined and historically often less credible than the earlier prisms.[281] The literary history of the dream of Gyges would suggest that the quotations of prophecies and other divinatory messages have easily grown

---

274 E.g., SAA 9 2.5 iii 23-25: *nakarūti ina sigarāti salmūti ina maddanāti ina pān šēpēšu ubbala* "I will bring enemies in neckstocks and vassals with tribute before his feet." Cf. SAA 9 7:12-13: [*šarrā*]*ni ša mātāti* [*tapīa*]*l tahūmāni tukallamšunu* [*hūl*]*ani ina šepišunu tašakkan* "[You shall ru]le over [the king]s of the lands; you shall show them their frontiers and set the courses they take."

275 Cf. Cogan & Tadmor 1977, 74.

276 Cf. also SAA 3 44:27: "At the mention of your name (*ina zikir šumīka*), which I made great, your troops go victorously wherever there is fighting with weapons."

277 Cogan & Tadmor 1977 date the edition in 665/4 ± one year (pp. 81-82), thus the Gyges episode must have happened between 668 and 665 (pp. 83-84; cf. also Grayson 1980, 230, 232).

278 See Cogan & Tadmor 1977, 77-78. Note that Prism A, which makes use of both E editions, mentions both *rakbû* and *mār šipri*.

279 On this problem concerning dreams, cf. Wilson 1980, 114; Grabbe 1995, 148.

280 See Grayson 1980, 245.

281 See Cogan & Tadmor 1977, 83; Tadmor 1983, 51.

from the minds of the writers of the inscriptions, especially if there is a considerable temporal distance between the events and the narratives.

However, in individual cases it is very difficult to judge whether the scribes have formulated divine messages out of their own imagination or whether they have utilized and, perhaps, interpreted written sources. If this is the case, temporal distance would constitute no problem. It has been noted earlier in this study that the inscriptions of Esarhaddon probably have profited from the interpretation of written prophecies, and there is no reason why this should not also be the case during the reign of Assurbanipal who also let prophecies be written down for archival purposes.

The comparison of Assurbanipal's inscriptions with contemporary prophecy is impeded by the fact that only a few prophecies (SAA 9 7-11) from his time have been preserved, and not even these few pieces of evidence directly coincide with the inscriptional references:

- The fragments SAA 9 10 and 11 are too badly damaged to be datable.[282]
- SAA 9 9 is dated by eponym to the year 650 which means that the tablet was composed during the Šamaš-šumu-ukin revolt, but the inscriptional narratives concerning that war do not make any reference to this utterance. However, the above cited response of the god Aššur to Assurbanipal's report on the Šamaš-šumu-ukin revolt seems to presuppose a prophetic encouragement (SAA 3 44 r. 22: "I spoke to you [with] my divine word and you acted").[283]
- Elam is mentioned in SAA 9 7.[284] The text includes a reference to the Palace of Succession which would imply a date before the accession of Assurbanipal[285] – unless this reference belongs to a quotation of an earlier prophecy (lines 2-11), as has been recently suggested by Weippert.[286] Since the prophecy was written down, its eventual early date would not have prevented its reinterpretation for later purposes. However, the inscriptions display no explicit knowledge of this prophecy.
- Finally, SAA 9 8 consists of words (*dibbī*) concerning Elam:

  dibbī [ša elam]āji kî an[nî ilu?] iqabbi mā att[alak at]talka hamšīšu šiššīšu iq[ṭib]i iddāti mā issu muhhi [nar]'anti attalka mā ṣerru ša

---

[282] The preserved lines of SAA 9 10 do not mention the name of Assurbanipal; the dating is due to the name of the prophetess, Dunnaša-amur, from whom SAA 9 7 also derives; see Parpola 1997c, LXXI who notes that SAA 9 11 r.4-5 "intriguingly remind one of the theophany reported to Assurbanipal before the war against Teumman (...) Could this be the original letter reporting it?"

[283] Cf. also the dream in A iii 118-127 above, pp. 55-56.

[284] *[m]ā šanītu laqbâkka kî Elamtu Gimir agammar* "Secondly, let me tell you: I will finish the land of Gomer like (I finished) Elam."

[285] Parpola 1997c, LXX dates it before Assurbanipal's introduction to the Palace of Succession in 672 because the act of investiture, the girding of the royal diadem (*pitūtu* line 7), is referred to as if it had not yet happened. Contrary to what Laato 1996, 183 asserts, I did not connect SAA 9 7 with the Šamaš-šumu-ukin war but, rather, noted that its addressee is Assurbanipal as the crown prince (1993, 229).

[286] Weippert 1997c, 153-157.

> *ina libbīša assadda abtataq u mā nar'antu ahtepi*
> *u mā Elamtu ahappi emūqšu issi kaqqir isappan mā kî annî Elamtu agammar*
>
> Words [concerning the Elam]ites.
> [*God*[287]] says as follows:
> "I have go[ne and I ha]ve come."
> He said (this) five, six times, and then:
> "I have come from the [m]ace. I have pulled out the snake which was inside it, I have cut it in pieces, and I have broken the mace."
> And (he said):
> "I will destroy Elam; its army shall be levelled to the ground. In this manner I will finish Elam."

There is no verbatim quotation of these words in the inscriptional sources and the mace and snake metaphor is unique; nevertheless, these oracles certainly illustrate how the *šipir mahhê* mentioned in the Teumman passage may have looked. The prophetic speeches included in this text may originally be connected with any of Assurbanipal's several campaigns against Elamite kings (Urtaku, Teumman, Humban-haltaš III). If the words really reflect the total decline of the political status of Elam and are not to be read as conventional propaganda, then the war against Teumman in 653 would provide the best alternative.[288]

In sum, the inscriptions of Assurbanipal indeed refer to prophecies and even quote them a couple of times; however, the prophecies addressed to him that we know are apparently not identical to those quoted. There remain two explanations for this fact: either the draftsmen of the inscriptions formulated the "prophecies" freely, using conventional phraseology, or they used sources that have not been preserved or at least not yet identified by modern scholars. The actual existence of prophetic activity and a general belief in its divine authorization is a prerequisite for both explanations: even fabricated quotations of prophecy presupposed a prototype in actual life to be substantially credible and stylistically consistent.[289]

The five extant tablets containing prophetic speeches give us just an inkling of the extent of prophetic activity during the reign of Assurbanipal. Thanks to the supplementary evidence provided by a few inscriptional references, the perspective can be broadened a little. Even though the available prophetic speeches addressed to Assurbanipal cannot be proved to have any direct

---

[287] There is room for one sign only, which means that divine names consisting of DINGIR + another sign are excluded.

[288] Parpola 1997c, LXX notes the fact that the war was triggered by the Elamites while Assurbanipal was worshiping Ištar of Arbela (B v 15-23) – "an insult provoking not only the anger of the king but of the goddess as well."

[289] Cf. Millard 1985, 131: "Même si... le récit entier [scil. the dream concerning the campaign against Teumman] est une fiction littéraire élaborée dans le but de grandir le roi, ou une mise en forme de la prière initiale du roi, il présente, néanmoins, une suite d'événements que le lecteur ancien pouvait accepter."

literary relationship to the inscriptions, the views of prophecy provided by the two sets of sources are not mutually exclusive but, on the contrary, complement each other to a high degree. The dual evidence substantiates the view of prophecy as an established institution at the time of Assurbanipal who evidently regarded the prophets at least as highly as his father did.

CHAPTER THREE

A PROPHET AMONG THE MILITARY

Text

SAA 7 9 r. i 20-24
(K 8143 + 80-7-19,105 / ADD 860)

20 ^{md}MAŠ.MAŠ–GIN–PAB LÚ.EN–GIŠ.GIGIR
21 ^{md}PA–MAN–PAB LÚ.GAL–*ki-ṣir* A–MAN
22 ^{m}*ú-a-za-ru* LÚ.*qur*-ZAG AMA—MAN
23 ^{m}*qu-qi-i* LÚ.*rag-gi-mu*
blank space of one line
24 PAB 4 *mu-še-bi di-ka-ni-a-a*

Nergal-mukin-ahi, chariot owner; Nabû-šarru-uṣur, cohort commander of the crown prince; Wazaru, bodyguard of the queen mother; Quqî, prophet; in all, 4: the 'residences' of the Dikanaeans

Background & Prophecy

Not much of profit can be gained from this text, except the fact that we can now add another new entry to our list of the proper names of the prophets. The name Quqî, which seems to be of West Semitic origin,[290] differs from the other names familiar to us, the majority of which are strongly symbolic and closely attached to the role of the person as a prophet (*Issār-lā-tašīјaṭ, Sinqīša-āmur, Ilūssa-āmur, Rēmutti-Allati, Urkittu-šarrat; Mullissu-kabtat* etc.).[291]

The excerpt belongs to a lodging list that originally consisted of about one hundred names. It was probably compiled on the occasion of some major event in Nineveh in which a great number of people from different parts of the empire took part – for example the ceremony arranged by Esarhaddon in order to conclude the succession treaty on behalf of his sons in 672, or some other comparable occasion.[292] If Nabû-šarru-uṣur, *rab kiṣri* of the crown prince is identical with the one appointed as chief eunuch by Assurbanipal (SAA 4 299),[293] then this event is likely to have taken place before his enthronement – or be the enthronement itself. Since the identification is not certain, its contribution to the dating of the text is, of course, not decisive.

---

290 This conclusion suggests itself because the names with the ending *-î* (with or without the hypocoristic *-ja*) tend to belong to persons of Aramean/Chaldean origin; cf. Naqīja, Sāsī(ja), Ṭābīja (ABL 527 r.5), Kabtīja (Sm 1700 r.3; see Dietrich 1968, 231-233), Damqî (SAA 10 352, cf. above); Danî (SAA 10 222:12) etc.

291 For the prophetic names, see Parpola 1997c, XLVIII-LII.

292 See Fales & Postgate 1992, XVII-XVIII and the remarks of Mattila 1990, 16, n. 5 concerning SAA 7 150; cf. also below, nn. 423 and 552.

293 Cf. Fales 1988, 118 and see below, pp. 148-149, nn. 554-555.

In the light of the above-discussed inscriptional references to the role of the prophets during the military campaigns it is not surprising to find a prophet among the military in an Assyrian list of persons. SAA 7 9 is a list of lodgings for mostly high officials, and it mentions the prophet Quqî together with three high-ranking officers who, according to their professional designations, are in the personal service of the court.

Even though this list hardly has much to do with any structure of the military bureaucracy,[294] the appearance of a prophet among commanders and bodyguards closely attached to the court is worth noticing. It is conceivable from the prophecies received during battles (e.g. SAA 9 1 and 8) as well as from the references to them in the royal inscriptions discussed previously in this study that the prophets, like haruspices,[295] constituted a part of the divinatory apparatus that followed the king to his campaigns and thus must have had a position within the military organization. One should remember, in any case, that the mentioning of one single prophet within the vast amount of Neo-Assyrian administrative documents does not warrant too far-reaching conclusions. Numerous as the extant lists of persons belonging to different classes are, one is tempted to ask why only one name with the designation "prophet" has found its way onto them.

---

294 Cf. the warnings of Fales & Postgate 1992, XIX.

295 See Starr 1990, XXX-XXXI.

CHAPTER FOUR

PROPHECY AND THE SUBSTITUTE KING RITUAL

4.1. Mar-Issar on the Burial of Damqî

Text

SAA 10 352
(= K 168 / ABL 437 / LAS 280)

Obv. ^{5} ^{m}[SIG$_5$-*i*] ^{6}DUMU LÚ*.ŠÀ.TAM *ša* A.GA.[DÈ.KI] ^{7}*ša* KUR–*aš-šur*.KI KÁ.DINGIR.KI : [*ù*] ^{8}KUR.KUR *ka-li-ši-na ib-i*[*l*$^{?}$*-u-ni šu-u*] ^{9}*ù* MÍ.É.GAL-*šú* MI *š*[*a* UD-*x*-KÁM *a-na*] ^{10}*di-na-a-ni ša* MAN EN-*iá* [*ù a-na ba-laṭ* Z]I.⌜MEŠ⌝ ^{11}*ša* ^{md}GIŠ.NU$_{11}$–MU–GI.[NA *im-tu*]*-tu* ^{12}*a-na pi-di-šú-nu a-na* ⌜*šim-ti*⌝ *it-ta-lak* ... ^{22}[*a*]*-se-me ma-a pa-na-at né-pe-še an-nu-ti* ^{23}[M]Í.*ra-gi-in-ti tar-tu-gu-mu* ^{24}*a-na* ^{m}SIG$_5$-*i* DUMU LÚ*.ŠÀ.TAM *taq-ṭi-*[*bi*] ^{25}[*m*]*a-a* LUGAL-*u-ti ta-na-áš-ši* Rev. ^{1}[*ù*] *ra-gi-in-tu ina* UKKIN ^{2}*ša* KUR *taq-ṭi-ba-áš-šu ma-a ka-ki-šu* ^{3}*šar-ri-iq-tu ša* EN-*ia uk-ta-lim* ^{4}*ina* ŠU.2 *a-sa-kan-ka* NAM.BÚR.BI ^{5}*an-nu-ti ša ep-šú-u-ni i-sa-al-mu* ^{6}*a-dan-niš* ŠÀ-*bu ša* MAN EN-*iá lu* DÙG.GA-*šú*

> 5 [Damqî], the son of the prelate of Akka[d], who had ru[led] Assyria, Babylon(ia) [and] all the countries, [di]ed with his queen on the night o[f the xth day as] a substitute for the king, my lord, [and for the sake of the li]fe of Šamaš-šumu-uki[n]. He went to his fate for their redemption. ......
>
> 22 [I] have heard that before these ceremonies a prophetess had prophesied, saying to the son of the prelate, Damqî: "You will take over the kingship!"
>
> r.1 The prophetess had also said to him in the assembly of the country: "I have revealed the thieving polecat of my lord, and placed (him) in your hands." These apotropaic rituals which were performed succeeded well indeed; the king, my lord, can be glad.

Background

This letter of Mar-Issar, Esarhaddon's "eye and ear" in Babylonia,[296] belongs closely together with another letter, SAA 10 351, sent by the same person a little earlier. Both letters deal with the substitute king ritual that took place on occasion of the lunar eclipse in the month of Tebet (X), 671 in Akkad, the ancient Sargonic capital of Babylonia that was restored by Esarhaddon.[297] The cult of Akkad had been re-established when the statues of Ištar (or Lady)

---

296 On the system of "king's eyes and ears" as an intelligent service, see Parpola 1972, 31. On Mar-Issar see Landsberger 1965, 38-57; Parpola 1983 (nos. 275-297); 1993, xxvf; Pečírková 1985, 165-167; Frame 1992, 90-91. Even if the name of the sender is broken away, the attribution of SAA 10 352 to Mar-Issar presents no problem since the letter belongs both thematically and orthographically together with SAA 10 351.

297 Cf. SAA 10 359:7-8 and see Frame 1992, 73-75.

of Akkad and other gods of Akkad returned from their exile in Elam on the 10th of Adar (XII), 674.[298]

In the first letter, SAA 10 351, Mar-Issar reports the entry of the substitute king (*šar pūhi*) into Akkad and his enthronement rituals on the night of the 20th of Tebet (II), 671 (= January 1, 670). That he had already been enthroned in Nineveh on the 14th of Tebet (X) (line 6) shows that he was crowned king of both Assyria and Babylonia. The re-enthronement was required because the right-hand lunar quadrant corresponding to Babylonia was also eclipsed – the eclipse was a total one – and thus afflicted Esarhaddon as the king of Babylonia.[299] Mar-Issar also recommends apotropaic (NAM.BÚR.BI) rituals for the protection of Esarhaddon and his sons for whom the eclipse portends evil – although the substitute king had already taken "all the celestial and terrestrial portents on himself" (lines 12-13).

In addition, two more letters are connected with the same ritual, both of them antedating those of Mar-Issar. In SAA 10 240, written on the 13th of Tebet (X), 671, the chief exorcist Marduk-šakin-šumi predicts that the lunar eclipse will take place on the 15th, gives an account of the *bīt rimki* rituals already performed due to this (lines 16-20), and suggests that somebody be enthroned as the substitute king (*memmēni nušēšib* line r.18) even before the eclipse occurs.[300] He also insinuates that the substitute should be a Babylonian this time (lines r.21-25):

> *assanamme mar*ʾ[*ē*] *Bābilī* [*šarru bēlī*] *ūda mī*[*nu ida*]*bbabūni* [*uš*]*annûni li*[*ptu ša d*]*ābibānūti lēp*[*ušū*]
>
> I am listening – [the king, my lord], knows the Babylonians and what they [pl]ot and [re]peat. (These) plotters should be af[flicted]!

The fragment SAA 10 377[301] also deals with the same event (lines 8-r.4):

> UD-14-KÁM *ana Nīnu*[*a*] *Adad-šumu-uṣur ēt*[*arab*] *issi Aššūr-nāṣir rab* [*x*] *Sāsî Urad-Ē*[*a iddubub*] *mā adu lā attal*[*û iškunūni*] *lūšib*

[298] According to the chronicles, the cult of Akkad was re-established at the end of the 7th year of Esarhaddon: MU.7.KÁM... *ina* ITI.ŠE ^{d}INNIN ⌜A⌝.GA.DÈ.KI *u* DINGIR.MEŠ *šá* A.GA.DÈ.KI TA KUR NIM DU.MEŠ-*nim-ma ina* ITI.ŠE UD.10.KÁM *ana* A.GA.DÈ.KI TU.MEŠ "In the 7th year... In Adar, Ištar of Akkad and the gods of Akkad returned from Elam and entered Akkad on Adar 10" (Grayson 1975a, 84:16-18). This, in spite of the opposite assertions of Landsberger 1965, 40 n. 57, makes it unnecessary to assume that Akkad should be identified with Babylon in SAA 10 352.

[299] See Parpola 1983, xxv.

[300] On the date of the letter and of the eclipse, see Parpola 1983, 176-177.

[301] As to this letter and to the role of Sasî in the conspiracy crushed a couple of months later, see below, pp. 144-145.

> On the 14th Adad-šumu-uṣur enter[ed] Nineveh and [spoke] with Aššur-naṣir, the chief [*eunuch*],[302] Sasî and Urad-E[a]: "Let him sit (on the throne) before the eclip[se occurs]."

This confirms that the substitute king was enthroned on the 14th (of Tebet), i.e., one day before the eclipse, as Mar-Issar had written in SAA 10 351.

SAA 10 352 had been sent at least a week later than SAA 10 240 but still during the 100 day period covered by the substitute king ritual as a whole,[303] that is, between the 1st of Shebat (XI) and 28th of Adar (XII), 671 (= January 12 and March 10, 670).[304] Mar-Issar now reports the death and the burial of the substitute king who appears to have been Damqî, *mār šatammi ša Akkad* "the son of the *šatammu*[305] of Akkad." He gives an account of the burial ceremonies as well as of apotropaic, *bīt rimki* and other rituals performed for the life of Esarhaddon. He also mentions that the people of Akkad got scared but were calmed down by him and his associates. Even the high officials of Babylonia are said to have become frightened.

It has been suggested with good reason that the people and officials were frightened because the substitute king was this time no simpleton from the common people but the son of a high Babylonian official. According to Landsberger who gives a vivid description of the letters and activities of Mar-Issar,[306] Damqî was the son of none other than Šumu-iddina, the *šatammu* of the Esaggil temple of Babylon.[307] This view, followed by some other

---

[302] For the problem with the title of Aššur-naṣir, cf. below, n. 546 and pp. 147-148.

[303] SAA 10 352 r.11-13: *ù ina* ŠÀ *du-ri* AN.MI ^{d}30 TE-*he*-⌜*e*⌝ DINGIR.MEŠ *i-ba-áš-ši a-na ka-qí-ri la il-lak* "still, during the (validity) period of the eclipse and the approach of the gods he [the king] may not go into open country." On the period of 100 days cf. SAA 10 220 r.4-6 and Parpola 1983, xxv; Bottéro 1992, 148.

[304] On the justification of this dating, see Parpola 1983, 270 and cf. ibid, XXV-XXVI. Note that the mentioning of Šamaš-šumu-ukin (line 11, together with Esarhaddon but without Assurbanipal!) implies a date post 672.

[305] The translation 'prelate' (or, as Landsberger puts it, 'bishop') is, of course, anachronistic and inaccurate to describe the office of *šatammu*, on which see Gallery 1980 (Old Babylonian period only).

[306] Landsberger 1965, 38-39: "Die Selbstsicherheit, die Kraft und die Farbenreichtum der Sprache fesseln noch heute den Leser dieser Briefe und erwecken Interesse an dieser düsteren Persönlichkeit... nur der Bischof (*šatammu*) von Babylon, der der Herrin von Akkad die täglichen Opfer darbringt, ist geeignet, an Stelle des Königs geopfert zu werden, wenn die Vorzeichen Böses für Akkad verkünden. Die Haare stehen uns zu Berge, wenn wir lesen, wie er den unschuldigen Sohn des Bischofs und seine Gattin opfert, nachdem der Bischof schon abgesetzt (und vermutlich gleichfalls hingerichtet) war; wie er, während 'die Versammlung des Landes' angstschlotternd zu Rate sitzt, eine Exstatikerin auftreten lässt, die in prophetischen Worten seine Massnahmen legitimiert..." Cf. Pečírková 1985, 166: "This is somewhat exaggerated; the attitude of Mār-Ištar towards Babylonia was the official attitude of the Assyrian king, his court and the administration, for whom Babylonia represented a difficult political problem and an unending source of unrest."

[307] Šumu-iddina appears as the šatammu of Esaggil (^{m}MU.SUM-*na* LÚ.ŠÀ.TAM É.SAG.ÍL) in a list of leading Babylonian officials that dates from the first or second year of Esarhaddon (Pinches 1939/41; cf. Landsberger 1965, 29-30). He is also the writer of the

scholars,[308] is, however, dependent on the undemonstrable assumption of Landsberger that Akkad be a cover name for Babylon.[309] If we do not accept this identification, then there is also no proof that the *šatammu* of Akkad could be identified with Šumu-iddina or, consequently, Damqî with his son.[310] Neither does the designation *mār šatammi* imply in itself that its holder would originally have been of a high social standing.

Mar-Issar indicates that the *šatammūtu* of Akkad had been given to a *saklu*, that is, to someone who did not originate from the Establishment of Babylonia[311] (lines r.13-15, 18-20):

> *šumma pān šarri bēlīja mahir kî ša ina pānīti saklu ana šatammūti lū paqīdi... kīm[a attalû] issakan māt Akkadî ilta[pat šû ana] dinānī šarri bēlīja lillik*
>
> If it suits the king, my lord, a common man should, as before, be appointed to the office of the *šatammu* ... When [an eclipse] afflicting Babylonia takes place, [he] may serve as a substitute for the king, my lord.

This suggestion of Mar-Issar has been interpreted as an implied excuse for the terrifying and scandalous performance of promoting the son of a real *šatammu* as the substitute king: let it never happen again![312] But it can also be understood as an encouragement to go on "as before" with the procedure that once had proved successful.

In fact, Mar-Issar does not see any problem in making a *šatammu* substitute king. Quite the contrary, he seems to be recommending that the person chosen as the substitute was first to be given the prominent status of *šatammu* to make him worthy of being promoted as the "king," as if this high office was nothing but a preamble to the fate of the substitute. This, however, is hardly what he is driving at. He rather points out that the *šatammu* should preferably be a

---

letter TKSM 21/676 (see below pp. 131-133). It is written almost a decade later than the list, but the contents of the letter leave little room for doubt that he still holds this position.

308 E.g., Bottéro 1992, 151.

309 There is no proof for the suggestion of Landsberger that Akkad could be used as an archaic cover name for Babylon (Landsberger 1965, 38-39 etc.); cf. above n. 298 and McEwan 1982, 12; Parpola 1983, 263-264; Wall-Romana 1990, 215-216.

310 Irrespective of the identity of the *šatammu* in SAA 10 352, it is worth noting that Šumu-iddina, *šatammu* of Esaggil, should not be identified with Šumu-iddina *šandabakku* of Nippur, whose son was placed in confinement about five years earlier; cf. SAA 10 112: 28-r.6 and below p. 138, n. 518.

311 Cf. ABL 1103: 6-r.1: *ina bīt ili ātamaršunu gabbu saklūte šunu memmēni issu libbi qinnāte ša Nīnua labirūte laššu* "I saw them in the temple: all are common people, none of them comes from the old families of Nineveh." For other occurences of the word, cf. CAD S 80; Landsberger 1965, 61 n. 114.

312 Bottéro 1992, 151: "Mâr-Ištar is thus making a report to the king, and perhaps the drama that he had initiated had left some bad memories, due to the personality of his victim. He seems more than once, if not to excuse himself, at least to justify himself, and especially to swear that he will not repeat what he has done, at least not in the same circumstances."

saklu, that is, a less risky alternative to be chosen as the substitute than someone of noble birth. Previously, it appears, the *šatammu* of Akkad was a a common man – not necessarily, or even plausibly, "simple, naïve, perhaps even somewhat 'retarded'"[313] but just a man without a noble lineage or renowned career – and, perhaps, without predecessors in this office. It is important to note that the cult of Akkad was re-established less than three years earlier[314] which means that there could not have been many holders of the *šatammūtu* of Akkad thus far – maybe just the one whose son was then executed as a substitute for the king. This would mean that he himself was a *saklu*, and when his son was executed, the next holder of the office was once again to be sought among the common men.

The question, though, arises why, then, the *son* of the *šatammu*, not he himself, was put to death? There are several ways to explain this problem.

The designation *mār šatammi* is usually translated literally "the son of the *šatammu*." Yet, since the word *māru/mar'u* sometimes also denotes a member of a professional group,[315] it could be maintained that *mār šatammi* actually means the *šatammu* himself, presenting Damqî as but one member in the chain of men who were appointed to *šatammūtu* only *ad hoc*, in order to let them go to their fate for the redemption of the king. Since, in reality, there was no such chain in Akkad and, on the other hand, *šatammūtu* as an office was surely not designed only for prospective substitute kings, this explanation lacks plausiblity. Thus it remains probable that Damqî really was the son of the *šatammu* of Akkad.

It could be argued *ex silentio* that the son was chosen because the father was already dead, but there is nothing in the sources that would support this supposition. He may have been still alive as well; it matters more that executing the son prevented the *šatammūtu* of Akkad from being passed on by inheritance and thus enabled the appointment of a new saklu to this office without the risk that a new powerful family would ensue from its holders in Babylonia. In any case, whether the father of Damqî was dead or alive, Mar-Issar's suggestions concerning the *šatammūtu* arrangements indicate that the office was vacant.

Why, then, did a high official, even without a noble origin, and not just any simpleton have to serve as the substitute? The advice of Mar-Issar should be understood against the background of the slightly earlier suggestion of Marduk-šakin-šumi that the "somebody" to be put on the throne should be a Babylonian (SAA 10 240 r.17-25). Despite the efforts of Esarhaddon to consolidate peace in Babylonia, local rebellions occurred here and there

---

313 Bottéro 1992, 147.

314 Cf. above n. 298.

315 Cf. *mār šā'ili amat ili* 'inquirer of oracles' SAA 2 6 § 10:117; *mār ušpari* 'weaver' Šurpu v 115; *mārē malāhi kalīšunu* 'all the skippers' Maqlû vii 9; *mār tamkāri* 'merchant' KAR 423 iv 59, 61; *mārē ummâni* 'scholars/masters' Borger 1956 (§ 53) 82:22; 83:24; *mārē bārâni* 'haruspices' Borger 1956 (§ 53) 82:21; 83:25.

throughout his reign.[316] Obviously the chief exorcist, who was entitled to suggest and choose the substitute king, considered it necessary to teach the separatist Babylonians (*dābibānu*) a lesson, and Mar-Issar encourages the king to go on with this policy. Executing a son of a high official – even if he was a *saklu* – reminded the Babylonians of their status. Hence it is no wonder that not only the people of Akkad but the "prelates and delegates" (*šatammāni qēpāni*) of all Babylonia got scared: there was a clear political message embedded in the religious ritual.

To this should be added that the ritual described here was already the second one within four months; the previous substitute king met his fate in Akkad in the month of Tishri (VII), 671.[317] The lunar eclipse was always an evil portent that signified disturbance of the sensitive equilibrium of heaven and earth. If it occurred repeatedly within a short period of time, the people had every reason to be afraid even if there was nothing exceptional in the substitute king ritual. Even the king himself could not feel secure as long as the whole period of 100 days required by the ritual was not over. It is the purpose of Mar-Issar to affirm to Esarhaddon that the elaborate rituals have succeeded according to expectations and the king "can be glad" even if the danger is not yet quite over.

Prophecy

In addition to the successful rituals, the king is reassured with a flashback to the appearance of a prophetess (*raggintu*) which occurred when the substitute king was still alive (lines 22-r.4). The mentioning of the prophetess is a kind of parenthetic note in the middle of the account of the rituals. Obviously Mar-Issar has remembered this event when writing about the apotropaic rituals subsequent to the death of Damqî and his wife and considered it worth mentioning as an additional proof of the divine justification of the election of the substitute king.

All that is quoted of the sayings of the prophetess is divine affirmation of the true kingship of Damqî. The quotations are certainly not to be understood as the personal attitudes of the prophetess but as divine words, probably those of Ištar as the Lady of Akkad,[318] transmitted by the prophetess. Obviously the prophecy is cited here to show that the unusual choice of the substitute was the divine will and not just an arbitrary decision of the earthly magnates, no matter what people may think about it.

---

[316] See the detailed description of Frame 1992, 64-101.

[317] The political difficulties caused by this fact have been noted by Mayer 1995, 395.

[318] Cf. line r.18 and note that the Lady of Akkad, once deported to Elam from where she was returned to Akkad (cf. SAA 10 359:4ff), is called Ištar of Akkad in the chronicles (cf. above n. 298).

The statement "You will take over the kingship!" (*šarrūti tanašši*)[319] expresses the divine election and the legitimacy of the accession of the substitute king. The same would also apply to the second quotation: "I have revealed the *ka-ki-šu sar-ri-iq-tu* of my lord[320] and placed (it/him) in your hands." Unfortunately, the meaning of this statement is unclear since the crucial words *kakkišu sarriqtu* are grammatically as well as semantically enigmatic and cannot be translated with certainty. The words constitute an object for the verb *uktallim,* and the latter word obviously qualifies the former. The apparent incongruity of gender may be explained by interpreting *kakkišu* as a term, the feminine gender of which is indicated only by the feminine attribute;[321] this assumption is corroborated by the fact that the only attested plural form of this word is feminine (*kakkišāti* SAA 9 1.7 v 3; cf. below). This does not, however, resolve the semantic problem: What do these words mean? While *kakkišu* most probably stands for a mustelid (a polecat or a weasel[322]) there are at least two alternatives for the word *sarriqtu.*

If *sarriqtu* can be connected with *zarriqu* 'glittering,'[323] then the prophetic word could describe delivering of the symbols of power to the substitute king – in this case something like an image of a mustelid made from a precious metal. If this be the case, the two prophetic quotations would belong together signifying an enthronement act in which the prophetess plays a central role as the mediator between the god(dess) and the substitute king.

There exists, however, a more plausible way to decipher this *crux interpretum.* If we read the initial sign of the line r.3 as *šar* instead of *sar* we arrive at *šarriqtu*, a derivative of *šarāqu* 'to steal' (cf. *šarrāqu* 'thief').[324] Thus, *kakkišu šarriqtu* could be understood as a derogatory term for the adversary or the enemy of the substitute king ('the thieving polecat' – which is idiomatic and iconic in English as well as Akkadian). This interpretation may be supported by the fact that the *Übergabeformel* "putting the enemies into the hands of the king" (*ina qāti šakānu*) and related affirmations belong to the standard phraseology of the Neo-Assyrian prophecies.[325] Furthermore, the word *kakkišu*, together with *pušhu* (perhaps the name of a rodent or insecti-

---

[319] Cf. SAA 9 1.8 v 22-23: *šarrūtu ikkû danānu ikkūma* "The kingship is yours, yours is the power!"

[320] For this form of address, even within a quotation of a prophecy, see below p. 103.

[321] Cf. GAG §§ 60d, 61n.

[322] So AHw 422 with reference to the Aramaic *karkuštā* (see Dalman 1938, 208); cf. also von Soden 1956, 107; Landsberger 1965, 48.

[323] See CAD Z 69; AHw 1030, 1515-1516, but cf. Landsberger (1965, 48 n. 84), according to whom "dieses durch Jahrzehnte als Gemeingut der Assyriologie geltende Verb muss aufgegeben werden."

[324] So von Soden in AHw 1188 ("diebisch"). For the model *parris(t)* see GAG § 55m.

[325] Cf. SAA 9 2.4 ii 32-33: *uhajjāṭa lā kēnūti ina qāt šarrīja ašakkan* "I will search out the disloyal ones, and I will put them into the hands of my king" and, for the sake of comparison, Judg 20:28; 1 Sam 23:4; 1 Kings 20:3; 22:12,15. On this phrase, see also Weinfeld 1977, 183-184; van der Toorn 1987, 69, 73-74.

vore)[326] has undisputedly this kind of connotation in the prophecy of Issar-beli-da''ini to the king's mother[327] (SAA 9 1.7 v 3-7):

> *kakkišāti pušhāti ša idabbabūni ina pān šēpēšu ubattaqšunu*
>
> I will cut the conspiring weasels and shrews to pieces before his feet.

Quite obviously the same imagery is used by the prophetess quoted by Mar-Issar.[328]

Mar-Issar indicates both the time and place of the prophetic sayings that, nevertheless, may not belong to one and the same situation. Rather, we have to do with two distinct quotations. The second one is said to have been proclaimed "in the assembly of the country" (*ina puhur ša māti*) which refers to a public occasion, presumably in Akkad, the inhabitants of which are mentioned in the letter. The "assembly of the country" may be comparable with the assemblies (UKKIN/*puhrum*) of the cities which from the Early Dynastic to the Old Babylonian period were institutions of a kind of "primitive democracy," forums for popular debate and decision, as well as legal affairs in Babylonia.[329] Even if these assemblies had hardly any political significance remaining in the first millennium, they may still have had a ceremonial role. In this case, the assembly seems to be attached to some phase of the substitute king ritual. Since the eclipse afflicted all Babylonia, it concerned the whole country.

The first quotation, "You will take over the kingship," is more problematic to locate. As such it could have been appropriately proclaimed at the enthronement ceremony, but this is probably not the case because the prophecy is said to have been uttered "before these rituals" (line 22: *pānat nēpēše annūti*). Which rituals are referred to here? Clearly not only the enthronement[330] and the burial of the substitute king but also the *namburbû* and *bīt rimki* rituals, exorcisms (*nēpēšu*) and other ceremonies mentioned just before and right after the flashback about the prophetess. What is of particular interest here is that the process of *bīt rimki* ('ablution house'), the purpose of which was to "wash away" the sins of the king (not the substitute but the actual king) on the occasion of the lunar eclipse, took several days and had in this case begun *already before* the eclipse became visible and the substitute was chosen (SAA 10 240:5-16, 14-20).[331] If the prophetess really had trans-

---

326 AHw 883: "eine Ratte?"

327 Cf. above, p. 23.

328 Cf. also the heavily restored lines SAA 9 4:3-4: [*ka-ki*]*š-a-ti* ⌜*ú*⌝-[*ba*?-*ra*? *ina* IGI] GÌR.2-*ka* ⌜*a*⌝-[*kar-ra-ar*] "I will [catch... and wease]ls, (and) I will [cast them before] your feet."

329 See Jacobsen 1943; 1957, 99-109; Postgate 1992, 80-81. The best example is the homicide trial at Nippur for which see Jacobsen 1959 and Postgate 1992, 278. In the later third millennium, even the king has demonstrably been chosen by the assembly of Kish (Jacobsen 1978/9, 6).

330 Thus Landsberger 1965, 47.

331 See Parpola 1983, 176-177.

mitted the divine promise of kingship to Damqî before the ritual process was started (and "before" does not stand for "before their completion"), it means that the substitute had been looked for in good time before the eclipse became a current problem. This may not have been the standard procedure, but it concurs with the remarkably early suggestion of the chief exorcist Marduk-šakin-šumi that the substitute be chosen – and among the Babylonians for that matter. Who knows if he already had a prophetically ascertained candidate called Damqî in his mind? Be that as it may, the suggestion of the chief exorcist and the citation of prophecy by Mar-Issar are equally motivated: the Babylonians needed to be reminded of their mortality, and it was the divine will that they were made to learn it in this way. Once again, prophecy proved to be an advantageous tool for those in power.

The letter is also remarkable because it is the only existing evidence of prophetic activity within the substitute king ritual. We do not know if the prophets always appeared on this occasion; the way Mar-Issar puts it ("I have heard...") would suggest the opposite. This, however, applies only to the first utterance which is likely to have taken place before the whole ritual and thus not in the presence of Mar-Issar, perhaps not in public at all.[332] The second prophecy uttered "in the assembly of the country" may well have been witnessed by him. In any case, it is quite consistent that a prophet had a function in the substitute king ritual as the prophets demonstrably had in the actual enthronement ceremonies. We have at our disposal a collection of five prophetic oracles (SAA 9 3) that are all attached to the enthronement of Esarhaddon and demonstrate the role of the prophetic word in different stages of the ritual.[333] The oracles are proclaimed either to the people or to the king in the presence of the public (SAA 9 3.2 i 27-30 and 3.3 ii 27-28, 32):

> *[sitam]meā marʾē māt Aššūr [šarru nakar]šu iktašad [šarrakūn]u nakaršu [ina šapil šē]pēšu issakan*
>
> [List]en, O Assyrians! [The king] has vanquished his enemy. [You]r [king] has put his enemy [under] his foot.
>
> *ṭuppi adê anniu ša Aššur... ina pān šarri errab... ina pān šarri isassiū*
>
> This covenant tablet of Aššur enters the king's presence... and they read it out in the king's presence.

Accordingly, in SAA 10 352 the prophetess speaks to the substitute king "in the assembly of the country" and proclaims his victory over his enemies.

---

[332] For the sake of comparison it can be noted that the in the Hebrew Bible kings are sometimes designated by prophets in private, before the public recognition of their kingship; cf. 1 Sam 9:26-10:1 (Saul); 16:1-13 (David; cf. the dynastic oracle in 2 Sam 7); 2 Kings 9:1-11 (Jehu) – unlike 1 Kings 1:32-40 (Solomon).

[333] For the date, cf. above n. 108.

The triumph over enemies is an essential factor in the accession to the throne; in fact, it appears to be a prerequisite for the enthronement.[334] One might wonder, of course, how the substitute king had already managed to get enemies, but one should also remember that he was not there as himself but as a personification and embodiment of the actual king: he "ruled" and died *as* the king whose sins in this way were removed.[335] This is why the exultation over the vanquished enemies must have also belonged to the substitute king ritual that imitated the actual coronation ceremonies. Since the function of the prophets on this occasion was the proclamation of the victory (cf. SAA 9 3.2; 3.3), it is only natural that a prophetess made a similar appearance in the substitute king ritual, too.

---

[334] Note that, even if the "enemy" was quite real, as in the case of Esarhaddon, i.e., his rebellious brothers, the "ideology of *nakrūtu* plays such a large role in Assyrian historiography, and gives origin to so many recurring literary images, exactly because it constitutes the counterpart of the values assigned by the authors to Assyrian kingship ideology" (Fales 1982, 425).

[335] For the ideology of substitution, see Parpola 1983, XXIV-XXV; 1993b, 54-55; Bottéro 1992, 142-143.

4.2. Should Adad-ahu-iddina Let the Throne Go?

Text

LAS 317
(= K 540 / ABL 149; not included in SAA 10)

Obv. ^{1}*a-na* LUGAL EN-*ia* ^{2}ARAD-*ka* ^{md}IM–PAP–AŠ ^{3}*lu-u šul-mu a-na* LUGAL EN-*iá* ^{4}*aš-šur* ^{d}NIN.LÍL ^{d}PA ^{d}AMAR.UTU ^{5}*a-na* LUGAL *be-lí-ia* ^{6}*lik-ru-bu* ^{7}[M]Í.^{d}NIN.LÍL–AD–PAP *ra-gi-in-tú* ^{8}*ša ku-zip-pi ša* LUGAL ^{9}*a-na* KUR URI.KI *tu-bi-lu-ni* ^{10}[*ina*] ⸢É⸣.DINGIR *ta-ar-tu-g*[*u-u*]*m* ^{11}[*ma-a* GIŠ].GU.ZA TA* É.[DIN]GIR
Rev. 5 lines unreadable
^{6}G[IŠ].⸢GU.ZA⸣ [*l*]*u ta-lik* ^{7}*ma-a* LÚ.KÚR.MEŠ ^{8}*ša* LUGAL-*ia ina lìb-bi* ^{9}*a-ka-šad mu-uk* ^{10}*ša la* LUGAL EN-*ia* ^{11}GIŠ.GU.ZA *la a-dan* ^{12}*ki-i ša* LUGAL *be-lí* ^{13}*i-qa-bu-u-ni* ^{14}*ina pi-it-te ne-pu-uš*

> ^{1} To the king, my lord, (from) your servant Adad-ahu-iddina: Good health to the king, my lord! May the gods Aššur, Mullissu, Nabû and Marduk bless the king, my lord.
> ^{7} The prophetess Mullissu-abu-uṣri who took the king's clothes to Akkad, has prophesied [in the te]mple: "[The] throne from the te[mp]le [...]
> *(Break)*
> $^{r.6}$ [Le]t the throne go, I shall catch my king's enemies with it." I said: "Without (the permission of) the king, my lord, I shall not give up the throne."
> ^{12} We will act according to the instructions of the king, my lord.

Background

Nothing is known about Adad-ahu-iddina who appears only in this letter and, possibly, in three further documents.[336] It is discernible from the contents of the letter that he holds a managerial position within the temple administration, since the moving of the temple throne, i.e., one of the most precious objects in the temple, appears to be under his authority. It cannot be concluded with certainty in which temple he is serving, but Ešarra, the Aššur temple of Assur, suggests itself,[337] not only because Aššur and Mullissu precede the otherwise more common Nabû and Marduk in the blessing formula, but also because that temple boasted the king's throne and the enthronement of Esarhaddon was celebrated there (SAA 9 3.1-3).

---

[336] The datable documents from the time of Esarhaddon and Assurbanipal include an individual with this name only as a slave owner in ADD 310:1, 6, 16, and as a witness in ADD 173 r.7 and ADD 622 r.5.

[337] Cf. Parpola 1983, 329.

The letter is written due to the appearance of a prophetess (*raggintu*) called Mullissu-abu-uṣri who prophesied (*tartugum*) something concerning the throne. The prophecy is quoted in the letter but, to our misfortune, most of its content is broken away.

The request of the prophetess: "Let the throne go, I shall catch my king's enemies with it" (*kussiu lū tallik nakarūti ša šarrīja ina libbi akaššad*) recalls a ritual described by Marduk-šumu-uṣur in his letter to Assurbanipal from the year 667 (SAA 10 174). When Esarhaddon was on his way to conquer Egypt, a ceremony was arranged on the outskirts of Harran in a temple of cedar specially built for this occasion.[338] When the king entered the temple, a crown (or two?)[339] was placed on his head and it was said to him: "You will go and conquer the world with it" (*tallak mātāti ina libbi takaššad*, line 14).[340] Both the throne and the crown serve as symbols manifesting the supreme and global rule and the presence of the person to whom they are given by the gods. It is not indicated who uttered the words quoted in the letter; in the text they are introduced with the mere particle *mā*. Against the background of LAS 317 r.6 it is not excluded that they were proclaimed by a prophet.

The preserved lines also let us know that the prophetess has "taken the king's clothes to Akkad" and now she states as the divine will that the throne should also be taken out from the temple. The taking of the king's clothes (*kuzippī*) to Akkad probably implies that the throne would belong to the objects that should be conveyed to Akkad for some purpose. Nevertheless, Adad-ahu-iddina is reluctant to let the throne go and asks the king's permission for its tranference – perhaps hoping for a negative answer but, naturally, submitting to the king's will (*kî ša šarru iqbûni nēpuš*).[341]

But why all this transportation of precious things? It has been pointed out that Mullissu-abu-uṣri may be identical with the prophetess of SAA 10 352 who prophesied on the occasion of the substitute king ritual in the month of Tebet (X), 671.[342] Thus, the taking of the king's clothes to Akkad as well as the intended transference of the throne could be connected with the very same ritual. If LAS 317 is connected with the preparations of the ritual described by Mar-Issar in SAA 10 351 and 352, then these items may have accompanied the substitute king from Nineveh to Akkad where he was enthroned for the second time. This may have happened in a ceremonial process during which

---

[338] For this text, see also below, pp. 123-124.

[339] The word is completely destroyed, but the word 'crown' suggests itself because the god Sin is seated in the temple wearing two crowns (2 AGA.MEŠ *ina* SAG.DU *š*[*ak-nu*], line 12). It can be imagined that when Esarhaddon enters into the temple, one (or both) of them are given to him as a symbol of his power over the world.

[340] Cf. also SAA 10 111 r.21-23: *ina kussīka ašbāta nakarūtēka takammu aiābīka takaššad u māt nakarīka tašallal* "Sitting on your throne, you will vanquish your enemies, conquer your foes and plunder the land of your enemy." See below, pp. 100-101.

[341] Cf. the same phrase in SAA 10 293:31-32.

[342] Von Soden 1956, 102, followed by Landsberger 1965, 49; Parpola 1983, 329.

the prophetess had a role to play.[343] Admittedly, this cannot be proved with absolute certainty, but there are at least two points strongly suggesting that a substitute king ritual – either the one described in SAA 10 352 or another one – is referred to here.

First, Akkad, the ancient Sargonid capital, was the city where the substitute kings were enthroned when the right-hand lunar quadrant, corresponding to Babylonia, was eclipsed during the reign of Esarhaddon who was the king of both Assyria and Babylonia.[344] If the king's throne was needed in Akkad, someone was expected to sit on it – if not the king, then the substitute king!

Secondly, a letter of the exorcist Adad-šumu-uṣur (SAA 10 189) concerning an earlier substitute king ritual itemizes a number of royal insignia. Just like Adad-ahu-iddina in LAS 317, Adad-šumu-uṣur is awaiting the instructions of the king before he takes any action (lines 6-12, r.6-8):

> *ina muhhi šar pūhi ša Akkadi ana šēšubi ṭēmu liškunu ina muhhi lubussi ša šarri bēlīja kuzippi ša ana ṣalam šar pūhi ina muhhi gāgi [ša hurā]ṣi haṭṭi kussî... mīnu ša šarru bēlī iqabbûni*
>
> Concerning the substitute king of Akkad,[345] the order should be given to enthrone (him). Concerning the clothes of the king, my lord, and the garments for the statue[346] of the substitute king, concerning the necklace [of go]ld, the sceptre and the throne... What is it that the king, my lord, commands?

This letter proves that the king's clothes and the throne, among other things,[347] belonged to the substitute king ritual. The throne was needed for the coronation, of course, and not just any chair was good enough. It had to be *the actual* royal throne because the whole personality of the king was transferred to the substitute, while the king as a "farmer," stripped of all royal insignia, went through elaborate purification rituals. Accordingly, the function of the garments was not just to dress the substitute king: by robing himself in them he took the sins of the ruling king upon himself and died, not only instead of him, but *as* him. The document in which the eclipse omens

---

[343] Thus Bottéro 1992, 150. Since the transfer of the substitute from Nineveh to Akkad, according to SAA 10 351, took only five days, it presumably took place by boat; see Wall-Romana 1990, 216.

[344] See Parpola 1983, XXIII, XXV, 428-429.

[345] ⸢*šá*! *a*!⸣-*ka*-⸢*di*!⸣; thus according to the collation of Parpola in LAS 2 and SAA 10 instead of the reading *ša* NINA!.KI (von Soden 1956, 104; Lambert in Landsberger 1965, 45).

[346] The "statue" actually means the substitute king himself as a living person; cf. SAA 10 90:5 and Parpola 1983, 305-306.

[347] The fragment SAA 10 312 that mentions "the bath" (*rimku* cf. SAA 10 189:13) – apparently belonging to the *bīt rimki* ritual (cf. SAA 10 352:18) – may be a remnant of a copy of the same letter: *ina ugu ri-in-ki mi-i-nu ša* LUGAL *be-lí* ⸢*i*⸣-*qab-bu-ni* "Concerning the bath, what is it that the king, my lord, commands?"

and other evil portents were written down was attached in the clothes to make sure that they kept constantly affecting the substitute.[348]

Prophecy

One interesting point among many others in this short letter is the attitude of the temple official towards the prophetic word. The prophetess is hardly acting fully unprompted. Certainly she could not possibly take along the king's clothes without due permission – on the contrary, she must have been authorized to transfer some royal insignia to Akkad. Presumably the conveying of the throne away from the temple was beyond her assignment – but it is not she herself who wants it to go. The verb *ragāmu* implies that the prophetess is not giving her personal opinions but proclaiming a divine message concerning the throne. This is why Adad-ahu-iddina, disagreeable as the idea might sound to him, cannot repudiate it straight away but has to ask the king's opinion. It is remarkable, even if at the same time very understandable, that in the actual decision-making the clear instructions of the king outweigh the prophetic utterances, the origin of which is difficult to control. The temple official cannot reject the divine word proclaimed by a prophetess but he can give up the responsibility of its interpretation to the king. In any case, the attitude of Adad-ahu-iddina reflects certain suspicions about the competence of the prophets as well as the authority of the words spoken by them.

---

[348] SAA 10 12 r.5-8: *ittimāli ussašmešūma aqṭadad ina qannīšu artakas* "Yesterday I made him (= the substitute king) hear them (= the signs) again, and I bent down and bound them in his hem."

CHAPTER FIVE

PROPHECY AND THE SCHOLARS

5.1. The Distress of Urad-Gula

Text

SAA 10 294
(= K 4267 / ABL 1285)

Rev. [30][*ù ina* M]U.AN.NA MEŠ-*ia ma-a a-na ši-bu-ti tak-šu-da tu-kul-ta-ka lu-u man-nu* [31][*ina* IGI *x la*]-*a mah-rak el-li a-na* É.GAL *la-a tar-ṣa-ak* : LÚ.*ra-ag-gi-mu* [32][*as-sa-ʾa-al*? SI]G$_5$? *la-a a-mur ma-ah-hur ù di-ig-lu un-ta-aṭ-ṭi* [33][*ša* LUGAL *be-lí*]-*iá a-ma-ár-ka* SIG$_5$: *na-as-hur-ka maš-ru-ú*

> [30][Also] I am [50?] years (already) and they say: "Once you have reached old age, who will support you?" [The *king*] is not pleased with me; I go to the palace, I am no good;
> [31][I turned to] a prophet (but) did not find [any hop]e, he was adverse and did not see much. [O king] my [lord], seeing you is happiness, your attention is a fortune!

Background

The letter SAA 10 294 has been thoroughly discussed by Parpola,[349] so it suffices here to describe the writer and content only in broad outline, paying special attention to the lines crucial for the understanding of Neo-Assyrian prophecy.

In this letter we meet an ill-treated scholar who complains of his lot with good reason. Once having been one of the confidants of the crown prince, he now finds himself completely edged out: "Now, following his father, the king my lord has added to the good name he has established, but I have not been treated in accordance with my deeds; I have suffered as never before, and given up the ghost" (23-25). Frustrated by repeated setbacks and suffering from poverty and dishonor he pleads with the king for at least some attention. Humiliated as he is altogether, he does not ask for anything more than a pair of draught animals and a spare suit of clothes (r.34-35). His beasts had died two years earlier (r.13-14), and he feels ashamed of going on foot (r.17-18). Heavily in debt, he cannot afford "a pair of sandals and the wages of a tailor" (r.27-29). Add to this an unhappy marriage and the failure to beget a son (r.24-25) and the distress is total.

To all appearances, the outcast who pours out his troubles in this exceptionally long (85 lines!), very skillfully written and polished letter is the well

[349] Parpola 1987a. Cf. also Hurowitz 1993 who concentrates on the literary topoi of the letter common to the Hebrew Bible.

known Urad-Gula,[350] son of the king's exorcist Adad-šumu-uṣur, who already appears as "deputy of the chief physician" in a purchase document from the time of Sennacherib (SAA 6 193 r.8 from 681-II-12)[351] and who made a career as an exorcist in Esarhaddon's court.[352] Urad-Gula had also served the crown prince Assurbanipal who knew him from the time he was a child (r.37). However, as becomes evident from this letter, he fell out of favor with Assurbanipal as soon as the latter ascended the throne, possibly for personal reasons.[353] Despite the repeated petitions of the father Adad-šumu-uṣur (SAA 10 224:16-r.8 from the year 667 and SAA 10 226 r.6-12 from the year 666), Assurbanipal never allowed Urad-Gula to stay in his entourage, even if this favor was subsequently granted to Adad-šumu-uṣur himself together with his nephews and cousins (SAA 10 227 r.15-16).[354] Urad-Gula's own efforts also went down the drain: the nonchalant answer of the king to his previous letter (r.3-4) and the humiliating walk back home from Assur (or Arbela) where the king summoned an exorcist from Ekallate instead of him (r.14-17) had disheartened him completely.[355]

This letter, written probably in ca. 664,[356] seems to be Urad-Gula's last, desperate attempt to be recognized by the king, whom he takes pains to convince, not only by the affecting story of his life, but also by means of literary perfection. Apart from being of a very high scribal quality in general, the letter contains several allusions to literary works[357] showing the writer's profound knowledge of the learned tradition which is certainly not intended to remain unnoticed by Assurbanipal, who himself boasted of his own erudition in the scriptures. Quite recently, Karel van der Toorn has demonstrated

---

[350] Even though the first line of the letter indicating the sender is broken away, the handwriting, orthography, idiolect and the story itself leave no doubt that writer is Urad-Gula (Parpola 1987a, 268-269).

[351] Considering this, it sounds like a hyperbole when he states that he initially, in the days of the king's father (i.e., Esarhaddon) was "a poor man, son of a poor man, a dead dog, a vile and limited person" (lines 14-15).

[352] Besides the present one, five of his letters to Esarhaddon (SAA 10 289-293), and one letter from the king to himself (SAA 10 295) have been preserved. In addition, he is mentioned in SAA 10 194 r.9, 257 r.8 and in BAK 498 r.10-11 (Hunger 1968, 135) where he appears as the son of Adad-šumu-uṣur. In a colophon of a Neo-Babylonian astronomical text from 650/649 [^{m}ÌR]-$^{⌈d⌉}$*gu-la* LÚ.⌈A.ZU⌉ "[Urad]-Gula the physician" is mentioned, presumably indicating the previous owner of the tablet before its incorporation in the royal library (K 2077+ s.2; see Pingree & Reiner 1974/77, 51; Parpola 1983, 452-453).

[353] According to Parpola (1987, 270-271), Urad-Gula gives the impression of a "negative-minded, habitual complainer" (SAA 10 289, 290) whose "snooping around" Assurbanipal may have disliked. The miscarriage of a royal child reported in SAA 10 293 might also have contributed to his ousting.

[354] On the chronological order of these documents see Parpola 1987a, 270.

[355] Hurowitz 1993, 16-17 refers to Eccl 10:7 as a description of an equally abnormal situation: "I have seen slaves on horseback and nobles walking on the ground like the slaves."

[356] For this date, and for the impossibility of an earlier date, see Parpola 1987a, 270.

[357] See Parpola 1987a, 272-274.

that Urad-Gula actually assumes the role of the protagonist of *Ludlul bēl nēmeqi*, the "righteous sufferer" who was totally abandoned by each and every one in the court but whose fate finally was changed by Marduk.[358] Obviously the king is supposed to take heed of the message.

Prophecy

Turning to a prophet (*raggimu*) seems like clutching at a straw in a hopeless situation. Urad-Gula seems to make mention of it in this context to show that there were not many options left for him. Urad-Gula is no longer a young man[359] and he has been reminded that: "Once you have reached old age, who will support you?" All the disappointments notwithstanding, he still regards the king as the only opportunity: "Seeing you is happiness, your attention is a fortune!" Since seeing the king is his final goal and he continues to be completely ignored at the palace, he tries something else: he goes to see a prophet. It is clear from the context that this was not just like falling back on a soothsayer for a therapeutic purpose, or to satisfy curiosity about future events. Rather, he regarded the prophet as the last quarter from which he could expect help in his efforts to gain the king's approbation.

It is difficult to conclude in concrete terms what Urad-Gula expected from the prophet. Did he want him to do some string-pulling: to say a good word for him before the king or otherwise use his influence over Assurbanipal who was not only versed in scriptures but also receptive to prophetic words? Or did he ask for a favorable oracle concerning himself that could have been transmitted to the king as a divine recommendation? Or perhaps he only wanted to hear divine encouragement such as "Fear not, Urad-Gula, the gods are with you"? Since he talks about a vision (*diglu*) he is likely to have asked for one; but what kind of a vision? Certainly he wanted the message to reach the king's ears. That he would have expected an oracle mentioning himself expressly appears dubious, considering that the extant prophecies at our disposal never mention any individuals except the king, the queen mother or the crown prince – but this fact may be simply due to another: only the prophecies addressed to court members have been preserved. Nothing else is left from the prophets' contacts with private persons except the letter of Urad-Gula which, though, is an indisputable document of the existence of such contacts.

---

[358] Paper read at the Annual Meeting of the Society of Biblical Literature in San Francisco, Nov. 24, 1997 (van der Toorn 1997b). I am grateful to Prof. van der Toorn for the opportunity of seeing the text of the paper before its publication.

[359] The preserved text does not indicate his exact age, and even the destroyed beginning of the line did not necessarily include any numerals. The [50?] suggested by the translation is, of course, a pure conjecture, but may not be far from the truth. If Urad-Gula was in his mid-twenties as the deputy of the chief physician in 681 – he could hardly be much younger in a demanding office like that – he is now, about two decades later, approaching his fifties.

All in all, the letter warrants at least the following conclusions:

i) A prophet was visited by a private person. Even if the prophets were mouthpieces of the gods in the first place and not consultants on private affairs on a personal level, the letter shows that divine words could be requested not only by the royal family but also by other people. That all prophetic oracles did not come spontaneously but could be queried on occasion[360] is confirmed in the existing oracles; cf. SAA 9 1.8 v 14-15: *kî tahhurīninni mā*... "Because you implored me, saying: ..."

ii) The visit was a total disaster. For whatever reason – maybe because of the status of Urad-Gula as a persona non grata in the court, or because he was a scholar – the prophet was "adverse" (*mahhur*), irritated perhaps, and did not deliver a convincing oracle if anything at all; *diglu untaṭṭi* means literally "he lacked a vision" and may also denote his defective power of seeing a vision.[361] Urad-Gula, thus, gives the impression that the failure to receive a divine message resulted from the reluctance and incompetence of the prophet.

iii) On the other hand, being abandoned not only by people but also by the gods can be seen as an additional feature of the role Urad-Gula is playing: the turning to the prophet fits well into the role of the "righteous sufferer" assumed by him as a means of convincing Assurbanipal of his desperate need of rehabilitation. The protagonist of *Ludlul bēl nēmeqi* is likewise disappointed at the performances of the diviners, whether he had consulted a haruspex (*bārû*), a dream interpreter (*šā'ilu*), an incantation priest (*mašmaššu*) or an exorcist (*āšipu*) (lines i 43-44, 52; ii 4-7, 108-113):[362]

> My god (*ilu*) has forsaken me and disappeared,
> My goddess (*ištaru*) has failed me and keeps at a distance...
> The omen of the *bārû* and *šā'ilu* does not explain my condition.
>
> I called to my god, but he did not show his face,
> I prayed to my goddess, but she did not raise her head.
> The *bārû* with his inspection has not got to the root of the matter
> (*arkat ul iprus*),
> Nor has the *šā'ilu* with his libation elucidated my case.
>
> My complaints have exposed the *mašmaššu*,
> And my omens have confounded the *bārû*.
> The *āšipu* has not diagnosed the nature of my complaint,
> Nor has the diviner put a time limit (*adannu*) on my illness.
> My god has not come to the rescue in taking me by the hand,
> Nor has my goddess shown pity on me by going at my side.

---

360 A practice well attested in the Hebrew Bible, mostly with a king as the inquirer: 1 Sam 9:9; 28:6; 1 Kings 22:5ff; 2 Kings 3:11ff; 19:1-7//Is 37:1-7; Jer 21:1ff; 38:14ff; 42:1ff.

361 See AHw 169 (sub *diglu* 1b) for other occurrences of *diglu* + *maṭû*. Cf. also the biblical references to a general lack of visions in 1 Sam 3:1 (*'ēn ḥāzôn nipraṣ*) and Mi 3:6 (*laylâ lākæm mē-ḥāzôn*).

362 Lambert 1960, 32-33, 38-39, 44-46.

Even though *Ludlul bēl nēmeqi* does not mention a prophet – to which the *šāʾilu* actually comes very close[363] – it seems obvious that the prophet in Urad-Gula's letter has the role of the diviner whose expertise is of no avail. Being an exorcist himself, Urad-Gula would have chosen a representative of a branch of divination other than his own.

iv) The reference to the visit in the present context serves the ends of the letter of Urad-Gula who would hardly tell the king about his turning to the prophet without a purpose. At first sight it may seem counter-productive even to mention the unsuccessful query: if the gods would not help him, how was the king expected to do so? But the gods did not always answer the king himself,[364] and in this case even the prophet is presented as averse to doing his job. Obviously Urad-Gula demonstrates his being abandoned by absolutely everyone in trying to arouse the sympathy of the king – all the more because he goes on with the direct appeal for material help, hoping that the king would "soften" (*lēṭib*) his heart. Presumably he is hoping that the king would take the hint and think about the divine favor which was finally granted to his literary precursor in *Ludlul bēl nēmeqi*, a story that the king was expected to know. Urad-Gula follows here the strategy of his father Adad-šumu-uṣur who also bewailed his loneliness and managed to make pity stir in the heart of the king.[365] But Urad-Gula was given no mercy then, and nothing indicates that this letter would have caused his situation to become any better.

---

363 See above, p. 10, and below, pp. 160-161.

364 Cf., e.g., SAA 10 362 r.8-10 and also 1 Sam 28:6: "[Saul] inquired of the Lord, but the Lord did not answer him, whether by dreams or by Urim or by prophets."

365 SAA 10 226 r.13-19: "My eyes are fixed on the king, my lord. None of those who serve in the palace like me; there is not a single friend of mine among them to whom I could give a present, and who would accept it from me and speak for me." The answer of the king is quoted in SAA 10 227:16-17, r.15-16: "May your heart become happy now, may your mind no longer be restless... I have gathered you, your nephews and your cousins, you belong now to my entourage." For a similar petition, cf. also SAA 10 334 r.9-18 (Nabû-ṭabni-uṣur to Esarhaddon).

5.2. Bel-ušezib Nurses a Grievance

Text

SAA 10 109
(82-5-22, 105 / ABL 1216)

Obv. 7 *[a-n]a-ku* $^{md+}$EN–*ú-še-zib* ARAD-*ka* UR.[KU]-*ka ù pa-lih-ka [x x x x]* 8 *d[i-ib]-bi ma-a'-du-tu i-ba-áš-ši šá i-na* NINA.KI *áš-mu-ú k[i-i ú-kal-li-mu]* 9 *am-me-ni re-eš* LÚ.*ra-ag-gi-ma-nu* MÍ.*ra-ag-gi-ma-a-tu x[x x x x]* 10 *[šá* LÚ].MAŠ.MAŠ *i-na pi-ia ap-ri-ku-ma a-na šul-mu šá* DUMU–LUGAL *be-lí-i[a]* 11 *[al-li]-ka la-pa-ni da-a-ku ú-še-zi-ba-am-ma a-na* URU.*a-ši-t[i ah-li-qa]* 12 *a-na* UGU-*hi da-a-ki-ia ù da-a-ku šá* ARAD.MEŠ-*ka* UD-*mu-us-s[u id-bu-bu]* 13 *ù it-tu šá* LUGAL-*ú-ti šá* ^{md}*aš-šur*–ŠEŠ–SUM-*na* DUMU–LUGAL *be-lí-[ia]* 14 *a-na* ^{m}*da-da-a* LÚ.MAŠ.MAŠ *ù* AMA–MAN *aq-bu-ú um-ma* $^{m⌈d⌉}$*aš-šur*–ŠEŠ–SUM-*na* 15 TIN.IR.KI *ep-pu-uš* É.SAG.ÍL *ú-šak-lal ù ia-a-[ši x x x x]* 16 *am-me-ni a-di* UGU-*hi šá en-na* LUGAL *re-eš-a la iš-ši*

> 7 I am Bel-ušezib, your servant and your dog who fears you [...].
> 8 Why [did *the king, my lord* sum]mon prophets and prophetesses w[hen I *disclosed*] the many [th]ings I had heard in Nineveh, (while) [I, who] blocked the exorcist with my mouth and [we]nt to pay homage to the crown prince my lord, who evaded execution [by fleeing] to the *Tower*, whose murder along with your servants [was plotted] every day, and who told the omen of the kingship of my lord the crown prince Esarhaddon to the exorcist Dadâ and the queen mother, saying: "Esarhaddon will rebuild Babylon and restore Esaggil, and [*honor*] me" –
> 16 why has the king up until now not summoned me?

Background

The writer of this letter is Bel-ušezib,[366] the well-known Babylonian astrologer who, judging from the distribution of the preserved documents, maintained a closer contact with the king Esarhaddon than any other Babylonian scholar. The present one included, he is the author of 13 preserved letters (SAA 10 109-121)[367] which report not only astronomical observations but also political and military events accompanied by respective suggestions of

---

366 The beginning of line 7 reads *[a-n]a-ku*! (cf. Dietrich 1970, 63 n. 6, confirmed by the collation of I. L. Finkel in SAA 10), thus leaving no doubt of the identity of the author even if the beginning of the letter is broken away. For basic information on Bel-ušezib and his correspondence see Dietrich 1968, 233-242; 1970, 62-68.

367 Compare the list of Dietrich 1970, 63 with the SAA edition which adds CT 54 258 as no. 117 (the author's name is preserved on line 1) and ABL 1183 as no. 119 to the group; on the other hand, CT 54 63 (= K 4684), identified by Dietrich as a letter of

what measures should be taken by the king. For instance, Esarhaddon's war against the Manneans in 675 is followed by the keen interest of Bel-ušezib (SAA 10 111-113, see below pp. 96-101). He also informs the king about an alleged conspiracy in Nippur (SAA 10 112:28ff, see below p. 138) and proposes appointments of high officials (SAA 10 116; 118), among them nobody less than Adad-šumu-uṣur who was to become Esarhaddon's exorcist and one of his closest advisors (SAA 10 110).

Bel-ušezib is said to display a greater interest in politics than in astronomy,[368] and this may be true, but it is important to note that astronomy and politics were not distinct areas which both happened to interest him; on the contrary, they were perceived as having a close connection. Being understood as signs of the divine determination, the constellations of stars provided a serious epistemological option in interpreting existing conditions, and their observation formed a part of "a set of socially defined and structured procedures for producing (notional) knowledge in a society from what are presumed to be extra-human sources."[369] The expertise on astronomy required extensive studies in the tradition consisting of an immense number of observations and omens compiled and handed down by earlier generations of scholars.[370] That Bel-ušezib is one of the scholars well versed in this tradition is evident from his regular quotations of the canonical omen series[371] and from his ability to apply this learning to concrete circumstances. His letters are an illustrative combination of astronomical skill, political counsel and personal ambition, and they also serve the modern historian with manifold information, the one in hand being especially rewarding in this respect.

The proper understanding of the letter requires the idea that it was not the superstitiousness or gullibility of the king but his confidence in the scholarly

---

Bel-ušezib, is included among the unassigned letters as no. 372.

Bel-ušezib is mentioned in an unassigned astrological report from the year 678 (SAA 8 502 r.12). A person with the same name appears in SAA 7 1 i 16 a list of experts at court, but since this person is listed among exorcists, he is hardly identifiable with the Babylonian astrologer. Furthermore, a person called Bel-ušezib appears in SAA 11 156 r.8, a list of scholars working on the palace libraries of Nineveh from the late years of Esarhaddon, among eight others "who are assisting their masters" in working on a scholarly series. This piece of data is difficult to reconcile with the career of the renowned astrologer, especially because other members of the group seem to be held as hostages in Nineveh (cf. below pp. 136-137).

368 Starr 1990, XXXIV.

369 Cryer 1994, 121-122 on divination in general; Dietrich (1970, 66) uses a more straightforward language: "Die Politik folgt (oder hat zu folgen) dem Lauf der Gestirne."

370 An illustrative example of the (presupposed) recognition of learnedness and scholarly tradition is the letter of the scholar Marduk-šapik-zeri (SAA 10 160) who first gives an account of his own learning (which he calls "my father's profession" *dullu ša abīja*), consisting of both performing rites and reading the canonical scholary works like Enuma Anu Enlil, Šumma izbu and Šumma alu (lines 36-46), and then recommends twenty apprentices of his own, all competent in the same tradition (lines 37ff).

371 E.g., SAA 10 109 r.14-15; 110:3-5; 111:3-8; 112:21, 23; 113:3-4, 6-8; 114:3-4, 10-s.1; 116:5-11; 117:4-5; 119:3ff; 121:3ff; cf. the edition of Enuma Anu Enlil by Weidner 1944/69.

tradition (and his crucial role in the religion and ideology advocated by and implied in it) that made him trust and consult a scholar.[372] Since, on the other hand, the career of a scholar was wholly depedent on the king's favor, he constantly had to demonstrate his experience and erudition in the professional lore as well as his absolute loyalty to the king. It was of vital importance for a scholar to be summoned[373] by the king, not only to receive professional recognition but also to make a decent living and retain an appropriate social standing. As we have just seen, the royal correspondence includes complaints and petitions of scholars who feel themselves disregarded by the king.[374] Bel-ušezib nurses a grievance because the king Esarhaddon has summoned prophets and prophetesses but not him – in spite of all the services and support he had given to Esarhaddon at the risk of his own life when the king was still crown prince. After all, he had been the one who told the subsequently realized omen of kingship of Esarhaddon to the exorcist Dadâ and the queen mother (lines 7-21). Bel-ušezib reminds the king of the scholarly duty imposed by the king's father to report all portents, even the unfavorable ones, that may occur (lines 22-r.13)[375] and then quotes a "sign of kingship," obviously the one he had mentioned earlier (lines r.14-15; cf. lines 14-15). The rest of the letter is damaged to the extent that its contents remain obscure;

---

[372] Once the "proto-scientific" nature of the Mesopotamian divinatory lore has been duly acknowledged, its representatives are no longer regarded as primitive predictors of the future or purveyors of superstition; cf. Oppenheim 1966, 40: "Outside the realm of folklore, the Mesopotamian diviner is not a priest, but an expert technician and, first of all, a scholar. And I mean a scholar in a rather modern sense..." See also Parpola 1983, XX-XXI; 1993a, XXVII; Starr 1990, XXX-XXXV; Bottéro 1992, 134-137; Cryer 1994, 124ff. Pečírková 1985, 158-159 explains Esarhaddon's extensive correspondence with the scholars by the political difficulties: "It is no wonder that in this troubled political situation Asarhaddon sought support in the tradition which symbolized the stability of royal power and which at the same time could reassure him that his actions were in accordance with the wishes of the gods."

[373] The Akkadian expression for the king's summons is *rēšu našû* "raise the head," a semantically varied compound (cf. Hebrew *nāśāʾ rōʾš*) which in this context has approximately the meaning "to employ"; see CAD N/2 107-108 (sub *našû* A 6 c).

[374] The best examples are the letter of Urad-Gula (SAA 10 194) and the petitions of his father Adad-šumu-uṣur on behalf of his son and himself (SAA 10 224, 226). Cf. also SAA 10 171:4-r.4: "[As) the king last year summoned [his scholars, he did not] summon me with [them], (so) I wrote to the palace: 'The apprentices whom the king appointed in my charge have learned *Enuma Anu Enlil*; what is my fault that the king has not summoned me with his scholars?' The king said: 'Have no fear, I will summon you.' But when I departed from there, up to now the king has not summoned me. Now the king has summoned scribes great and small, but the king has not sum[moned] me..." This letter demonstrates the importance of able students for the reputation of a scholar; cf. SAA 10 160 where Marduk-šapik-zeri does no longer speak for himself ("Let the king, my lord, summon me, and if I am to die, let me die") but for his apprentices.

[375] That this duty was taken seriously is evident from the frustration of Balasî who is not able to answer the king's inquiry: "Nothing has risen; I have seen nothing... With deep anxiety, I have nothing to report" (SAA 10 45:4-15, s.2-3). Another scholar, who cannot answer the king's question concerning a solar eclipse, steers clear of it by affirming his proficiency in stargazing (SAA 10 170).

perhaps Bel-ušezib gives here an account of a recent (similar?) sign which has given occasion to write the letter.

For the historical interpretation of the letter, the lines quoting the "sign of kingship" are of paramount importance. As recognized by Labat,[376] the text quoted is the apodosis of an omen from Enuma Anu Enlil 56, which is preceded by the protasis: "If a *bibbu* approaches a *bibbu*." Parpola has shown[377] that this pertains to the conjunction of Mercury, the star of the crown prince, and Saturn, the star of the king,[378] and suggested that Bel-ušezib in this particular case refers to the conjunction that occurred on the 8th of Sivan (III) (= May 18), 681. A brief look at the circumstances at that time shows that this date matches well indeed the historical data as well as the information given by Bel-ušezib in this letter.

As we already know, Esarhaddon, appointed the crown prince of Assyria in the month of Nisan (I), 683, had been sent by his father Sennacherib to a "secure place" in the Western provinces because his brothers had turned against him for the reason that Esarhaddon had replaced his elder brother Arda-Mullissi as the crown prince.[379] If the omen observed by Bel-ušezib is identifiable with the above-mentioned conjunction, it becomes clear why he reported it to the exorcist Dadâ and the queen mother: while Esarhaddon was out of reach at that time, the queen mother Naqija resided in Nineveh working for her son.[380] The reference to the "many things" that Bel-ušezib had "heard in Nineveh" (line 8) suggests that the information given by him was not entirely of astronomical nature. It appears that during his exile Esarhaddon had supporters in Nineveh who had an ear to the ground and kept the queen mother informed about what was happening[381] – and not without risk, for that matter, if the claims of Bel-ušezib about his life having been in danger are true. When the brothers finally concluded their "treaty of rebellion" (*adê ša sīhi*)[382] and murdered Sennacherib on the 20th of Tebet (X), 681 (= January 10, 680),[383] Esarhaddon very soon got enough support to move against them with the result that the brothers fled the country, Esarhaddon marched

[376] Labat 1959, 117.

[377] Parpola 1980, 179-180, 182.

[378] Cf. SAA 8 95:3-4, 7: "Saturn is the star of the sun... Sun is the star of the king."

[379] See above, pp. 18-21.

[380] This is evident also from the prophetic oracles received by Naqija during the exile of Esarhaddon (SAA 9 1.7; 1.8; 5); cf. above, pp. 22-2428.

[381] If this historical interpretation is correct, then there is no need to assume that the city of Ninâ in Southern Babylonia would be meant here instead of Nineveh (Dietrich 1970, 68); this does not mean, however, that this city did not exist at that time (cf. also Brinkman 1977, 319).

[382] Thus the letter ABL 1091 (line 4) which confirms that Arda-Mullissi actually was responsible for the murder of his father; see Parpola 1980 and cf. above, p. 21, nn. 80-81.

[383] For the date, see Grayson 1975a, 81:34-35.

to Nineveh and ascended the throne in the month of Adar (XII), 681 (= February/March, 680).[384]

Thus, the first part of the omen, according to which a son of the king will rebel against him but will not seize the throne but a "son of nobody" will become king instead and restore the temples, was already true when the constellation was observed by Bel-ušezib, and the second part of it materialized when Esarhaddon was enthroned (even though he was not a "son of nobody"). Since he had hardly managed to restore any temples so far, the third part of the omen was still waiting for its realization; Bel-ušezib, as a Babylonian, interpreted this part of the omen as referring to the rebuilding of Babylon and its main temple Esaggil (line 15) – a work that Esarhaddon tried to accomplish during the remainder of his reign.[385]

Considering all his efforts that contributed to the victory of Esarhaddon, as well as his astronomical skill that enabled him to reveal the divine will concerning his kingship, the expectations of Bel-ušezib of becoming employed by the newly enthroned king were by no means exaggerated. The letter was probably written soon after the enthronement[386] but long enough for him to become impatient at the silence of the Palace. The letter of Bel-ušezib is "a good test of the ruler's short memory as regards good omens":[387] he was aware that if he could not refresh the ruler's memory, he would soon find himself in oblivion. Even though there are no records of Bel-ušezib before the time of Esarhaddon, his self-assertive style as well as his reminiscences of earlier days imply that he already had a position in the court of Sennacherib. It may have been quite normal that a new king was free to choose his officials and servants and even the scholars did not automatically continue their service under the new king. Bel-ušezib, however, considers his merits too weighty to become totally disregarded.

Prophecy

Bel-ušezib contrasts his fate with that of the prophets and prophetesses who, according to him, have indeed been summoned by the king. He clearly gives the king to understand that this was a sign of the undervaluation of his achievements and his profession altogether. By reminding the king of the "sign of kingship" he apparently underlines the importance of the learned

---

384 Borger 1956 (§ 27) 43-45:63-86.

385 For Esarhaddon's efforts to restore Babylon, see Brinkman 1984, 72-76; Frame 1992, 67-78. This responsibility was also imposed on him by prophetic words; cf. SAA 9 2.3 ii 24-27 and see above pp. 33-34.

386 This can be concluded not only from the way Bel-ušezib writes about the past events which he apparently supposes to be still fresh in memory but also from the fact that a new conjunction of Mercury and Saturn occured in Iyyar (II) (May) 680, i.e., a couple of months after the enthronement of Esarhaddon in Nineveh; it may be this sign he refers to in lines r.16ff. See Parpola 1980, 179.

387 Lanfranchi 1989, 112.

tradition in revealing the divine determination – a tradition not shared by the prophets who employed totally different divinatory methods. It was the lack of the canonical scriptural tradition and the inductive interpretation of any observable omens that made prophecy a different kind of divination than astronomy or extispicy. It may be interpreted between the lines that the professional astrologer, for this reason, did not regard prophetic expertise to be of equal standard with scribal lore. That Bel-ušezib talks explicitly about prophets and prophetesses instead of using the masculine form in a gender-inclusive sense may reflect his strange feelings about female diviners being honored with royal audiences – as far as the existing sources correspond with the actual circumstances, there were plenty of women among the prophets but none among the other classes of diviners! In addition, leaving the "prophets and prophetesses" nameless indicates that their identities were a matter of complete indifference to the writer.

We do not know the position of the prophets in the Neo-Assyrian court before Esarhaddon, but it is not likely that he would have been the first king to make use of their services, since the prophetic tradition existed long before the Neo-Assyrian era and was, as far as can be concluded on the basis of the totality of preserved documents, closely attached to kingship. One thing is clear, however: Esarhaddon appreciated the prophets to the extent that he let their oracles be deposited in the royal archives, and the documents thus preserved leave no doubt about the activity of the prophets during his war against his brothers and in his enthronement. The largest collection of individual prophecies, SAA 9 1, consists of ten oracles all attached in one way or another to the turbulence of the year 681. The message of virtually every oracle is the rightfulness of his kingship: his divine election,[388] the legitimacy of his rule,[389] the defeat of his enemies[390] and the durability of his reign.[391] The five oracles collected in SAA 9 3 confirm the importance and appreciation of prophecy as the proclamation of the divine support of his reign.[392] The inscriptional references to prophecy in Esarhaddon's account

---

388 E.g., SAA 9 1.4 ii 20-33: "When your mother gave birth to you, sixty great gods stood with me and protected you. Sin was at your right side, Šamaš at your left; sixty great gods were standing around you and girded your loins. Do not trust in man. Lift up your eyes, look to me! I am Ištar of Arbela; I reconciled Aššur with you. When you were small, I took you to me."

389 Cf. SAA 9 1.8 quoted above (p. 22) and SAA 9 1.6 iv 5-6, 20 where he is called *aplu kēnu* 'rightful heir.'

390 E.g., SAA 9 1.1 i 6-14: "What wind has risen against you, whose wing I have not broken? Your enemies will roll before your feet like ripe apples. I am the Great Lady; I am Ištar of Arbela, who cast your enemies before your feet."

391 E.g., SAA 9 1.6 iv 14-17: "Esarhaddon! I will give you long days and everlasting years in the Inner City"; SAA 9 1.10 vi 27-30: "Your son and grandson shall rule as kings on the lap of Ninurta."

392 SAA 9 3.2 ii 3-7: "Aššur has given the totality of the four regions (*kippat erbetti*) to him. From sunrise to sunset there is no king equal to him." SAA 9 3.5 iii 20-22: "Did I not bend the four doorjambs of Assyria, and did I not give them to you? Did I not vanquish your enemy?"

of his rise to power (see above, pp. 14-34) likewise allude to prophetic activity and support both in the course of the war and on the occasion of the enthronement. During the civil war of the year 681, the queen mother Naqija appealed to Ištar through the prophets for divine help (SAA 9 1.7; 1.8; 5) while she also maintained contact with Bel-ušezib and, supposedly, with other scholars[393] loyal to her son.

All this makes it feasible to conclude that Esarhaddon actually had every reason to summon the prophets and prophetesses after his ascent to power. This certainly did not mean any underrating of other diviners, even if some scholars may have had to await the king's summons a little longer. At least in the case of Bel-ušezib the royal nonchalance, if there was any, was not of a permanent nature: his later correspondence demonstrates that he was to be summoned by Esarhaddon many times in the days to come.

393 As regards later times, this is certain (cf., e.g., SAA 10 16; 154; 313 r.1-7).

5.3. Bel-ušezib Quotes Prophecy

Text

SAA 10 111
(83-1-18, 1 / ABL 1237)

Rev. [19]LUGAL DINGIR.ME [d]AMAR.UTU *it-ti* LUGAL *be-lí-ia sa-lim* [20]*mim-ma ma-la* LUGAL *be-lí-ia i-qab-bu-ú ip-pu-uš* [21]*ina* GIŠ.GU.ZA-*ka áš-ba-a-ta* LÚ.KÚR.MEŠ-*ka* [22]*ta-kám-mu a-a-bi-ka ta-kaš-šad ù* KUR KÚR-*i-ka* [23]*ta-šal-lal* [d+]EN *iq-ta-bi um-ma a-ki-i* [24md]AMAR.UTU–DUB–NUMUN [m]AN.ŠÁR–ŠEŠ–SUM-*na* LUGAL KUR–*aš-š*[*ur*.KI][25]*ina* GIŠ.GU.ZA-*šú lu-ú a-ši-ib ù* KUR.[KUR] [26e]*gab-bi a-na* ŠU.2-*šú* ⸢*a*⸣-*man-ni* LUGAL*be-lí*-[*a lu-ú*] [27e]*ha-di-iš* LUGAL *a-ki-i šá i-le*-[ʾ*u-ú*] [28e]*li-pu-uš*

r.19 The king of the gods, Marduk, is reconciled with the king, my lord; whatever the king, my lord says, he can do. Sitting on your throne, you will vanquish your enemies, conquer your foes and plunder the land of your enemy.
23 Bel has said: "May Esarhaddon, king of Assyria, be seated on his throne[394] like Marduk-šapik-zeri, and I will deliver all the countries into his hands." The king, my lord, may rejoice over this![395]
26 The king may do as he deems best.

Background

Here we have another letter written by Bel-ušezib who has now become an established member of Esarhaddon's "inner circle" and represents himself accordingly. In his letters SAA 10 111 and 112 he advises the king on matters concerning the Manneans, against whom Esarhaddon fought in the mid-670's. The historical and astronomical details[396] warrant the dating of SAA 10 112, and thus also the previous letter, to the year 675. Together with a group of oracle queries (SAA 4 29-34), these letters serve as the most informative source for Esarhaddon's Mannean war. Unfortunately, however, Bel-ušezib does not write to serve the needs of a modern historian to reconstruct historical events. The chronological order of the letters SAA 10 111 and 112 cannot be determined with certainty. Generally, as the order of the SAA edition indicates, SAA 10 111 is understood as preceding 112, but Lanfranchi

---

394 Line 25 according to the collation of M. Dietrich (courtesy M. Dietrich). The SAA edition has *ina* GIŠ.GU.ZA *ù ina* ŠÀ *a-ši-bu*.

395 The end of line 26e according to the collation of M. Dietrich (courtesy M. Dietrich). The SAA edition has LUGAL ⸢EN⸣ *ni*-[*x x x*].

396 I.e., the capture of Sidon in 677/676 (13-15; cf. Grayson 1975a, 83:3; 126:12.14) and the partial eclipse of the moon (SAA 10 112:3-6); see Dietrich 1968, 234-235; 1970, 47.

has opted for the reverse order.[397] For the purposes of this study, this issue is not of prime importance.

SAA 10 112 indicates that Esarhaddon's army had already attacked the Manneans, captured forts and towns and plundered the open country when this letter was written (lines 8-11). Bel-ušezib, having observed a celestial portent – the sun and the crescent of the moon seen together on the 15th day (lines 3-7, 21-24)[398] – urges the king to go on with the campaign, referring to the fall of Sidon which carried the same portent in the previous year (lines 12-17). According to the interpretation of Bel-ušezib, this portent, indicating that "an enemy will attack a country" afflicted the Manneans – the "enemy," in this particular case, meaning Assyria.[399]

SAA 10 111 begins with quoting two meteor omens concerning the defeat of an enemy (lines 3-4 and 5-8), but he does not say whether or not he has already observed the respective phenomena in the sky. These quotations, drawn from canonical collections,[400] are followed by instructions concerning Esarhaddon's plans to invade Mannea.

As the letter continues, it appears that the king has been undecided about the campaign. The reason for this was the Cimmerians who had affirmed that they would not intervene if Esarhaddon invaded Mannea: "The Manneans are at your disposal, we shall keep aloof"[401] (*Mannāja ina pānīkunu šēpāni niptaras* lines 13-14). These words, however, should not be trusted , since the Cimmerians are barbarians who recognize no oath sworn by god and no treaty" (*zēr halgatî*[402] *šunu māmēti ša ili u adê ul idû* lines 15-16), that is, have not submitted themselves to the sovereignty of Esarhaddon by making an *adê* with him.[403] For this reason, the intentions of the Cimmerians should

[397] Lanfranchi 1989, 110-111. His arguments are as follows: 1) the sentence "I have written to the king, my lord" (*ana šarri bēlī altapra*; cf. the translation of SAA 10: "I am writing to the king, my lord") may refer to SAA 10 112; 2) the favorable forecasts of SAA 10 112 (lines 3-27) may find a confirmation in SAA 10 111 (lines 3-8, r.6-8); 3) the mention in SAA 10 111 r.5 about the repeated divine confirmation of the good fate may also refer to the omens mentioned in SAA 10 112. On the other hand, it speaks for the chronological priority of SAA 10 111 that in SAA 10 112:10 Esarhaddon's army is said to have plundered Mannean cities, whereas according to SAA 10 111:17-r.4, r.17-18 the king needs to be advised whether or not the cities should be invaded.

[398] On this omen, which was considered a good one if occuring on the 14th, but a bad one on the 13th, 15th and 16th day of the month, see Parpola 1983, 11, 83; Lanfranchi 1989, 101-102.

[399] As noted by Lanfranchi 1989, 105-109, Bel-ušezib explains the sun-moon omen in an inverted way and, for that reason, uses much energy in SAA 10 112:3-27 to convince the king of his interpretation. According to the accustomed standards, the omens observed by him would have been considered as portending evil for Assyria rather than for Mannea.

[400] Compare lines 5-8 with SAA 8 552.

[401] For the expression *šēpu naprusu*, see AHw 832 (sub *parāsu* N 1b).

[402] For the translation of *zēr halgatî*, see Cogan & Tadmor 1977, 80 n. 26; Fales & Lanfranchi 1981, 15 n. 12.

[403] Note that violating and disregarding the treaty is a standard feature of the ideological role of the enemy (Fales 1982; for the vocabulary, cf. also Weinfeld 1973, 193-196;

be tested by invading and plundering the countryside of Mannea and then drawing back. Should the Cimmerians stay away, the cities of Mannea could be invaded with total force (lines 17-r.4).

It is not entirely clear who should be understood as the implied speaker of lines 9-r.4 which include quotations from other speakers, too. While the arrangement of the SAA edition, to judge from the lack of quotation marks, seems to favor the interpretation that Bel-ušezib himself is giving military advice to the king,[404] Fales and Lanfranchi have put forward an alternative interpretation: lines 9-r.4 constitute an extensive quotation of a letter from Esarhaddon, containing excerpts of his earlier correspondence and asking for the opinion of Bel-ušezib.[405] The latter interpretation has the advantage of better explaining the continuation of the letter, in which Bel-ušezib actually refrains from detailed military instructions, drawing instead on his divinatory lore and ideological affirmations.

The major question of the letter, in any case, concerns the intentions of the Cimmerians, and Bel-ušezib is supposed to answer it on the basis of his scholarly, rather than military, expertise. He is anticipating a portent on the 15th day, that is, the moon seen together with the sun (lines r.6-9), to get a confirmation of the Cimmerians' keeping aloof. In the same breath he admits that he does not know "the exit and the entry of that country"; that is, being an astrologer and not a field marshal, he is not sufficiently informed about the actual circumstances of the battlefield (r.9-10). That is why he recommends the king to consult "an expert (*mūdû*) of the country" and by capturing deserters and questioning them; should no sign of the presence of the Cimmerians, or "Indareans,"[406] appear, then the cities of Mannea could be invaded (r.10-18).

A certain tension between ideology and practice is perceivable in the apparent discrepancy between the concrete instructions, implying the writer's uncertainty about the situation in the field, and the unconditional affirmations of the favor of Marduk. Obviously Bel-ušezib does not want to shoulder the responsibility for decisions beyond his competence and therefore advises the

---

Nissinen 1991, 180-186; 1993, 236-239). In this case, the enemies have not broken any treaty since they have not concluded one; but even the failure to make the treaty is enough to make them fit in with the image of the enemy.

[404] Thus also, e.g., Dietrich 1970, 64.

[405] According to Fales & Lanfranchi 1981, 27, lines 9-r.4 presuppose five phases of Esarhaddon's correspondence concerning the invasion of Mannea:

(i) The Cimmerians send their message that they will keep aloof (lines 12-14).
(ii) Esarhaddon's "war correspondent" writes to the king quoting the message of the Cimmerians and requesting the king's instructions.
(iii) Esarhaddon writes to his troops, quoting (i) and giving the instructions requested in (ii) (lines 9-22).
(iv) The "war correspondent" answers the king requesting further instructions.
(v) Esarhaddon writes to Bel-ušezib, quoting (i) and (iii) and asking whether the action should be undertaken with total force or not (lines 9-r.4).

[406] The Indareans, attested elsewhere only in ABL 1007 (see Parpola 1970b, 174), seem to appear here as a virtual synonym for the Cimmerians (cf. lines 12-14, r.1-2, 8).

king to consult people who are better informed on strategic and tactical matters. He does not know whether the Cimmerians are there or not; however, if evil omens concerning the Manneans are observable, then the Cimmerians probaby will not involve themselves (lines r.6-8; cf. SAA 10 112:4-8, 21-27). As a scholar and diviner, Bel-ušezib is trained in interpreting the divine will, thus he is entitled to encourage the king if the portents, according to his interpretation, give the green light. Lastly, the king does as he deems best (lines r.12, 27: *akī ša ile''û*), that is, his decisions are based on his own discretion which, in ideological terms, is identical with the divine judgment.

It may strike the modern reader as suspicious that Bel-ušezib keeps proclaiming the victory of Esarhaddon even if the actual situation is unstable and he is clearly aware of it. His suggestions are cautious enough to give the impression that he himself feels insecure about the campaign, in spite of repeated affirmations to the contrary. It is clear that the king cannot rush to Mannea without finding out in concrete terms whether or not a campaign is worth the risk that has to be taken, and this cannot be overlooked by a responsible adviser like Bel-ušezib. However, Bel-ušezib makes it plain that his expertise is that of an astrologer, not of a field strategist, and he is not there primarily to explain his personal scenarios for war but to interpret the divine will. He has learned the tradition in order to be able to intepret the will of the gods according to which the king should act as their image and representative. The destruction of Mannea is the will of Marduk; this is not to be doubted, according to Bel-ušezib. But even the king can fail in his decisions. Should an inconsistency occur between ideology and experience, the gods are not to be blamed, but the adviser himself may be on shaky ground. This compels him to be wary of excessive triumph in the interpretation of divine messages.

Prophecy

As a Babylonian, Bel-ušezib is most emphatic about the favor of Marduk of Babylon on Esarhaddon, and the way he describes the liaison between the god and the king is an ideal illustration of the royal ideology: The defeat of the Manneans is the will of Bel, or Marduk, who will deliver them into the hands of the king (lines r.4-5, cf. SAA 10 112:19-20) because "the king of the gods, Marduk, is reconciled (*salim*) with the king, my lord; whatever the king my lord says, he can do" (lines r.19-20). This means that heaven and earth are in perfect balance: the interests of the king are divine interests and his deeds are fully in accordance with the divine will. "You are the Marduk of the people" (SAA 10 112 r.31), writes Bel-ušezib to the king. This is why, "sitting on his throne," the king will vanquish his enemies, conquer his foes and plunder their land (lines r.21-23). The throne manifests the divinely sanctioned global rule of the king; it is the symbol of the will of Marduk which is realized in the achievements of Esarhaddon.

The idea of the throne as a symbol, if not an instrument, of divine power executed by the king is also put into words by the prophetess Mullissu-abu-uṣri: "Let the throne go, I shall catch my king's enemies with it" (LAS 317 r.6-9). This is not the only affinity between prophecy and the letters of Bel-ušezib. The idea of reconciliation between the gods and the king is cherished by the prophets, too.[407] Bel-ušezib's phraseology for vanquishing enemies (cf. also SAA 10 112:19-20) is very close to that used by the prophets[408] and, like the prophets, he sees the victory over enemies as a corollary of the idea of reconciliation.[409] In a different context his choice of words would not necessarily imply any specific contact with prophecy. However, Bel-ušezib does more than just express his thoughts by means of conventional phrases, he quotes divine words which to all appearances are prophetic ones (lines r.23-26):

> *Bēl iqtabi umma akī Marduk-šāpik-zēri Aššūr-ahu-iddina šar māt Aššūr ina kussīšu lū ašib u mātāti gabbi ana qātīšu amanni*
>
> Bel has said: "May Esarhaddon, king of Assyria, be seated on his throne like Marduk-šapik-zeri, and I will deliver all the countries into his hands."

That we are dealing here with prophetic words is not, of course, to be regarded as absolutely certain since this is not indicated by the writer; but the quotation fulfills the criteria of what may be called prophecy in this study. It refers to what Marduk has "said" (*qabû*), there is no indication of the use of any other methods of divination, and the words itself are well in line with the extant prophecies. The words of Bel read like a scriptural assertion of what has just been said, and it seems that Bel-ušezib wants to confirm his own words by citing divine ones that point to the same conclusion.

Marduk-šapik-zeri was the king of Babylon and the seventh ruler of the second dynasty of Isin (1081-1069).[410] His deeds included the rebuilding of the fortifications of Babylon and the restoration of the Ezida, the temple of Nabû, in Borsippa, which had suffered from Aramean intrusions in the early 11th century. He also entered into alliance with Aššur-bel-kala, the king of Assyria (1074-1057). That Marduk-šapik-zeri was still remembered in the Neo-Assyrian era four hundred years later is confirmed by a building inscription from his time dealing with the Ezida of Borsippa, which was recopied in

---

[407] SAA 9 1.4 ii 31: *Aššūr issīka usallim* "I reconciled Aššur with you"; SAA 9 2.5 iii 19-20: *māt Aššūr utaqqan ilāni zēnūti issi māt Aššūr usallam* "I will put Assyria in order and reconcile the angry gods with Assyria;" SAA 9 2.6 iv 19 [*x x x usa*]*llam* "[I will re]concile [...] Cf. SAA 9 2.3 ii 3: *māt Aššūr issīka u*[*sallam*] "I will re[concile] Assyria with you."

[408] Cf., e.g., SAA 9 1.1 i 12-14; 2.1 i 10-12; 2.2 i 22-23; 2.5 iii 31-32; 3.2 i 28-29; 3.5 iii 22, iv 17; 4:4; 5:7, r.3-5; 9:26-27; 11 r.4.

[409] Thus, e.g., SAA 9 2.5 iii 31-34: *ina libbi ū'a nakarūti ša šarrīja aka*[*šša*]*d māt Aššūr utaqqan šarr*[*ūtu ša*] *šamê utaqqan* "In woe I will vanquish the enemies of my king. I will put Assyria in order, I will put the kin[gdom of] heaven in order." Cf. SAA 9 2.3 ii 1-5; 11 r.4-5.

[410] On Marduk-šapik-zeri, see Brinkman 1968, 130-135, 334-335 and 1987/90; Longman 1991, 157-158; Frame 1995, 45-49.

the fifteenth year of Kandalanu,[411] the successor of Šamaš-šumu-ukin as the ruler of Babylon (633).[412] The comparing of Esarhaddon with this ancient Babylonian king, evidently, not only highlights the position of Esarhaddon as the ruler of Assyria and Babylonia but also expresses the hope that he, following the example of Marduk-šapik-zeri, will rebuild Babylon and its temples. A quotation of this kind, while advocating the Assyrian imperial ideology, implicitly reminds the king of his duties to the southern sister nation. That this was also a prophetic concern is evident from the oracles demanding the re-establishment of the cult of Esaggil.[413]

In the light of the previously discussed letter of Bel-ušezib (SAA 10 109) it might appear as somewhat odd that a scholar who once felt himself supplanted by the prophets is now apparently quoting one of their oracles. However, half a decade has passed and Bel-ušezib is now without any doubt one of the highest-ranking scholars, whose place in the entourage of Esarhaddon is not threatened. On the other hand, in spite of the difference in divinatory methods, there is no ideological discrepancy between Bel-ušezib and the prophets. As regards the stability of the throne of Esarhaddon as a symbol of reconciliation between the divine and human worlds, the concern of the prophets is identical with that of Bel-ušezib. Thus, from the ideological point of view, he had no difficulty in citing their words if they were concordant with the common imperial phraseology, no matter what he might have thought about them as persons and diviners. If he used written prophecies, they could be considered a part of the scholarly lore. It is noteworthy that the rehabilitation of the gods of Babylon was insisted on not only by Babylonians like Bel-ušezib[414] but also by prophets who actually came from Assur (SAA 9 2.1: [Nabû]-hussanni) and Arbela (SAA 9 2.3: La-dagil-ili). This is probably because the rebuilding of Babylon is seen as a sign of the reconciliation which, as long as the gods of Esaggil were in exile, could not be complete.

It can be observed that SAA 10 111 is framed with quotations from canonical astronomical collections at the beginning (lines 3-8), and from prophetic sources at the end (lines r.23-26).[415] These authoritative statements clearly serve as an "objective" support of Bel-ušezib's own suggestions concerning a specific political decision of current interest. As a skilled political adviser, he interweaves the learned tradition with his own reasoning in a confidence-building way.

---

[411] Whether or not Kandalanu should be identified with Assurbanipal is irrelevant here; for the pros and cons, see respectively Zawadzki 1988, 24, 57-62 and Frame 1992, 191-213, 296-306.

[412] The inscription is published by Frame 1995, 47-48.

[413] SAA 9 2.3 ii 24-27: "The gods of Esaggil languish in the 'steppe' of stirred-up evil. Quickly let two burnt offerings be sent out to their presence, and let them go and announce your well-being!"

[414] Cf. SAA 10 109 r.15.

[415] Note that Bel-ušezib elsewhere also quotes and interprets authoritative (non-prophetic) sources other than those of an astronomical nature (SAA 10 112 r.20-23, 29-33)

5.4. Banishment Based upon Prophecy

Text

SAA 10 284
(K 1033 / ABL 58 / LAS 213)

Obv. ^{1}*a-na* LUGAL EN-*ia* ^{2}ARAD-*ka* ^{md}AG–[SUM]–MU ^{3}*lu* DI-*mu a-na* L[U]GAL [EN-*i*]*a* ^{4} ^{d}PA *u* ^{d}AMAR.UTU *a-na* [LUGAL EN-*ia*] ^{5}*a–dan-niš a–da*[*n-niš lik-ru-bu*]
lines 6 and 7 unreadable; several lines broken away
Rev. ^{1}*k*[*i-m*]*a in-ta-ra-a*[*ṣ*] ^{2}*pa-ni am-mu-te* ⸢SIG$_{5}$⸣.MEŠ [*ša* LUGAL] ^{3}EN-*ia* TA* *pa-ni-šú li-is-*[*hu-ru*] ^{4}*ù ki-i ša* ^{d}15 *šá* N[INA.KI] ^{5} ^{d}15 *šá arba-ìl iq-ba-a*[*n-ni*] ^{6}*ma-a šá* TA* LUGAL *be-li-n*[*i*] ^{7}*la ke-nu-ni ma-a* TA* KUR–*aš-šur*.[KI] ^{8}⸢*ni*⸣*-na-sah-šu* : ⸢*ket-tu-ma*⸣ ^{9}TA* KUR–*aš-šur*.KI *li-in-ni-s*[*íh*] ^{10}*aš-šur* ^{d}UTU $^{d+}$EN ^{d}AG ^{11}DI-*mu šá* LUGAL EN-*ia* ^{12}⸢*liš*⸣*-ʾu-lu*

[1] To the king, my lord: your servant Nabû-[nadin]-šumi. Good health to the king, m[y lord]! May Nabû and Marduk very gr[eatly bless the king, my lord]! ......
[r.1] [I]f he has become troublesome, may that gracious face [of the king], my lord, tur[n] away from him! And inasmuch as Ištar of N[ineveh] and Ištar of Arbela have said: “We shall root out from Assyria those who are not loyal to the king, our lord!” he should really be banished from Assyria!
[10] May Aššur, Šamaš, Bel and Nabû feel concern over the health of the king, my lord!

Background

This letter is written by Nabû-nadin-šumi who was the chief exorcist after Marduk-šakin-šumi and served both Esarhaddon and Assurbanipal. He is the author of 15 preserved letters (SAA 10 273-288), this one being concerned with a male person whose loyalty to the king is seriously questioned. The chief exorcist considers his crime to be severe enough to be punished by banishment, and rests his argument on the words of the two main Assyrian manifestations of Ištar. Unfortunately, the crucial lines that probably would have indicated the name of the suspect as well as the problem connected with him, are totally broken away so that we cannot know anything of the concrete circumstances that occasioned the writing of the letter. This also makes its exact dating impossible.[416]

Obviously the unknown person in question, whatever he might be suspected of, has not been caught in the very act. The expression of Nabû-nadin-šumi is conditional: in case that[417] he proves to have caused trouble (*marāṣu*), then "the gracious face of the king" should "turn away from him," i.e., he would fall out of favor with the king.[418] What this means in actual terms depends on the interpretation of the verb *nasāhu*. The judgment "He should really be banished from Assyria" (*issu māt Aššūr linnisih*) corresponds exactly to the words of the Ištars of Nineveh and Arbela, according to whom those who are not loyal to the king shall be rooted out from Assyria by the goddesses (*issu māt Aššūr ninassahšu*). The verb *nasāhu* is used in both instances but its concrete meaning is not quite clear and does not have to be exactly the same in both cases. The semantic field of *nasāhu* with a human object ranges from transferring a person from one post to another to evacuation and deportation of people and even to their total extermination.[419] In the words of the goddesses the latter could originally be meant but their interpretation by Nabû-nadin-šumi seems to underline the words "from Assyria" in favor of a more lenient punishment, i.e., the banishment from the country. If this be the case (which is, admittedly, difficult to prove on the basis of the meager context alone) the crime of the person referred to would have been severe enough to be punished with banishment (which could be the consequence of any sign of disloyalty), without being a capital offence. It is not ruled out that Nabû-nadin-šumi is talking about a non-Assyrian person whom he believes to have spied or plotted on behalf of the king's enemies and should thus be sent back to his own country.

Prophecy

It is quite beyond doubt that Nabû-nadin-šumi refers to a prophetic oracle even though this is not explicitly mentioned. It quotes what Ištar of Nineveh and Ištar of Arbela have *said* (*qabû*), and does it in the form of direct speech.

---

[416] Parpola (1983, 208) suggests early 670, which is possible if the person in question was involved in the same conspiracy that ABL 1217, CT 53 17 and CT 53 938 deal with; see below.

[417] Either *ki-ma* or *šum-ma* could be read here; see the collation in SAA 10, p. 420.

[418] For phrases similar to *pānī ammūti damqūti ša šarri bēlīja* see Parpola (1983, 208) who understands the 'turning of the face' quite literally as implying a face-to-face encounter of the king and another person. If this is true, then the person referred to must have belonged to the few ones privileged to look at the king's face, i.e., to the higher staff of the court. If, however, the expression is used in a more metaphorical sense, this conclusion is less certain. For the occurrences of *pānī sahāru* see AHw 1007; cf. *pānī wabālu* (AHw 819, 1451); *pānī nadānu* (AHw 702) *būnī našû* (AHw 138). For Hebrew *hēšīb pānīm* cf. 1 Kings 2:16-17, 20; 2 Kings 18:24//Is 36:9; Ps 132:10; Ez 14:6; Dan 11:19; for *nāśā' pānīm* cf. e.g. Job 34:19; Lam 4:16; Num 6:26 etc.

[419] See AHw 750-752; CAD N/2 1-15.

The fact that the Ištars of Nineveh and Arbela call Esarhaddon "our lord" might look strange at first sight. It is obvious, however, that this oddity goes back to the courtesy of the writer of the letter. Even when quoting words of goddesses he, the humble servant of the king, may not give up the conventional form of address!

The reference to the words of the goddess(es) does not allude to any kind of inductive divinatory technique. This alone would justify the definition of the oracle as a prophetic one. The case becomes, however, even clearer when we take a look at an oracle of the prophetess Urkittu-šarrat from Calah, received by Esarhaddon, probably during his first regnal year[420] (SAA 9 2.4 ii 29-33):

> *akī tappala lā kēnūti abat Issār ša Arbail abat šarrati Mullissi adaggal assanamme uhajjāṭa lā kēnūti ina qāt šarrīja ašakkan*
>
> Thus shall you answer the disloyal ones! The word of Ištar of Arbela, the word of Queen Mullissu: I will look, I will listen, I will search out the disloyal ones, and I will put them into the hands of my king.

In this piece of prophecy the goddesses Ištar and Mullissu, who merge into one divine being, introduce themselves as a secret agent for Esarhaddon who looks and listens to the movements of the "disloyal ones" (*lā kēnūti*[421]), seeks them out (literally "weighs them in" *hiāṭu* D) and delivers them to the king. All this corresponds perfectly with the treatment of "those who are not loyal to the king, our lord" (*ša issi šarri bēlīni lā kēnūni*) in this letter where Nabû-nadin-šumi acts on behalf of the goddess(es), informing on a potential *lā kēnu*.

The letter documents a concrete case in which a counsellor of the highest rank (Nabû-nadin-šumi belonged to the "inner circle" of the scholars in Nineveh[422]) is recommending heavy action against a person under suspicion of disloyalty. The prophetic oracle is certainly not introduced as a mere suggestion of what could be done with the suspect but as a binding divine ordinance. On the other hand, as the prophecy is not concerned with any specific case, it comes within the jurisdiction of the king to determine on the people against whom the words of the goddess(es) should be directed. In this case the role of Nabû-nadin-šumi is crucial: he is the one who interprets the divine message, defines the conclusions that should be drawn from it and recommends to the king the respective action. The letter demonstrates that prophecy could be used as an effective political weapon against the real or potential adversaries of the king or of the establishment of the empire.

It is also noteworthy that a scholar, in this case the chief exorcist, is once again ready to draw on divinatory expertise of another kind than his own – and notably on prophecy which, again, shows that the scholars did not hesitate

---

[420] As to the dating of SAA 9 2 cf. Parpola 1997c, LXIX.

[421] The verb (*lā*) *kuānu* is the standard expression for (dis)loyalty, cf. SAA 2 1:5; 2 iii 24; 6 § 8:97, § 21 236, § 57 502; 11 r.3(?); 14 ii r.9.

[422] Cf. Parpola 1993, XXVI.

to turn to good account any divine words if they were ideologically acceptable and applicable to current interests. Prophecy might have been suspected by some scholars as a technique less flawless than the methods of divination based on inductive observation. Since prophecy, after all, shared the common royal ideology and underpinned the existing power structure, it was functionally in complete accordance with a scholarly occupation.

CHAPTER SIX

THE LETTERS OF NABÛ-REHTU-UṢUR

Texts

The following three letters, ABL 1217+CT 53 118, CT 53 17+107 and CT 53 938, are written by the otherwise unknown[423] Nabû-rehtu-uṣur. The letters belong both thematically and historically together; CT 53 938 is actually a partial duplicate of CT 53 17+107. They deal with the same persons and events – an alleged conspiracy of a certain Sasî and his adherents – and were probably written within a relatively short period of time. The letters form an indispensable piece of evidence in many respects. They are not only informative about some disputed historical events but also give a unique, though at the same time highly enigmatic, insight into different functions of prophecy.

It is my purpose here to inquire into the role and function of prophecy as represented by these letters. To perform this task it is necessary, however, not only to examine the plot of each letter but also to sketch out some conceivable historical circumstances behind their wording with the help of other documents related to them.

Unfortunately, the interpretation of the letters of Nabû-rehtu-uṣur is seriously impeded by their poorly preserved state and their implicit way of expressing things – obviously because the addressee of the letters is supposed to know well enough the immediate circumstances surrounding and motivating their writing. Thus, the modern reader is left without precise information about many important details such as the positions and the backgrounds of many of the persons involved, let alone the date of the events. The difficulties in the interpretation of the letters, together with the fact that they still lack an up-to-date edition[424] and that CT 53 17+107 and 938 have not been a matter of extensive discussion so far,[425] have led to divergent opinions on their significance as historical sources among the few who have taken them into consideration. The theory of a widespread conspiracy led by Sasî in Harran in the mid 670's, meticulously composed by Dietrich,[426] has been almost completely dismantled by Brinkman.[427] This alone motivates a reas-

---

[423] The writer of the letter may be identical with the Nabû-rehtu-uṣur who appears as a witness in legal documents from the years 679 (SAA 6 268:9) and 666 (SAA 6 314 r.27) but hardly with the insurrectionist mentioned by Aššur-etel-ilani in SAA 12 35:13 and 36:10; cf. Parpola 1983, 238 n. 408. The lodging list SAA 7 9 that may date from the year 672 (see above, pp. 64-65) includes a group of nine persons, among them Nabû-rehtu-uṣur who is in the queen mother's employ; his professional title is, unfortunately, broken away (SAA 7 9 ii 11: ^{md}PA–*re-eh-tú*–PAB LÚ.[*x* A]MA–MAN).

[424] The numerous misreadings of the ABL-edition of R. F. Harper are repeated by Waterman 1930, 344-347 which makes his translation largely unreliable. Excerpts of ABL 1217 are previously published by Dietrich 1970, 160-161 (lines r.3-5, 9-10; Nr. 58-59); Dietrich 1973, 39 (lines 1-13, r.2-5; translation only) and Parpola 1983, 239 nn. 412-417 (lines r.4-5 and r.2-3) and 464 (lines r.9-17; translation only). A complete German translation of ABL 1217, based on the transliteration and English translation of Simo Parpola, has been published in Nissinen 1996, 183-184.

[425] To the best of my knowledge, only Parpola 1983, 239, nn. 414 and 416, van der Toorn 1987, 78 and Nissinen 1996, 182-193 have referred to these letters.

[426] Dietrich 1970, 50-55.

[427] Brinkman 1977, 312-315.

sessment of the material, together with some sources so far overlooked, even if it cannot be promised that the new pieces of evidence might yield a final solution to the problem; many gaps that unavoidably remain cannot be filled without circumstantial evidence – and some speculation.

The complete text of each letter is displayed here in Simo Parpola's transliteration and translation.

ABL 1217 + CT 53 118
(82-5-22,108 + K 13737)

1 *a-na* LUGAL [EN-*i*]*a*
2 ARAD-*ka* ^{md}PA–*re-eh-tú*–PAB ^{d}EN ^{d}GA[ŠAN ^{d}PA ^{d}*taš-m*]*e-tum*
3 ^{d}15 *šá* URU.NINA ^{d}15 *šá* URU.*arba-ìl* UD.MEŠ [GÍD.M]EŠ M[U.AN.NA].MEŠ *d*[*a-r*]*a-ti*
4 *li-di-nu-nik-ka šá ina* ŠÀ *ṭa-ab-ti šá* AD$^{!}$-[*ka ina* ŠÀ *a-de-e šá* AD]-*ka*
5 *ù ina* ŠÀ *a-de-e-ka ih-ṭu-u-ni* ^{d}NIN$^{!}$.GAL [*x x x x* UN.ME]Š-*šu-nu*
6 MU-*šu-nu* NUMUN-*šu-nu* TA* ŠÀ É.GAL-*ka hal-li-qí*$^{!}$ *a-na* [*x x x x x lu*]
7 *tak-ru-ur* UN.MEŠ *ša* TA ^{m}*sa-si-i ú-du-u-*[*ni ár-hiš li-mu-tu x x x*]
8 *a-ni-nu* LUGAL *be-lí da-ba-bu šá* ^{d}NIN.GAL *ú-*[*da x x x x x x*]
9 *li-mu-tu* ZI.MEŠ-*ka* ZI.MEŠ *šá qin-ni-ka* [*še-zib x x x x x x*]
10 AD-*u*$^{!}$-*ka*$^{!}$ AMA-*ka lu šu-nu li-im-tu-*[*hu x x x x x x x x*]
11 ZI.MEŠ-*ka la tu-hal-la-qa* LUGAL-*u-tu* TA ŠU.2-*k*[*a la tu-še-li*]
12 *a-ni-nu* LUGAL *be-*⸢*lí*⸣ [*ina* Š]À *da-ba-bi* ^{d}NIN.[GAL *an-ni-e*]
13 *la ta-ši-*[*aṭ x x x*] -⸢*ú*⸣-*nim-ma* [*x x x x x x x x*]
14 *e-gír-tu* [*x x x x x*] *x x* [*x x x x x x x x x x*]
15 *ina* [*x x x x x x x x x x x x x x x x x x x x*]
uncertain number of lines broken away

CT 53 118
1′ [*x*] *x* [*x x x x x x x x x x x x x x x x x x x x*]
2′ *ma-a a-*[*x x x x x x x x x x x x x x x x x x x x*]
3′ *la ú-*⸢*ba-la*⸣ [*x x x x x x x x x x x x x x x x*]
4′ *ina* IGI-*šu iz-za-zu x*[*x x x x x x x x x x x x x x x*]
5′ *pi-i-šú-nu šá-ki-in* [*x x x x x x x x x x x x x*]
6′ *ka-a.a-ma-nu ina* UGU ^{m}*sa-s*[*i-i x x x x x x x x x x*]
7′ *ma-a ina* IGI LUGAL *dam-mì-iq ma-*[*a x x x x x x x x x x*]
8′ *le-pu-šú* TA* ^{md}PA–EN–[*x x x x x x x x x x x x x*]
9′ ta ^{m}SUHUŠ–^{d}PA L[Ú.*x x x x x x x x x x x x x*]
10′ ⸢TA LÚ⸣.GAL.MEŠ *š*[*a x x x x x x x x x x x x x x*]
11′ [*x x x*] *x*[*x x x x x x x x x x x x x x x x x*]
rest broken away

ABL 1217 Rev. beginning broken away
1′ *is–su-ri i-*⸢*ba-áš*⸣-[*ši x x x x x x x x x x x x x x*]
2′ *liš-ú-lu ma-a* GEMÉ *šá* ^{m}EN–PAB–PAB *ina*$^{!}$ *q*[*a-n*]*i šá* ⸢URU⸣.K[ASKAL].2 *ina* UG[U *x x x x*]
3′ *ma-a* TA* ŠÀ ITI.SIG$_{4}$ *sa-ar-ha-at ma-a da-ba-bu* SIG$_{5}$ *ina* UGU-*hi*

4′ *ta-da-bu-bu ma-a a-bat* ^{d}PA.TÚG *ši-i ma-a* LUGAL-*u-tu a-na* ^{m}*sa-si-i*
5′ *ma-a* MU NUMUN *šá* ^{md}30–PAB.MEŠ–SU *ú-hal-la-qa* LÚ.GAL–*mu-gi-ka*$^{?}$
6′ *ina šap-la* KÁ.GAL *šá* É ^{d}PA É ^{md}EN–PAB–PAB *liš-al* LÚ.*še-e-pi* [*šá*]
7′ GEMÉ *ina* É ^{m}*sa-si-i ú-bi-lu-ni lu-bi-lu-ni-ši dul-lu* LUGAL$^{?}$ [*x x x*]
8′ *ina* UGU-*hi-šá le-pu-šú* ^{m}EN–PAB–PAB TA* URU.KASKAL *lu-bi-lu-ni* ^{d}PA.TÚG [*x x x*]
9′ MU NUMUN *šá* ^{m}*sa-si-i šá* ^{m}EN–PAB–PAB *šá* UN.MEŠ *šá is-si-šú-nu ú-du-*[*u-ni*]
10′ *li-ih-li-iq* MU NUMUN *šá* LUGAL EN-*ia* ^{d}EN ^{d}PA *a-na* ⸢*ṣa*$^{!}$-*at*⸣ [UD.MEŠ *lu-ki*]*n-nu*
11′ TA* ^{m}*ar-da-a lid-bu-bu ma-a* UD.27.KÁM *ina nu-bat-ti ma-a a-na* [^{m}*sa*]-*si-i*
12′ LÚ.*šá*–UGU–URU ^{m}15–SUM–A LÚ.A.BA *ma-a si-mu-nu ha-*[*an-ni-u bé-et*]
13′ *il-li-ku-u-ni* TA* ^{m}*a-ú-ia-a-ni* LÚ.SAG *ni-*[*x x x x x x*]
14′ *ma-a* ^{m}15–SUM–A LÚ.A.BA *ma-a* ^{md}PA–KAR-*ir an-*⸢*ni*$^{!}$⸣-[*tú x x x x*]
15′ *ma-a* UD.28.KÁM *ma-a* ^{m}*sa-si-i mì-i-nu ina* UGU-*hi* ⸢*x x x*⸣ [*x x x x x x*]
16′ *ma*$^{?}$ *a*$^{!}$-*na*$^{!?}$ 2-*e* UD-*me* ^{m}*sa-si-i is-si-ka* ta* LÚ.[*x x x x x x x x*]
17′ *id-bu-bu ma-a a-*[*ta*]-*a mì-i-nu šá ta-m*[*u-ru-ni x x x x x x x*]
18′ LÚ.GAL–*mu-gi x*[*x x x x x x x x*] ERIM.MEŠ [*x x x x x x x*]
19′ ^{m}15–[SUM–A] LÚ$^{?}$.A$^{!}$.B[A *x x x x x*]
20′ [*x x x x x x* UN.MEŠ *š*]*a*$^{!}$ *is-si-šú-nu* TA* ^{m}*sa-si-i ú-du-u-ni* [*li-mu-tú*]
21′ [*x x x x x x* DUMU].MEŠ-*ka* ŠEŠ–AD.MEŠ-*ka* EN.NUN-*ka li-ṣu-ru*
22′ [*x x x k*]*a lu-pa-ah-*⸢*hi* ⸣-*ir* [*x x x x at-ta*]*tu-qu-nu ina* É.GAL-*ka ši-bi*
23′ [*x x*] *a-du* ⸢É⸣ [*la i-ha-ru-pu-ni* UN.MEŠ *li-mu*]-*tú* ZI.MEŠ-*ka še-zib*

1 To the king, m[y lord], your servant Nabû-rehtu-uṣur. May Bel and Be[let, Nabû and Tašme]tu, Ištar of Nineveh and Ištar of Arbela give you long days and ever[lasting years]!
4 Nikkal [*has revealed*] those who sinned against [your] father's goodness and your [father's] and your own treaty. Destroy their name and seed from your palace! [May] she cast [...]! [May] the accomplices of Sasî [*die quickly*].
8 Hear me,[428] O king, my lord! I *k*[*now*] the words of Nikkal. Let [the people] die! [Save] your life and the life of your family! Let [the goddesses...] be your father and your mother, and let them li[ft up[429]...]! Do not destroy your life, do not let the kingship [slip] from your hands!
12 Hear me, O king, my lord! Do not disregard [these] words of Ni[kkal! Let...] and [...] a letter [...] in [...]

[428] The word *anīnu* (cf. line 12 and CT 53 17 r.18, s.1) is hardly to be understood as a personal pronoun of 1. p. pl. but rather as an interjection similar to *anīna* or *annû* "behold" (cf. Hebrew *hinnê* and see AHw 51, 53); cf. ABL 1250 r.7: *a-ni-na* LUGAL *be-li* "Behold, O king my lord."

[429] The reconstruction of AHw 635 *li-im-tu-*[*tu* ?] 'let them die one after another' (*mâtu* Gtn) does not make sense in regard to the goddesses.

(Break; contd. in CT 53 118)

4 ... are staying in his presence [...] are making common cause [with ...]. 6 [They are] constantly [...] to Sas[î ...]: "Present yourselves in a good light with the king! Let [...] do [...] with Nabû-belu-[...] with Ubru-Nabû [...] with the magnates *w[ho...]*

(Break; contd. in ABL 1217, rev.)

r.1 Perhaps *ther[e is* ...] let them ask [...].

2 "A slave girl of Bel-ahu-uṣur [...] upon [...] on the outskirts of H[arran]; since Sivan (III) she is *enraptured* [430] and speaks a good word about him: 'This is the word of Nusku: The kingship is for Sasî! I will destroy the name and seed of Sennacherib!'"

6 Let your *squadron* commander question the household of Bel-ahu-uṣur under the gate of the Nabû-temple. Let the *ša šēpi* guards who brought the slave girl into[431] the house of Sasî bring her here, and let the *king* [...] perform a(n extispicy) ritual on her (account).

8 Let them bring Bel-ahu-uṣur from Harran and [...] Nusku. May the name and seed of Sasî, Bel-ahu-uṣur and their accomplices perish, and may Bel and Nabû establish the name and seed of the king, my lord, until far-off days!

11 Let them speak with Ardâ as follows: "On the 27th, at night, [*when*] the scribe Issar-nadin-apli at this particular moment went to Sasî the city overseer, [*did* ...] with the *eunuch*[432] Awyanu? [*Did*] the scribe Issar-nadin-apli [...] Nabû-eṭir? What did Sasî [...] concerning it on the 28th? Did Sasî speak with you and the [...] on the following day? Why have you [not reported] what you sa[w and heard]?" [*Let*] the *squadron* commander [...] men [...] the scrib[e] Issar-[nadin-apli ...].

20 The people w]ho conspire with them and with Sasî [should die! ...]. Let your [son]s and uncles guard you. Let [*me*] gather your [... As for you], stay in safety in your palace until [...]. [Let the people di]e! Save your life!

CT 53 17 + 107[433]
(= K 1034 + K 7395 + K 9204 + K 9821 + K 10541 + K 11021)

CT 53 17

1 *a-na* LUG[AL] EN-*ia*

---

430 In this translation by S. Parpola, the word *sa-ar-ha-at* is interpreted as an Aramaism, i.e., G stat. of a verb corresponding to the Syriac *šrḥ* 'to range,' Aph. 'to ravish, enrapture, fascinate, captivate'; Ethpa. 'to be immoderate, run riot, commit excesses, to be overjoyed, ravished with joy'; see Payne Smith 1902, 598.

431 Or: from (*ina* ablativum; see GAG § 114c, p. 164).

432 The title of Awyanu constitutes a problem since it can be read either LÚ.SAG "eunuch" or LÚ.*šaknu* "governor." A governor of Que with this name is attested in the eponym chronicle (see Millard 1994, 53) but, since his eponym year is as late as 655, he may be a different person. As to the name Awyanu, see Tallqvist 1914, 48.

433 Restorations partly from CT 53 938.

2 ARAD-*ka* ^{md}PA–*re*-⸢*eh*⸣-[*tú*–PAB ^{d}EN ^{d}]GAŠAN ^{d}⸢PA⸣ ^{d}*taš-me-tum*
3 ^{d}15 *šá* NI[NA.KI ^{d}15 *šá* URU.*arba-ìl* DINGIR.MEŠ]-*ka* (*šá*)
4 MU-⸢*ka*⸣ [*a-na* LUGAL-*ti iz-kur-u-ni šu-nu lu-bal-li-ṭ*]*u-u-ka*
5 *šá* [*ina* Š]À [*ṭa-ab-ti šá* AD-*ka ina* ŠÀ *a-de-e šá* A]D-*k*[*a u ina* Š]À *a-de-ka*
6 ⸢*i*⸣-*ha-ṭu-u-n*[*i šá ina* UGU ZI.MEŠ-*k*]*a* ⸢*i*⸣-[*da-ba-bu-u*]-*ni*
7 *šu-nu ina* ŠU.⸢2⸣-[*ka i-šá-ka-an-šú-nu*] MU-*šú-nu* [TA* KUR–*aš*]-*šur*.KI
8 TA* ŠÀ ⸢É⸣.[GAL-*ka tu-hal-la-qa*] *da-ba-bu an-ni-*⸢*ú*⸣
9 *šá* ^{d}NIN.LÍL [*šu-ú* LUGAL *be-lí*] ⸢*ina*⸣ ŠÀ-*bi lu la i*-[*ši-aṭ*]
10 *ina* UD.6.KÁM *šá* I[TI.APIN$^{?}$ *di-ig-lu*] ⸢*a*⸣-[*d*]*a-gal ma-a x*[*x x x*]
11 *ma-a ina* ŠÀ-*b*[*i x x x bi-da* EN–*a-de-e šá* LUGAL EN-*ia a-na-ku*]
12 *la–mu-qa-a.a la ú*-[*pa-az-za-ar di-ib-bi šá x x x x x*]
13 *ki-i šá a-mur-u-ni ina* Š[À *x x x x x x x x x x x x x x*]
14 *ak-ta-ra-ar a-na* M[UL$^{?}$].*ur-k*[*a-ti x x x x x x x x x x*]
15 LUGAL *be-li ú-da a-ki* ⸢É⸣ [*x x x x x x x x x x x x x*]
16 *ki-i an-ni-i ina* ŠÀ *e-gír-t*[*i-šú šá-ṭi-ir ma-a x x x x*]
17 *lu iṣ-ṣi-a* ⸢*ma-a x x x*⸣ [*x x x x x x x x x x x x*]
18 ⸢*x x x*⸣ [*x x x x x x x x x x x x x x x x x x*]
two or three lines broken away

CT 53 107

1′ [*x x x m*]*a-a* DUMU L[UGAL *x x x x x x x x x x x*]
2′ [*x x x ṣ*]*i a-na* DUMU.LU[GAL *x x x x x x x x x x x*]
3′ *ma*-⸢*a* TA⸣ *a-he-iš ú-sa-ma*-[*hu-ni x x x x x x x x x*]
4′ *i-qab-bi ma-a an-nu-ti is*-[*x x x x x x x x x x x x*]
5′ *ù ma-a* É.GAL *gab-bu* ⸢TA*⸣[*x x x x x x x x x x x*]
6′ *me-me-ni ma-a* DUMU.MÍ ^{m}*ba-am-ba*-⸢*a* ⸣[*x x x x x x x x x x*]
7′ *ù* ERIM.MEŠ $^{md!}$IM–⸢MU⸣–PAB ^{m}*ar*-[*da-a x x x x x x x x*]
8′ *iq-ṭi-bu-ni ma-a* ⸢*bar-tu*⸣ *e-pu*-[*šu x x x x x x x x*]
9′ *ma-a šu-ú ina* UGU ŠÀ-⸢*bi*⸣ *ir-ti-hi-i*[*ṣ x x x x x x x x*]
10′ *a-sa-kan ma-a šá* ^{d}EN ^{d}PA ^{d}15 *šá* U[RU.*x x x x x x x x*]
11′ *ur-ta-am-me ma-a šá ra-mì-ni-šú* [*x x x x x x x x x*]
12′ ^{d}15 *šá* NINA.KI *ma-a a*-⸢*x*⸣-*x* [*x x x x x x x x x x x*]
13′ *e-tap-šu ma-a ú-sa-hi-x*[*x x x x x x x x x x x x x*]
14′ [*ma*]-⸢*a*⸣ [T]A* ŠÀ É.[GAL *x x x x x x x x x x x x x*]
two lines and edge (two lines) broken away

CT 53 107 Rev.

1 [*x x x x x x x x x x x x x x x x x x x x x*]
2 [*x x x x x x x x x x x x x x x x x x x x x*]
3 [*x x x x x x x x x x x x x x x x x x x x x*]
4 *lu-ba-x*[*x x x x x x x x x x x x x x x x x x*]
5 *ki-i an-ni-i q*[*a-b*]*i ma-a ina* ⸢URU.KASKAL⸣[*x x x x x x x*]
6 *ma-a ina* UGU-*hi-ia a-ke-e ṭè-e-mu iš-kun* [*x x x*]
7 *ma-a iá-bu-tú šá la* ⸢*x*⸣-*e a*–⸢*dan*⸣-*niš ta-ta-aṣ*-[*ra*$^{?}$]
8 *ma-a* É.GAL *a-na* ⸢*x x x*⸣ *x*[*x x t*]*a-sa-kan ma-a šá x*[*x x x*]
9 ⸢*ma*⸣-[*a* ER]IM.MEŠ-⸢*ia*⸣ *x*[*x x x x x*] *x*[*x x x x*]*x a-na g*[*i*$^{?}$- *x x x*]
10 ⸢*x* ^{m}*sa*$^{?}$⸣-*si*-⸢*i*⸣ [*x x x x x x x x x x x x x x x x*]

11 *ta-ku-*⸢*la*⸣ [*x x x x x x x x x x x x x x x x x*]
12 *ma-a šu-nu* [*x x x x x x x x x x x x x x x x*]
13 TA* ^{m}*s*[*a-si-i x x x x x x x x x x x x x x x x*]
14 *lu-k*[*i x x x x x x x x x x x x x x x*]
a few lines broken away

CT 53 17 Rev.

1′ *ši* [*x x x x x x x x x x x x x x x x x x x x*]
2′ *ma-a* [*x x x x x x x x x x x x x x x x x x x*]
3′ *ma-*⸢*a*⸣ [*x x x x x x x x x x x x x x x x x x*]
4′ ⸢*šá*⸣ [*x x x x x x x x x x x x x x x x x x x x*]
5′ x[*x x x x x x x x x x x x x x x x x x x*]
6′ [*x x x x x x x x x x x x x x x x x x x x x*]
7′ Z[I.MEŠ *x x x x x x x x x x x x x x x x x x x x*]
8′ ZI.M[EŠ *x x x x x x x x x x x x x x x x x x x x*]
9′ [*ina* I]GI LÚ.GAL–⸢SAG⸣ [*x x x x x x x x x x x x x x x*]
10′ ZI.MEŠ-*ka še-zib ár-*[*hiš x x x x x x x x x x x x*]
11′ *ši-i* ^{m}*sa-si-i a* ⸢*na*⸣ *x*[*x x x x x x x x x x x x x*]
12′ [^{m}*mi*]*l-ki*–ZÁLAG ^{m}ARAD–15 *is-s*[*i-šú x x x*] ⸢*ú*⸣-[*x x x x*]
13′ [*x*]-*šá-ʾa-al-šú-nu* UN.MEŠ *a*[*m–mar x x*]*x-ti is-si-šú-nu* ⸢*ú- du*⸣-[*u-ni*]
14′ [*l*]*i-iq-bu-nik-ka* ⸢UN$^{?}$⸣.[MEŠ *an-nu-t*]*i li-mu-tú la ta-pa-làh*
15′ ^{d}EN ^{d}PA ^{d}NIN.LÍL [*is-si-ka*] *iz-za-zu ár-hiš* UN.MEŠ
16′ *li-mu-tú* ZI.MEŠ-*k*[*a še-zib*] ⸢*e*⸣-*gír-tú an-ni-tú lu ši-ip-tú*
17′ *ina* UGU-*hi-*⸢*ka*⸣ *i-*⸢*ma*⸣-[*x ár-hi*]*š* UN.MEŠ *li-mu-tú*
18′ *a-du la i-ha-*⸢*ru*⸣-[*pu-u-ni*] *a-ni-nu* LUGAL *be-li*
19′ ZI.MEŠ-*ka ba-l*[*i-iṭ* ERIM$^{?}$.MEŠ *š*]*a* ^{m}*sa-si-i*
20′ *šu-ub-tú ú-*[*se-ši-bu x x x*] *is-si-ni*
21′ *i-da-bu-u*[*b ma-a a-du la i-h*]*a-ru-pu-ni*
22′ *ma-a a-ni-*[*nu x x x x*]*x-šú*

Left Edge CT 53 107 + 17

1 *a-ni-nu* LUGAL [*be-li*] ⸢^{d}EN$^{!}$⸣ *a-n*[*a x x x x*] KUG.GI NA$_{4}$.MEŠ *šá ka-a.*⸢*a*⸣-[*m*]*a-nu* ^{m}LÚ-*x*[*x x*]*x*
2 *lu-bi-*⸢*lu*⸣ [*at-ta tu*]-*qu-nu a-*⸢*na*⸣ [*sa-ri-ir* ZI].MEŠ-*ka lu-ur-rik ra-*[*man*]-*ka ú-*⸢*ṣur*⸣ KI.MIN KI.MIN
3 ZI.MEŠ-⸢*ka*⸣ [ZI.MEŠ *šá*] ⸢*qin*$^{!}$⸣*ni-ka* [*še-zib x x* LÚ].SAG.MEŠ ZI.MEŠ-*ka še-zib* [K]I.MIN KI.MIN
4 ŠÀ-⸢*ba*⸣-*k*[*a ṣa-ab-t*]*a* ⸢*x*⸣ *hu un x*[*x x x is-si-ka l*]*i-zi-zu* ŠÀ$^{!}$-*ba-šú-nu ga-mur-*⸢*ak*$^{!}$⸣-*ka*

[1] To the ki[ng], my lord: your servant Nabû-re[htu-uṣur. May Bel and] Belet, Nabû and Tašmetu, Ištar of Ni[neveh and Ištar of Arbela, your] gods (who) [called] you by name [to kingship, keep] you a[live]!

[4] Those who sinned against [your father's goodness, yo]ur fa[ther's and] your own treaty, and who p[lo]t [against yo]ur [life, shall be placed] in [your] hands, [and you shall delete] their name [from As]syria and from [your pa]lace.

[8] This is the word of Mullissu; [the king, my lord,] should not be

ne[glectful] about it.
10 On the 6th of [*Marchesvan* (VIII)] I had a vi[sion]: "[...] in the midst [...]." [I am bound by the treaty of the king, my lord]; I cannot c[onceal it ...]. Just as I saw, in [...] I have put, *discree*[*tly*...].

The king, my lord, knows, that [...] as follows in the lette[r: "...] should have ...[...]

(Break; contd. in CT 53 107 Obv.)

1 [...] the *crown pr*[*ince*...] to the *crown prin*[*ce* ...] are in league with one another [...] he says: "These [...]" and: "The whole palace [is] with [...] anything; the daughter of Bambâ [...] and the men of Adad-šumu-uṣur and Ar[dâ......] have said to me: "They are making a rebellion [...]" He has become confident in (his) heart [and is saying:] "I have set [...]." He has rejected what Bel, Nabû, Ištar of Ni[neveh and Ištar of Arbela have ...ed], and [...] of his own. Ištar of Nineveh says: "[...] have done [...] from [your] pal[ace...

(Break; contd. in CT 53 107 Rev.)

r.4 may ... [...] It r[ead]s as follows: "In Harran [...] What orders has he given [*to you*] about me? [...] The word of my *father has become* very [...]. You have turned the palace into a [...]. My men [...] *Sasî* [...]. I trust in [...] They [...] with *Sasî* [...] *let him e*[*stablish*...]

(Break; contd. in CT 53 17 Rev.)

r.7 the l[ife of ...] the lif[e of ... in the pres]ence of the chief eunuch [...] Save your life! [Let the people die] qu[ickly! ...] Sasî to [...] Milki-nuri and Urad-Issar [...] with [*him*].
13 Interrogate them! Let them tell you the [...] people who conspired with them, and let [these] people die! Have no fear; Bel, Nabû and Mullissu are stan[ding with you]. Let the people die quickly, and [save] your life! May this letter *be a spell*, it will [...] upon you! Let the people die before they *get ahe*[*ad*] (of you).
18 Hear me, O king my lord! Save your life! [The *men* o]f Sasî have [set] an ambush, [saying: "The moment the king] will speak with us, we shall [*kill*] him [before he gets ahead] (of us)."
s.1 Hear me, O king [my lord]! Bel [...] Let the [...] bring gold and precious stones ... [As for you, ke]ep in safety, [pray to...] and let him prolong your life. Take care of yourself, ditto ditto (= let the people die quickly)!
3 [Save] your life and [the life of] your family! Save your life [*from the hands of* the e]unuchs! Ditto ditto. Brace yourself! Let the [...] stand [with you]; they are loyal to you.

CT 53 938[434]
(= 83-1-18,508)

Obv.
1 [*a-na* LUGAL EN-*ia*]

[434] Restorations partly from CT 53 17; cf. Parpola 1983, 239 n. 416.

2 [ARAD-*ka* ^{md}PA–*re-eh-tú*–PAB ^{d}EN ^{d}GAŠAN ^{d}PA ^{d}*taš-me-tum*]
3 [^{d}15 *šá* UR]U.NINA ^{d}15 *šá* [URU.*arba-ìl* DINGIR.MEŠ-*ka šá* MU-*ka*]
4 [*a-na* LUGAL]-*ti iz-kur-u-ni šu-n*[*u lu-bal-li-ṭu-u-ka šá ina* ŠÀ]
5 [*ṭa-ab-ti*] *šá* AD-*ka ina* ŠÀ *a-de-e š*[*á* AD-*ka u ina* ŠÀ *a-de-ka*]
6 [*i-ha-ṭu-u-ni*] *šá ina* UGU ZI.MEŠ-*ka* ⸢*i*⸣-[*da-ba-bu-u-ni*]
7 [*šu-nu ina* ŠU.2-*k*]*a i-šá-ka-nu-šú-nu* ⸢MU⸣-[*šú-nu* TA* KUR–*aš-šur*.KI]
8 [TA* ŠÀ É.GA]L-*ka tu-hal-la-qa da-ba-bú* [*an-ni-ú*]
9 [*šá* ^{d}NIN.LÍ]L *šu-ú* LUGAL *be-li ina* ŠÀ-*bi lu l*[*a i-ši-aṭ*]
10 [*ina* UD.*x*.KÁM *š*]*á* ITI.APIN *di-ig-lu a-da-gal ma-a* [*x x x*]
11 [*ma-a ina* ŠÀ-*bi x x x x t*]*a*$^{?}$-*bi-da* EN–*a-de-e šá* LU[GAL EN-*ia a-na-ku*]
12 [*la–mu-qa-a.a la ú-pa-az-z*]*a-ar di-ib-*[*bi šá x x x x x*]
rest broken away

Rev. beginning broken away
1′ [*x*]*x x*[*x x x x x x x x x x x x x x x x x*]
2′ *ša ina* É.GAL-*ka* ⸢*ep-šu* ⸣-*u-n*[*i x x x x x x x x x*]
3′ *la iš-me la ú-da a-* [*na x x x x x x x x*]
4′ PI.2-*ka lu la ta-sa-hu-r*[*a x x x x x x x x x*]
5′ *hal-lu-qi a-na* [*x*]*x da x* [*x x x x x x x x*]
6′ ⸢*ù* ⸣ ^{m}*ba-am-ba-a a-* [*x x x x x x x x x x x*]
7′ [*x*]*x* [*x*] ⸢*ú* ⸣-*nu la ta-* [*x x x x x x x x x x*]
two lines broken away

Side
1 [*x x x x x x x x x x*]-*tú ú-qa-*[*x x x x*]
2 [*x x x x x x x x x x*] ⸢*x x* ⸣ [*x x x x x*]
two lines broken away

1 [To the king, my lord: your servant Nabû-rehtu-uṣur. May Bel and Belet, Nabû and Tašmetu, Ištar of] Nineveh and Ištar of [Arbela, your gods who] called [you by name to kings]hip, [keep you alive]!

4 [Those who sinned against] your father's [goodness, your father's and your own] treaty, and who p[lot] against your life, shall be placed in yo[ur hands], and you shall delete [their] name [from Assyria and from] your p[alace].

8 [This] is the word of [Mullis]su; the king, my lord, should not be ne[glectful] about it.

10 [On the 6th o]f Marchesvan (VIII), I had a vision: "[...] *spend the night* [...]." [I am] bound by the treaty of the ki[ng, my lord]; I cannot c[onceal] the thi[ngs that ...].

(Break)

r.2 which have been done in your palace [...] he has not heard, and does not know [...] to not turn away your attention [...] to destroy...[...] and Bambâ [...] do not [...] their [...]

Background

The Message of the Letters

We can now make an attempt to rough out an outline of the substance of the three letters. The best-preserved text, ABL 1217, will be used as a skeleton supplemented by the information obtainable from the more fragmentary letters CT 53 17 and 938.

Lines 1–4: The greeting of the letter indicates that it is addressed to the king who as "the seed of Sennacherib" (line r.5) can only be Esarhaddon.[435] The unique god-list, consisting of a triad of two divine couples (Bel & Belet, Nabû & Tašmetu) and two main Assyrian manifestations of Ištar, seems to be typical of Nabû-rehtu-uṣur since it appears in all three letters (cf. CT 53 17:2-3 and 938:2-3).

Lines 4–7: The subject matter of the letter is introduced by referring to people "who have sinned against your father's goodness and your father's and your own treaty" (*ša ina libbi ṭābti ša abīka ina libbi adê ša abīka u ina libbi adêka ih(aṭ)ṭūni*). This phrase is repeated in all three letters of Nabû-rehtu-uṣur (cf. CT 53 17:5-6 and 938:4-6)[436] and it corresponds to the standard treaty phraseology well known from Neo-Assyrian treaties and other documents as the parallelism of *ṭābtu* "goodness" and *adê* "treaty" as well as the use of the verb *haṭû* "to sin" clearly show.[437] By using this language the writer was able to demonstrate his subservience to the king as well as his political correctness.[438] The treaties of the Assyrian king did not only concern the vassal kings but also the Assyrian and Babylonian citizens who were obliged to observe the treaty stipulations. For the citizens this meant above all the claim of absolute loyalty towards the king and the crown prince and the obligation to report, to seize and even to kill any instigators of insurrection.[439]

Moreover, the phrase is not purely ideological but also has historical implications. The people of Assyria were made to swear a treaty oath by the

---

[435] Cf. ABL 442 r.1-2: *at-ta* NUMUN.MEŠ GIN *ša* ^{md}30–PAB.MEŠ–SU "You [Esarhaddon] are the true seed of Sennacherib."

[436] The remnants of the lines indicate that the phrase is originally almost word-for-word the same in all three cases.

[437] Cf. Parpola and Watanabe 1988, XVI-XXIII; Nissinen 1993, 238 and further, e.g., Weinfeld 1973; Fox 1973 and Johag 1977.

[438] Cf. the similar use of the same phraseology by Urad-Nanaya in SAA 10 316 19-r.4: "Because of this speech of the king, Aššur and the great gods bound and handed over to the king these criminals who plotted against the (king's) goodness (*ina muhhi ṭābti idbubūni*) and who, having concluded the king's treaty (*adê ša šarri*) together with his servants before Aššur and the great gods, broke the treaty (*ina libbi adê ihṭūni*). The goodness of the king (*ṭābtu ša šarri*) caught them up."

[439] This obligation is incessantly repeated in the treaties; cf. SAA 2 3:2-6; 4:4-9; 6 §§ 6, 8, 10, 12, 13 etc.; 8 r.2-27; 9:6-16, 29-37; 13:10-17.

great gods on the occasion of the investiture of both Esarhaddon (683) and Assurbanipal (672) as crown princes. These events are recorded in the inscriptions of Esarhaddon and Assurbanipal[440] and the treaties themselves have been preserved and published as SAA 2 3 and SAA 2 6, respectively.[441] There is every reason to believe that these are actually the two texts referred to as "your father's and your own treaty." This conviction gains in likelihood if we take a closer look at the phraseology utilized in the letter. The divine ordinance concerning the people who break the treaty is that the king will destroy their name and their seed from his palace (*šumšunu zara'šunu issu libbi ekallīka halliqi*, cf. CT 53 17:7-8 and 938:7-8: *šumšunu issu māt Aššūr issu libbi ekallīka tuhallaqa*). This expression (cf. also lines r.5, 9-10) shows such a close resemblance to the phraseology of one specific text – SAA 2 6 alias the Succession Treaty of Esarhaddon, concluded on the occasion of the investiture of Assurbanipal and Šamaš-šumu-ukin as crown princes in the month of Iyyar (II), 672 – that an influence of this text on the language of the letters of Nabû-rehtu-uṣur may be assumed.[442] This, together with the mentioning of the crown prince in CT 53 107:1, gives us a terminus post quem for the dating of the letter, so that it must have been written between Iyyar (II), 672 and Marchesvan (VIII), 669, when Esarhaddon died.[443]

Nabû-rehtu-uṣur claims to have had a "vision" on the 6th day of the month of Marchesvan (VIII) (*ina* UD.6.KÁM *ša Arahšamna diglu addagal* CT 53 17:10 and 938:10). This implies that the letters cannot have been written in this month – and not in the following month either as this would probably

[440] Borger 1956 (§ 27) 40-41:8-22.; 1996, 15-16, 208-209: A i 8-34//F i 7-32 (cf. Streck 1916, 2-5).

[441] See Parpola 1987b, 163-164 and Parpola & Watanabe 1988, XXVIII-XXIX.

[442] In this particular treaty – unlike the other preserved treaties – the verb *halāqu*, "disappear" (D "make disappear, destroy") occurs very often together with *šumu* and *zar'u* ("name" and "seed"). Cf. SAA 2 6 § 12:140-141, § 13:161, § 22:255-256: MU-*šu-nu* NUMUN-*šu-nu ina* KUR *la tu-hal-laq-qa-a-ni* "You shall destroy their name and their seed from the land"; § 26:315: MU-*šu* NUMUN-*šu ina* KUR *la tu-hal-laq-a-ni* "You shall destroy his name and his seed from the land"; § 45:435-436: MU-*ku-nu* NUMUN-*ku-nu ina* KUR *lu-hal-liq* "(May Zarpanitu...) destroy your name and your seed from the land"; § 66:538-539: MU-*ku-nu* NUMUN-*ku-nu* NUMUN *ša* DUMU.MEŠ-*ku-nu* DUMU.MÍ.MEŠ-*ku-nu* TA* KUR *li-ih-liq* "May your name, your seed, and the seed of your sons and your daughters disappear from the land"; § 67:543-544: [NUMU]N-*ku-nu* NUMUN.MEŠ *šá* D[UMU?.MEŠ-*ku-n*]*u* [TA?] UGU *pa-ni ša kaq-qa-ri li-ih-liq* "May your [see]d and the seed of y[our] s[ons] disappear [from] the face of the land"; § 105:661: MU-*ku-nu lip-ši-ṭi* NUMUN-*ku-nu ina* KUR *lu-hal-liq* "(May Nabû...) erase your name and destroy your seed from the land." Cf. also the inscription of Esarhaddon concerning his rise to power, composed in 673: *an-nu kab-tú e-mid-su-nu-ti-ma ú-hal-li-qa* NUMUN-*šu-un* "I imposed a heavy punishment upon them (= insurrectionists) and destroyed their seed" (Borger 1956 [§ 27] 45:10-11).

In addition, "life" (*napšutu*) occurs together with *halāqu* in SAA 2 6 § 25:292-293: *ina* ŠÀ-*bi a-de-e-ku-nu la ta-ha-ṭi-a* ZI.MEŠ-*ku-nu la tu-hal-la-qa* "Do not sin against your treaty and annihilate yourselves."

[443] The date of Esarhaddon's death is recorded in the chronicles (Grayson 1975a, 86:31; 127:29). As to the dating of the letter, cf. Parpola 1983, 239 n. 412 over against earlier attempts.

have been referred to as "the last month." Most probably the letter was written still in the same year, otherwise the writer would have spoken about "last year." Thus, we arrive between the months of Tebet (X) and Adar (XII); the only possible years are 672/671, 671/670 and 670/669.

The "vision" (*diglu*), the substance of which has not been preserved, has obviously led Nabû-rehtu-uṣur to the conviction that something evil is being done to the king in his own palace.[444] It appears that a person called Sasî, together with some people allied to him, has come under Nabû-rehtu-uṣur's suspicion. Since the "vision" he has kept himself informed about the activities of the suspects in order to keep the treaty on his own behalf and report the disloyal ones to the king (EN–*a-de-e šá* LU[GAL EN-*ia a-na-ku*] "[I am] bound by the treaty of the ki[ng, my lord]" CT 53 938:11; cf. CT 53 17:11).[445] What he writes corresponds so well with the stipulations of the Succession Treaty of Esarhaddon that one cannot escape the idea the he was familiar with them. The general obligation to report any conspiracy is expressed in the treaty as follows (SAA 2 6 § 12:130-146):

> If anyone should speak to you of rebellion and insurrection (*sīhu bārtu*) (with the purpose) of ki[lling], assassinating, and eliminating Assurbanipal, the [great crown] prince designate, son of Esarhaddon, king of Assyria, your lord, concerning whom he has concluded (this) treaty with you (*ša ina muhhīšu adê issīkunu iškunūni*), or if you should hear it from the mouth of anyone, you shall seize the perpetrators of insurrection and bring them before Assurbanipal, the great crown prince designate.
> If you are able to seize them and put them to death, then you shall destroy their name and seed from the land (*šumma... šumšunu zaraʾšunu ina māt lā tuhallaqāni*). If, however, you are unable to seize them and put them to death, you shall inform before Assurbanipal, the great crown prince designate, and assist him in seizing and putting to death the perpetrators of rebellion.

Obviously, now, Nabû-rehtu-uṣur is fulfilling this obligation in his letter, revealing something that is prohibited in the same treaty with the following words (SAA 2 6 § 19:212-213):

> You shall not hold an assembly to adjure one another and give the kingship to one of you.

Nabû-rehtu-uṣur does exactly what he is obliged to do according to these stipulations. As it seems to be impossible for him to seize and kill the conspirators by himself, he informs on them in order to let the king's officials do it. He makes every endeavour to convince the king of the grave danger and

---

[444] Even if the frequent references to *ekallu* often occur in broken contexts, many of them give the impression that the king is in danger in his own palace; cf. ABL 1217:6, 21-22; CT 53 118:7; CT 53 17 s.3-4; CT 53 107:5, r.8; CT 53 938 r.2ff.

[445] Cf. SAA 10 199:18-22: "Is it not said in the treaty as follows: 'Anyone who hears something (but) does not inform the king...' Let them now summon him and question him!"

uncover the alleged conspiracy of Sasî and his accomplices. He is certain that these people have laid an ambush ([*ṣābāni š*]*a Sāsî šubtu u*[*ssēšibū...*] CT 53 17 r.19-20) for the king[446] and are only waiting for the right moment to seize the opportunity to assassinate him.

The fate of those who break the treaty is proclaimed in the name of the goddess Nikkal (^{d}NIN.GAL) – or, in the case of CT 53 17 and 938, Mullissu (^{d}NIN.LÍL). It may be asked if any difference should be made between these two goddesses or if they just appear as manifestations of Ištar, as Mullissu frequently does in prophetic oracles and other Neo-Assyrian texts.[447] As we shall see below, the reference to Nikkal instead of Mullissu in ABL 1217 is explicable in the light of the fact that an alleged oracle of Nusku, another Harranean deity, is cited on the reverse of the letter (r.4-5).

Obviously an oracle of Nikkal/Mullissu is referred to in the letters since all of them warn the king against neglecting "this word of Nikkal/Mullissu" implying that an oracle has just been quoted (CT 53 17:8-9 and 938:8-9: *dabābu anniu ša Mullissi šū šarru bēlī ina libbi lū lā i*[*šīaṭ*]; ABL 1217:12-13: *šarru bēlī* [*ina li*]*bbi dabābi ša Nik*[*kal annie*] *lā tašī*[*aṭ*]). The quotations do not have to be literal ones – we may have to do with paraphrases by the writer as well. Since it would be atypical for a prophetic oracle to mention names of any individuals except the king himself,[448] the words *nīšī ša issi Sāsî ūdû*[*ni...*] can hardly belong to any oracle but express the conviction of Nabû-rehtu-uṣur that the words of Nikkal apply to Sasî and his allies. The writer of the letter applies the general rule expressed in the divine words ("those who break the treaty will be destroyed") to a specific case.

Lines 8–11: The writer attempts to inspire the king with confidence by assuring him that he knows the words of Nikkal (*dabābu ša Nikkal ū*[*da...*]). He may mean the preceding text, but it is not excluded that what follows could also be paraphrased from divine words. The complete wording and syntactic structure of the following text is difficult to reconstruct, but the message is clear enough: the adversaries of the king will die but the king (together with the royal family) will save his life and his kingdom will be guarded by divine powers. All this is in complete accordance with the interminable flow of similar affirmations in the prophetic oracles, e.g. SAA 9 2.5 iii 22-23, 26-27:[449]

> *dāme ša nakarūte ša šarrīja atabbak šarrī anaṣṣar... anāku abūka ummaka birti agappīja urtabbika*

---

[446] For *šubtu* in the meaning of "ambush" cf. SAA 1 175:16; 244:9; SAA 5 33 r.12.

[447] E.g., SAA 9 2.4 ii 30: *abat Issār ša Arbail abat šarrati Mullissi* "The word of Ištar of Arbela, the word of Queen Mullissu"; cf. also SAA 9 7 r.6; SAA 9 9 r.1-3; SAA 3 31:8-9; 3 7:11-12 and see Weippert 1985, 64 and Nissinen 1993, 228.

[448] The preserved prophetic oracles (SAA 9) never mention the names of the enemies of the king or of the people disloyal to him; cf., however, the prophecy against Ahšeri, the king of Mannea, quoted in Assurbanipal's Prism A iii 5-7; see above, pp. 43ff.

[449] Cf. also SAA 9 1.2 i 30-35; 1.6 iv 5-19; 2.3 ii 1-5; 2.4 ii 31ff.

> I will shed the blood of my king's enemies. I will protect my king... I am your father and mother. I raised you between my wings.

The expression *abūka ummaka lū šunu* "let them be your father and mother" (line 10) is especially noteworthy since it recalls the above-cited words of Ištar: *anāku abūka ummaka* "I am your father and mother." This also gives us a hint of the goddesses as the possible antecedent of *šunu*.

Lines 12ff: The writer urges the king not to be neglectful of the word of Nikkal (cf. CT 53 17:8-9 and 938:8-9: *dabābu anniu ša Mullissi šū šarru bēlī ina libbi lū lā išīaṭ*). Then he obviously enters into his particular subject. He mentions a letter (*egir*[*tu*]) of which we are left without any information because the rest of the text is broken away. It is obvious, however, that the data gathered by Nabû-rehtu-uṣur, who apparently does not live in the midst of the storm, is based on his correspondence with people on the spot. CT 53 17:16 also refers to a letter as a source of information (*kî ina libbi egirt*[*i...*] "as follows in the lette[r...]")[450] and CT 53 107 apparently mentions some of his informers.

CT 53 118:2–10: Whether or not the text of this fragment has anything to do with the above-mentioned *egirtu*, cannot be known. The few preserved words do not reveal much of the contents of the missing text, except that something concerning Sasî is or has been done continually (*kaiamānu ina muhhi Sās*[*î...*]). Presumably he has been told to playact the loyal servant of the king (*ina pān šarri dammiq*) and Nabû-rehtu-uṣur makes an effort to uncover him as a fake. A couple of proper names, Nabû-bel-*x* (mdPA–EN–[*x x*])[451] and Ubru-Nabû (mSUHUŠ–dPA LÚ.[*x x*])[452] have been partly preserved on the fragment but nothing can be deduced about the role and position of these persons except that they seem to be presented as collaborators of Sasî.

ABL 1217 r.2–5: The principal manifestation of the disloyalty of Sasî and his adherents is now laid bare: Nabû-rehtu-uṣur discloses that a "slave girl" (*amtu*) of a certain Bel-ahu-uṣur has appeared on the outskirts of Harran (*ina q*[*ann*]*i ša H*[*arrāni*])[453] and delivered a "good word" (*dabābu damqu*)[454] from the god Nusku according to which Sasî would take over the kingship:

---

[450] Whether he refers to a letter written by himself because of the vision he had just had or to his correspondence with other people, is not clear.

[451] Proper names beginning with Nabû-bel(u)- are very common in Neo-Assyrian sources (e. g. Nabû-belu-uṣur, mayor of Nineveh SAA 6 86; 87; Nabû-belu-uṣur, mayor of Dur-Šarrukku SAA 6 283; Nabû-bel-šumati, governor of the Sealand ABL 839 [cf. Dietrich 1970, 36-39] etc.) so that the person mentioned here is extremely difficult to identify.

[452] The name Ubru-Nabû is attested in documents ranging from the time of Tiglath-Pileser (SAA 6 19 r.14) and Sargon (SAA 1 244 r.5; SAA 6 11 r.11) through the 680's (SAA 6 155 r.7; 262 r.6; 263 r.4) down to the year 671 when a person called Ubru-Nabû appears in a document as keeper of rams, oxen and donkey stallions belonging to Remanni-Adad, Assurbanipal's charioteer (SAA 6 296:5). A person with the name Sasî is one of the witnesses of this document (line r.5).

[453] Cf. SAA 10 174:11 (below, p. 123).

[454] As there is nothing "good" for Esarhaddon in the oracle, *dabābu damqu* should be

abat Nusku šī mā šarrūtu ana Sāsî mā šumu zar'u ša Sīn-ahhē-riba uhallaqa

This is the word of Nusku: The kingship is for Sasî. I will destroy the name and seed of Sennacherib.

What we have here demonstrates that not all prophecy was favorable to the king but could also be used against him – a peril fully reckoned with in the Succession Treaty of Esarhaddon (SAA 2 6 § 10:108-109, 116-119; cf. below):

šumma abutu lā ṭābtu lā de'iqtu lā banītu... ina pî raggimi mahhê mār šā'ili amat ili lū ina pî naphar ṣalmat qaqqadi mal bašû tašammāni...

If you hear any evil, improper, ugly word... from the mouth of a prophet, an ecstatic, an inquirer of oracles, or from the mouth of any human being at all...

The oracle of Nusku is indeed diametrically opposed by the words of Nikkal at the beginning of the letter, and it becomes obvious why that particular message of Nikkal is chosen to be cited there. Nabû-rehtu-uṣur responds to the prophecy with another prophecy – on the presumption, of course, that the words delivered by the "slave girl" are regarded as a pseudo-prophecy. Likewise in CT 53 107 he wants to prove that Sasî has become self-reliant enough to reject the divine legitimation of the kingship of Esarhaddon and seize the throne for himself (CT 53 107:9-11):

šū ina muhhi libbi irtihi[*ṣ* ...] *assakan mā ša Bēl Nabû Issār ša* [...] *urtamme ša raminīšu* [...]

He has become confident in (his) heart [and is saying:] "I have set [...]." He has rejected what Bel, Nabû, Ištar of [... have *said/decreed*], and [...] of his own.

The ambitions of Sasî are then, it seems, repudiated with a word of Ištar of which no readable line is preseved (lines 12ff). The reference to the gods identical with the triad in the salutations of Nabû-rehtu-uṣur's three letters, Bel, Nabû and Ištar,[455] probably alludes to the words of these gods as the divine guarantee of Esarhaddon's rule. Interestingly enough, the same triad of gods appears with the same function in the prophecy of Bayâ SAA 9 1.4.[456]

understood in the same sense as *šulmu* "oracle of salvation" ("Heilsorakel") in SAA 9 3.2 ii 8; 3.3 ii 26.

455 Parpola, who equates Ištar with the biblical Holy Spirit (1997c, XXII-XXIII) would find here an analogy of the Holy Trinity: Father, Son and the Holy Spirit.

456 SAA 9 1.4 ii 16-20, 30-33, 38-39: *lā tapallah Aššūr-ahu-iddina anāku Bēl issīka adabbūbu gušūrū ša libbīka aharrīdi... anāku Issār ša Arbail Aššūr issīka usallim ṣeherāka attaṣakka lā tapallah na''idāni... anāku Nabû bēl qarṭuppi na''idāni* "Fear not, Esarhaddon! I am Bel. (Even as) I speak to you, I watch over the beams of your heart... I am Ištar of Arbela; I reconciled Aššur with you. When you were small, I took you to me. Do not fear; praise me!... I am Nabû, lord of the stylus. Praise me!"

It is certainly not by chance that a woman from the neighborhood of Harran delivers an oracle in the name of Nusku. The cult of Nusku was centered in this particular city. In the Neo-Assyrian period Nusku was seen as the son of Sin, the moon-god, who was also worshipped in Harran and whose cult was actively promoted by the Neo-Assyrian kings, perhaps in the interests of the Assyrian political and cultural expansion to the West.[457] In the Sin temple of Harran, Ehulhul, there was a chapel of Nusku called Emelamanna, at least in the time of Assurbanipal.[458] In this context it is noteworthy that Nusku seems to have been virtually equated with Nabû at Harran.[459] Hence, the message of the Nusku oracle may be compared with a curse in the Succession Treaty of Esarhaddon, the wording of which has a close affinity with both the Nusku oracle against Esarhaddon and the phraseology of Nabû-rehtu-uṣur (SAA 2 6 § 105:660-661):

> *Nabû nāši ṭuppi šīmti ilāni šumkunu lipšīṭi zara'kunu ina māt luhalliq*
>
> May Nabû, bearer of the tablet of fates of the gods, erase your name, and destroy your seed from the land.

This certainly gave Nabû-rehtu-uṣur who, as has been assumed, knew this treaty, enough reason to curse "the name and the seed" of the conspirators.

Furthermore, it is quite consistent that Nabû-rehtu-uṣur in ABL 1217 refers to the words of Nikkal instead of Mullissu whose words are quoted in his other letters: Nikkal was the consort of Sin and likewise worshipped in Harran.[460] Nabû-rehtu-uṣur thus contrasts the words of the Harranean goddess against the alleged oracle of the Harranean god. In addition, the roles of the goddesses overlap to the point that both Mullissu and Nikkal can be seen as manifestations of the Goddess who in Assyria is most frequently called Ištar but who in Harran was invoked as Nikkal.[461] Thus, as it seems, the triad Bel, Nabû and Ištar has its Harranean equivalent in Sin, Nusku and Nikkal.

---

457 Thus Holloway 1995, 307; cf. the reservations of Uehlinger 1997, 320.

458 See Borger 1996, 143 C i 85-90. On the basis of Assurbanipal's inscriptional account it is difficult to fathom whether or not Emelamanna existed before his reign. Assurbanipal claims to have rebuilt the temple in his first year, but Tadmor 1981, 23 prefers to date it to the year 664 when the text was composed. If SAA 10 14, dating from Tammuz (IV) 670/669, actually refers to the restoration of Ehulhul and its chapel of Nusku (cf. Parpola 1983, 12), then the work must have been at least in preparation at the beginning of his reign.

459 See Lewy & Lewy 1948, 149-150; Gadd 1958, 40; Drijvers 1980, 144; Green 1992, 33-34.

460 For the cults of Sin, Nikkal and Nusku in Harran in the Neo-Assyrian era, see Postgate 1972/75, 124-125; Seux 1976, 318, 340, 373, 377, 388; Parpola 1983, 11-12; Green 1992, 19-43; Lipiński 1994, 171-192; Holloway 1995, 287-291 and, especially for the goddess in Harran, Green 1996. The divine couple Sin and Nikkal is very common, e.g., in treaties (SAA 2 2 vi 8; 3:7, r.2) and in blessings of letters; sometimes Nusku is also invoked together with them; cf. SAA 10 343:5-6; 346:8.

461 Ištar and Sin even appear together on a few cylinder seals as if Ištar had "replaced" Nikkal as the divine consort of the Moon god (cf. Uehlinger 1997, 321 with illustrations

That the word against Esarhaddon was proclaimed "on the outskirts of Harran" (*ina q[a-n]i šá* ⌜URU⌝.K[ASKAL]) is not purely coincidental either. According to a letter of Marduk-šumu-uṣur to Assurbanipal from the year 667 (SAA 10 174:10-16)[462] it was precisely "on the outskirts of Harran" where Esarhaddon, on his way to Egypt in the month of Nisan (I), 671, arranged a spectacular demonstration of his rule in a newly built temple:[463]

> When the father of the king, my lord, wen[t] to Egypt, a temple of cedar was bu[ilt] outside the city of Harran (*ina qa-an-ni* URU.KASKAL). Sin was seated upon a staff, with two crowns on (his) head, and the god Nusku stood before him. The father of the king, my lord, entered; he placed [the crown(s)?] on his head, (and it was said to him:) "You will go and conquer the world with it!" [So he we]nt and conquered Egypt; the king, the lord of kings (= Assurbanipal), will conquer the rest of the countries [which] have not submitted to Aššur and Sin.

In the letter of Marduk-šumu-uṣur this ritual was a symbol of the global rule of Esarhaddon as well as a favorable omen for Assurbanipal who at that time still ruled over Egypt. From the local point of view, however, the ritual and the temple of cedar in which it was performed represented a manifestation of the presence of the Assyrian king in Harran – eventually accompanied by a prophecy, provided that the words "You will go and conquer the world with it" are proclaimed by a prophet which is not certain but should not be excluded either.[464] On the other hand, the coronation of Esarhaddon in the presence of the double-crowned[465] representation of Sin and Nusku also demonstrated the legitimation of the Egyptian campaign by the Lord of Harran whose status in the Western provinces was high. Presumably the presence of the king was

---

19 and 20). It is also noteworthy that The Doctrine of Addai, a Christian source from the late 4th century CE, refers to the goddess of Harran as Bath Nikkal, "daughter of Nikkal" – which Ištar actually was in the Mesopotamian divine genealogy! See Green 1996, 91-94 and Drijvers 1980, 143.

[462] As to this letter, cf. Parpola 1983, 100 and Uehlinger 1997, 316-318.

[463] There are records of two temples of Sin in the vicinity of Harran. The fourth century CE author of the Historia Augusta states that Caracalla was returning from a temple of the moon god outside Harran when he was assassinated. In the village of Asagi Yarimca, four miles north of Harran, a stele with the disc and crescent emblem of Sin was discovered in 1949, possibly on the location of a temple (see Green 1992, 27-28). It can only be speculated whether either of these two temples could be traced back to the temple erected by Esarhaddon.

[464] Cf. above, p. 79.

[465] According to Redford 1992, 360, this was "a sure sign that this double uraeus diadem of Egypt would soon grace his bow." Spalinger 1976, too, has seen the two crowns of Sin as representing the Egyptian double crown, i.e., the crowns of Upper and Lower Egypt (cf. Onasch 1994, 161). However, Spalinger has recently opted for the two horns of the (crescent) moon as a closer parallel (a private communication to Chr. Uehlinger; cf. Uehlinger 1997, 318, n. 97); as to the horns of the crescent moon see also Loretz 1985.

subsequently symbolized by erecting large statues of the king and of the crown princes around the statue of Sin, the "lord of the crown."[466]

It seems obvious that the supposed word of Nusku has been uttered by the "slave girl" at this very location. If this is true, then the prophecy against Esarhaddon must have been proclaimed after Nisan (I), 671; Nabû-rehtu-uṣur mentions the month of Sivan (III), not necessarily as the date of the word of Nusku, but as the beginning of the prophetic activity of the "slave girl." Whoever was behind the oracle could not possibly have chosen a better spot for their purposes. The prophecy proclaimed against the king would have been a sign of open rebellion anywhere, but its symbolic effect must have been tremendous at the place where the presence of the king was manifested in connection with a campaign that became a victorious conquest – all the more so if the coronation of Esarhaddon in the temple of cedar was accompanied by a prophecy.

Since the oracle of Nusku is said to have been delivered by a person referred to as *amtu*, the question arises if she was actually the one who transmitted the alleged words of Nusku or if she only informed others about the oracle uttered by someone else. There are good grounds for assuming that the "slave girl" indeed acted as the prophetess, even if this is not explicitly stated. It is she who was claimed to have "spoken" the oracle (*tadabbubu*) and who has been captured – perhaps having been caught in the very act of speaking the oracle – and brought into the house of Sasî. Whether or not she actually was a prophetess is difficult to judge, however. The appellation *amtu* does not have to be understood literally since it may be a defamatory designation of the person whom the writer does not want to call a prophetess.

Lines r.5–8: Nabû-rehtu-uṣur moves on to suggestions about what should be done with the people under suspicion. He advises the king to let the *rab mūgi* question the household of Bel-ahu-uṣur "beneath the great gate of the temple of Nabû" (*ina šapla bābi rabie ša bēt Nabû*). This would mean that he wants the case to become public knowledge – perhaps because rumors about it have been circulated widely enough already.

It appears that Bel-ahu-uṣur must be brought from Harran where he seems to reside. The city of Harran is mentioned also in CT 53 107 r.5 where it obviously is part of a quotation from a letter concerning the plot of Sasî:

> *kî annî q*[*ab*]*i mā ina Harrān...*
>
> It r[ead]s as follows: "In Harran [...]"

---

[466] Cf. SAA 10 13 r.2-17: "If it [is acceptable] to the king, my lord, the large royal statues should be erected on the right and the left side of the [Moon] god. The statuettes of the king's sons should be s[et up behind] and in front of the Moon god. The Moon, lord of the cr[own] (EN *a*-[*ge-e*]), will [then] every month without fa[il], in rising and [setting], unceasingly send h[appy] signs of long-lasting days, steady reign and increase in power to the king." Although Parpola 1983, 10, dates this letter only approximately in the years 672-669, it is most probably connected with this event (thus also Uehlinger 1997, 318).

The "slave girl" of Bel-ahu-uṣur who also made her appearance in the environs of Harran has already been brought before the authorities by the guards. That Nabû-rehtu-uṣur makes no suggestion that she be executed is in accordance with the Succession Treaty of Esarhaddon in which only the denunciation of the "prophet, ecstatic and the inquirer of oracles" is stipulated (§ 10) whereas the conspirators are to be put to death right away (§ 12). A noteworthy detail in this context is his proposal for a *dullu* (line r.7; probably an extispicy ritual[467]) on account of the "slave girl." Is Nabû-rehtu-uṣur still wavering about whether or not the alleged oracle of Nusku should be considered a genuine one? If this is the case, then we would have here the only Neo-Assyrian case of "checking" the accuracy of a prophecy by means of another divinatory method.[468] Nevertheless, in the context of the Neo-Assyrian royal ideology, it would be as counter-productive to inquire whether a prophecy against the king is true as it would be to ask if the gods really are gods. What we have here is rather a proposal for inquiry about the existence of the conspiracy and the role of Sasî in it; inquiries of this kind are well known (SAA 4 139-148), many of them being connected with the political turbulence of the years 670/671.[469] It is also possible that the inquiry might look into the connection of the conspiracy with Harran and the Harraneans.

Lines r.9-10: Nabû-rehtu-uṣur hardly considers the possibility that Nusku himself could have said anything like the oracle alleges. He declares instead that the name and seed of Sasî, Bel-ahu-uṣur and their adherents will perish whereas the name and seed of the king will be established by Bel and Nabû forever. Since a word or two is broken away after the name of Nusku at the end of line r.8 the syntactic position of the name remains unclear; possibly Nusku will destroy the conspirators[470] and thus fulfill the words of Nikkal cited at the beginning of the letter.

Lines r.11-19: Nabû-rehtu-uṣur suggests the settling of the case be continued with a conversation with Ardâ who is supposed to have detailed information about the moves of Sasî and his accomplices and thus appears as the key witness. Since Ardâ is not to be interrogated (*ša'ālu*) but just "talked with" (*dabābu*) he is perhaps not looked upon as one of the suspects but rather as the informer who has denounced the plot to the authorities. This can also

---

[467] The word *dullu* often means a service for the king (cf. SAA 1 147:5: *ša ina Milqia dulli šarri eppaššūni*) but this meaning is excluded here. Rather, *dullu* would mean a ritual performed on account of the woman, as is the case in a letter addressed to the mother of the king (SAA 10 313:6-12): *qallatu ša ina bēt Šamâ ša ina pānīja paqdatu ultu dulla ša attalû ibaššû ina muhhīša inneppuš* "The slave girl in the house of Šamâ who was entrusted to my care – once the ritual of the eclipse becomes timely, it will be performed on her." Cf. further SAA 10 315:17-19: *šumma ina pān šarri bēlīja mahir bārâni dullu ina muhhi lēpušū* "If it suits the king, my lord, let the haruspices perform an extispicy on account of this."

[468] For this practice in Mari, see, e.g., Noort 1977, 84-86.

[469] Cf. Starr 1990, LXIII.

[470] Note, however, that the subject of *lihliq* (G instead of D) should be the fixed expression "name and seed."

be seen in CT 53 107:7-8 where Ardâ seemingly appears as an informer together with some other people:[471]

> *ṣābāni Adad-šumu-uṣur Ar*[*dâ...*] *iqṭibûni mā bārtu eppu*[*šū...*]
>
> The men of Adad-šumu-uṣur and Ar[dâ...]Íhave said to me: "They are making a rebellion [...]."

The nature of the questions suggested by Nabû-rehtu-uṣur imply that Ardâ belonged to the immediate circle of Sasî. He is supposed to know about Sasî's meetings and conversations with other persons on specific days. He also seems to be reproached for not having reported (all?) the things he saw and heard (*atâ mīnu ša tām*[*urūni...*]).

In this connection yet more persons involved in the alleged conspiracy are exposed: Issar-nadin-apli the scribe,[472] Nabû-eṭir,[473] Awyanu the eunuch (?) and the "city overseer" (LÚ.*ša*–UGU–URU/*ša-muhhi-āli*). The last mentioned appellation is preceded by the name of Sasî himself, thus it may (but does not have to) be his professional designation. Nabû-rehtu-uṣur apparently suggests that the *rab mūgi* should send his troops to capture and interrogate all these persons (line r.18; cf. CT 53 17 r.13).

The gallery of persons mentioned by Nabû-rehtu-uṣur is expanded by several other names in CT 53 17+107 and 938: Bambâ (CT 53 938 r.6)[474] and his daughter (CT 53 107:6), Milki-nuri and Urad-Issar[475] (CT 53 17 r.12). All of these names occur in broken contexts and the roles of their bearers remain obscure. The daughter of Bambâ may appear together with the men of Adad-šumu-uṣur and Ardâ as an informer,[476] whereas Milki-nuri and Urad-Issar seem to belong to the adherents of Sasî who should be interrogated (*ša'alšunu* CT 53 17 r.13). More significant is the mentioning of the chief eunuch (*rab ša-rēši* CT 53 17 r.9) whose name is not preserved but who may be connected with the eunuch (?) Awyanu mentioned in ABL 1217. On the basis of the closing lines of CT 53 17 it seems probable that Nabû-rehtu-uṣur

---

[471] Unless Ardâ is not to be understood as an object of the action or information of "the men" of Adad-šumu-uṣur (i.e., the king's exorcist who certainly remained loyal to the king). If this be the case, then Ardâ cannot be treated as an informer but as one of the traitors.

[472] A scribe with the same name appears as the keeper of some contracts of the royal charioteer Remanni-Adad from the year 666 (SAA 6 311 r.7; 314 r.24; 315 r.7; 316 r.14). Note that in SAA 6 314 the following persons are listed among the witnesses: Sasî, mayor of *x* (r.10), Adad-šumu-uṣur, chief [exorcist] (r.12) and Nabû-rehtu-uṣur (r.27)!

[473] Hardly to be identified with Nabû-eṭir, the governor of the Sealand (cf. Dietrich 1970, 50 n. 1).

[474] Possibly, though not certainly, to be identified with the vizier Banbâ whose eponym year was 676 and who thus is mentioned in many documents dating from that year (e. g. SAA 6 210, 212, 226, 239, 274).

[475] Two persons with this name appear as witnesses together with one called Nabû-rehtu-uṣur in a document from the year 679 (SAA 6 268 r.7.9).

[476] Cf., however, n. 471 above.

considers some of the eunuchs to be involved in the plot, perhaps even as its leading figures (CT 53 17 s.3):

> [*issu qātē ša ša*]*-rēšāni napšatka šēzib*
>
> Save your life [*from the hands of* the] eunuchs!

Lines r.20-23: The letter ends with phrases typical of the letters of Nabû-rehtu-uṣur: "Let those people die!" (*nīšī... limūtū* cf. CT 53 17 r.10, 14, 15-16, 17) "Save your life!" (*napšatka šēzib* cf. CT 53 17 r.10, 16, 19, s.3) These exhortations make it clear that the writer believes the conspiracy of Sasî and his accomplices constitute a mortal danger to the king. The incessant repeating of these words produces a somewhat magical effect, and Nabû-rehtu-uṣur indeed uses the words as a spell to protect the king against the traitors (CT 53 17 r.15-17):

> *arhiš nīšī limūtū napšatk*[*a šēzib*] *egirtu annītu lū šiptu ina muhhīka...*
>
> Let the people die quickly! [Save] your life! May this letter be a spell, it will [...] upon you.

The Conspiracy of 671/670

The historical course and scene of the conspiracy exposed by Nabû-rehtu-uṣur is extremely difficult to reconstruct on the basis of the data obtainable from his partly broken letters. Even though no less than fifteen different persons (Sasî, Nabû-bel-*x*, Ubru-Nabû, Bel-ahu-uṣur and his "slave girl," Ardâ, Issar-nadin-apli the scribe, Awyanu the eunuch (?), Nabû-eṭir, Adad-šumu-uṣur, Bambâ and his daughter, the chief eunuch, Milki-nuri and Urad-Issar) and a few dates ("on the 6th of Marchesvan (VIII)"; "since Sivan (III)"; "on the 27th – on the 28th – on the following day") are provided, we do not gain much from all these particulars because most of the names occur in broken contexts and the dates do not reveal the year in which the events have taken place. The basic idea is clear, however: the firm conviction of Nabû-rehtu-uṣur that the life of the king is threatened by a conspiracy, the leader of which was Sasî; that a (pseudo)prophecy has been uttered against his kingship; and that most of the above-mentioned persons, including the chief eunuch and other eunuchs, belong in one way or another to the accomplices of Sasî.

It must be stressed that the letters of Nabû-rehtu-uṣur in the first place document his personal view of the events which does not necessarily have to be in complete accordance with the historical reality. This is why the letters should, if possible, be supplemented with other sources in order to sharpen the picture of their historical background.

1) That an attempted coup d'état really took place during this period of time, in Nisan (I), 670, to be precise,[477] is confirmed by the chronicles of Esarhaddon by the following entry:[478]

> MU.11.KÁM *šarru* (*ina*) *Aššūr rabiānīšu ma'dūtu ina kakki iddūk*
>
> In the eleventh year the king of (in) Assyria put many of his magnates to the sword.

We learn nothing about who these magnates were and why they were executed. Presumably they were too many to be listed within the limits of the chronicler's telegraphese.

Since neither the chronicles nor the inscriptions include any records of other revolts against Esarhaddon between 672 and 669, the texts dating from this period of time and presupposing a conspiracy against him are most probably to be connected with this event, provided that no data prove otherwise. Following this rule, the letters of Nabû-rehtu-uṣur must be dated between Tebet (X), 671/670 and Nisan (I), 670. This date is corroborated also by the apparent connection between ABL 1217 and the events of Nisan (I) 671 described in SAA 10 174:10-16 (see above, pp. 123-124).

2) There also exists an unusually large group of oracle queries concerning potential insurrections against the king (SAA 4 139-147) as well as the loyalty of individual appointees to office (SAA 4 150-180).[479] According to Starr, the entire group largely belongs to the years 671-670. The great number of appointment queries is probably due to the large-scale executions which "may account for the numerous vacancies open to prospective aspirants to office whose loyalty was being tested by means of divination."[480]

3) There are a few letters that are best explained as presupposing the executions of 670.

The letter of the chief physician Urad-Nanaya to Esarhaddon (SAA 10 316) must be viewed against the background of the chronicles and the letters of Nabû-rehtu-uṣur. The letter certainly postdates the year 672 since it presupposes the joint rule of the king and the crown prince (lines r.12-14). Using

---

[477] This date is confirmed by the observation of Larsen 1974, 22 concerning the unusual eponym date in a purchase document (SAA 6 286:11) dating from Nisan 670: ITI.BARAG *lim-mu ša* EGIR [m]ITI.AB-⌜*a*⌝-[*a*] "Month Nisan, eponym year of (the official) after Kanunayu." This kind of eponym date is used in the midst of political turbulence which has prevented the choice of the new eponym.

[478] Grayson 1975a, 86:29; 127:27.

[479] SAA 4 156:2-8 is a good representative of the wording and concern of these queries: "Should Esarhaddon, king of Assyria, appoint [the ma]n whose name is written in this papyrus and placed before your great divinity, [to the po]sition which is written in [th]is papyrus? If he appoints him, [as] long as he holds this position, will he instigate an insurrection and rebellion against Esarhaddon, king of Assyria, and [Assu]rbanipal, the crown prince of the Succession Palace?"

[480] Starr 1990, LXIII; cf. also Mayer 1995, 396.

idioms of the standard treaty phraseology, the writer refers to people who have recently plotted against the king (SAA 10 316:19-r.4):

> *issu pān dabābi anniu ša šarri annūti parriṣūti ša ina muhhi ṭābti idbubūni adê ša šarri ina pān Aššūr u ilāni rabūti issi urdānīšu iškunūni ša ina libbi adê ihṭūni Aššūr u ilāni rabūti uktassiū ina qāt šarri bēlīa issaknūšunu ṭābtu ša šarri taktašassunu*
>
> Because of this speech of the king, Aššur and the great gods bound and handed over to the king these criminals who plotted against the (king's) goodness and who, having concluded the king's treaty together with his servants before Aššur and the great gods, broke the treaty. The goodness of the king caught them up.

It appears that the attempted coup had been uncovered while the king was suffering from an attack of illness (cf. lines 7ff). This had made him so suspicious of all his servants that even those not involved with the conspiracy had to make every effort to convince the king of their loyalty.

The post-mortem on the plot seems also to be in progress in SAA 10 199, a letter from Adad-šumu-uṣur dealing with an informer who had not had the courage to lay his information in due time. This letter, too, alludes to a recently overcome fit of illness that more or less coincided with the plot.[481]

As Esarhaddon demonstrably suffered a severe fit of illness in his early 11th regnal year[482] it may be assumed with Parpola that both letters refer to the incident recorded in the chronicle entry cited above.[483]

The executions of 670 may be referred to in two further letters which, unfortunately, are badly damaged. Since CT 53 249 is probably addressed to the crown prince (line 2: ⌜*a*⌝-*na* DUMU–LU[GAL]) it must be dated between 672 and 669; if a joint rule of the king and the crown prince may be assumed from the wording,[484] then the letter can be regarded as contemporaneous with SAA 10 316. As far as can be concluded from the fragmentary text, it first reminds the king of the loyalty of the writer[485] and then refers to a "charioteer" (*mukīl appāti*) and "third men" (*tašlīšāni*), perhaps in order to reveal

---

481 SAA 10 199 r.16-18: *ūmâ kî šarru innaššarūni iqṭebīa ana šarri bēlīa assapra... ūmâ rēssu liššiū lišʾulūšu* "Now that (the illness of) the king is being taken away, he (finally) spoke out to me, and I wrote to the king, my lord... Let them now summon him and question him."

482 See Parpola 1983, 59-60 on the date of SAA 10 43.

483 Parpola 1983, 238.

484 Even if the crown prince is the addressee of the letter, the writer continuously speaks to the "king, my lord" (lines 3, 4, 8).

485 Lines 4-7 (transliteration by S. Parpola): LUGAL *be-lí em*-⌜*mar* LÚ*⌝.ARAD *ša* [TA EN-*šu*] ⌜*ke*⌝-*nu-ú-ni* LÚ*.ARAD *ša* ⌜*x*⌝ *ša* EN-*š*[*ú x x x* L]Ú*.ARAD *ša* UGU É–⌜EN.MEŠ⌝-*š*[*ú i-ma-qa-tu-ni i*]-*mu-tú-u-ni* "The king, my lord, (can) see: (I am) a servant who is loyal [to his lord], a servant who [...] of his lord, a servant who [falls and] die[s] on behalf of the house hi[s] lords [...]."

alleged insurrectionists who are still at large.[486] ABL 1364, a letter from the time of Assurbanipal, recalls three officers, Šulmu-ereš the charioteer, Dadi-ibni the "third man" and Adad-remanni the weaver, who have been sentenced to death by Esarhaddon.[487]

4) A miscellaneous group of mostly anonymous letters inform against persons that have allegedly made themselves guilty of suspicious or conspirational acts: ABL 445; 1245; 1308; CT 53 44; 46 and 78+426. The first mentioned four letters even include the name Sasî and will therefore be discussed later. The remaining three letters are void of absolute dating criteria; thus their connection with the executions of 670 cannot be verified. In any case they expose alleged mutinies against the king and, interpreted against the background of other documents, have at least a chance of belonging to the same historical crisis.

CT 53 46 is a long letter from the time of Esarhaddon concerning acts of disloyalty performed by a group of named persons in Guzana, a province and a city between Harran and Nineveh.[488] Since the city of Harran plays a role in the events around 671/670, it is not excluded that the affairs in Guzana, which is not so far away from Harran, are also connected with these events.[489] The names mentioned in this letter do not appear in other documents discussed here; it is noteworthy, however, that one of them, called Qurdî, has the title *mukīl appāti*.[490]

The letter CT 53 78+426 deals with people who appeal to the king (*ina* UGU LÚ.ERIM.MEŠ *ša a-bat–šar-ra-a-*⌜*te*⌝ [*i-zak-ka-ru-u-ni*] line 1).[491] The anon-

---

[486] Lines 7-12 (transliteration by S. Parpola): *ú-ma-a* ⌜*šúm-ma ina*⌝ [U]GU *x*[*x x x x* LÚ*.D]IB–PA.MEŠ LÚ.3-*šú*-MEŠ *ina* IGI LUGAL E[N-*ia x x x x x*]-*u-ni lu-u-sa-li ša ina* UGU GIŠ.[*x x x x x* LÚ*.D]IB–PA.MEŠ 2 LÚ.3-*šú*-MEŠ *ina* U[GU *x x x* MU.MEŠ-*šú*]-*nu liš-ṭu-ru ba-si l*[*u x x x x x x x x x* ^{m}]^{d}PA–*mu-še-zib* [*x x x x x x x*] "Now if on [... the ch]arioteers and the 'third men' [com]e before the king, [my] lo[rd...] let him... [the ch]arioteer and two 'third men' [... The names of] those who [...] should be written in order to [...] Nabû-mušezib [...] ..."

[487] Lines r.1-6 (transliteration by S. Parpola): ^{m}DI-*mu*–APIN-*eš* LÚ.*mu-kil*–KUŠ.PA.MEŠ ^{m}U.U–DÙ LÚ.3.U5 ^{m}10–*rém-a-ni* LÚ.UŠ.BAR *ša* TA* *pa-ni du-a-ku* TA* *pa-ni* AD-*ka ih-liq-u-ni* "Šulmu-ereš the charioteer, Dadi-ibni the 'third man' and Adad-remanni the weaver who, in order to escape being killed fled from the presence of your father..."

[488] On this letter, see Fales 1980, 142-146; on Guzana, cf. Becking 1992, 64-65.

[489] See Fales 1980, 142 n. 7.

[490] Written exceptionally LÚ*.*mu-kil*–KUŠ.*a-pa-a-ni* (line 21). Other persons concerned are Kutî the scribe (LÚ*.A.BA line 2), Tutî (LÚ*.[*x x*] line 2), Adad-killanni the priest (LÚ*.SANGA line 3), Tarṣî the scribe of Guzana (LÚ*.A.BA *ša* URU.*gu-za-na* line r.12), Zazâ the wife of Tarṣî (line 5), Niri-Ya'u the chief of accounts (LÚ*.GAL–NÍG.SID.MEŠ line 4) and Palṭi-Ya'u (L[Ú*.*x x*] line 4). Both last mentioned names are of Hebrew origin (Albright 1958, 36; Becking 1992, 67); cf. the names *Nēriyyâ/Nēriyyāhû* (cf. Noth 1928, 167; Tallqvist 1914, 176) and *Palṭî/ Pĕlaṭyâ/Pĕlaṭyāhû* (cf. Noth 1928, 38, 156, 180; Tallqvist 1914, 179).

[491] Thus according to the reconstruction of Parpola; for this letter, see also Fales 1980, 148 whose reconstrucion and translation is different: *ina* UGU LÚ.ERIM.MEŠ *ša a-bat šar-ra-*⌜*a-t*⌝[*e*$^{?}$ *im-hu-ru-ni*] "As regards these people who [received roy]al letters..."

ymous writer gives suggestions on how the king should proceed with these likewise anonymous people (lines 2-6):

> L[Ú.UN.MEŠ *an-nu-te*] *li-li-ku-u-ni li-iq-*⌜*bi*⌝*-ú* ⌜*ina de-e*⌝*-n*[*i-*(*šú-nu*) LUGAL *be-lí*] *le-ru-ub a-bu-tú š*[*a*] *ina* IGI LUGAL *mah-ra-tu-*[*u-ni*] *ina* ŠU.2-*šú li-ṣi-bat ša* [*in*]*a* IGI LUGAL EN-*iá la mah-r*[*a-tu-u-ni*] LUGAL *be-l*[*í lu*]-⌜*ra*⌝-*am-mi*

> May [these people] come and speak up. May [the king, my lord,] familiarize himself[492] with their cases and seize upon the matter that is accept[able] to the king. What is not acce[ptable] to the king, my lord, the king, my lo[rd may] drop.

The writer, assuming that the persons in question try to conceal their designs, is confident that they will be uncovered (lines r.1-5):

> [*i*]-*lak a-na me-eh-ri-šu i-qa-bi ma-a ina* IGI LUGAL-*ma la-qa-bi ú-la* LUGAL *be-lí bir-te* IGI.2.MEŠ *ša* LÚ.GAL.MEŠ *ina* UGU-*hi lu-ma-di-du bi-is i-šam-me-ú* UN.MEŠ *ma-a*ʾ-[*d*]*u-te i-la-ku-u-ni ṣa-hi-it-tú ša* LUGAL EN-[*ia*] *ina da-ba-bi ma-a*ʾ-*di ta-na-mar*

> He will [g]o to his comrade and say: "I want speak in front of the king(, too)!" Alternatively, O king, my lord, the magnates should be given accurate instructions about it. Then many people will hear it and come, and the desire of the king, my lo[rd], will be realized in the words of many (people).

The general character of this letter does not warrant any specific dating; suffice it to say that a connection with the case of 670 is by no means excluded.

5) A further hint at the events of 671/670 is provided by a letter from Šumu-iddina, *šatammu* of the Esaggil temple of Babylon, to Esarhaddon (TKSM 21/676).[493] This letter dates from the year 670[494] and deals with the actions of Mar-Issar, the agent of Esarhaddon in Babylonia and the author of the above-discussed letter SAA 10 352. The letter of Šumu-iddina is connected with the reconstruction of Esaggil described more or less contemporaneously by Mar-Issar himself in SAA 10 354.

The letter of Šumu-iddina does not mention any conspiracy, attempted or crushed, but it does tell about eunuchs (*ša-rēši*) that have escaped from Assyria and sought shelter in Babylonia. Šumu-iddina has taken one of them into custody while two others have managed to slink out with the help of an anonymous royal delegate (*qīpu*)[495] to Borsippa, outside his jurisdiction.

---

[492] Literally: "enter" (*erābu*).

[493] Published and translated by Landsberger 1965, 8-13 on the basis of the copy of Muazzez Çığ.

[494] For the date of TKSM 21/676 and its relations to SAA 10 354 and 358 see Parpola 1983, 278, 282-284.

[495] As to the position of *qīpu* cf. Landsberger 1965, 30, 36-37.

Šumu-iddina now asks the king to depute someone to bring them from Borsippa before it is too late. He himself promises to take care of the arrested eunuch (lines 33-49):

> *ù i-qab-bu-ni um-ma* 2 LÚ.SAG.MEŠ *ul-tu* KUR *ᵈaš-šur ki-i ih-li-qu-ni* LÚ.*qí-i-pi ina* É-*šú ip-te-sím-šú-nu-ti ù en-na a-na* BÁR.SIPA.KI *il-ta-par-šú-nu-ti a-na-ku ul a-šal-laṭ-ma ul-tu* BÁR.SIPA.KI *ul ú-še-ṣa-a ki-i pa-an* LUGAL EN-*iá mah-ru* LÚ.DUMU–*šip-ri šá* LUGAL *it-ti-šú-nu lil-li-kam-ma a-šar áš-bu li-bu-ku-ni a-di la i-šem-mu-ú-ma a-na a-šar šá-nam-ma il-la-ku* LÚ.SAG *šá* LUGAL EN-*a iš-pu-ra aṣ-ṣa-bat-su a-du-u ina* ŠU ᵐDUMU–ᵈ15 *ú-šu-uz-za-ku ki-i ša dul-la-ni nu-uq-ta-at-tu-ú it-ti-iá ab-ba-kaš-šu*
>
> I have also been told that the royal delegate has hidden in his house two eunuchs after their flight from Assyria, and that he has now sent them to Borsippa. It is not within my power to get them from Borsippa. If it suits the king, my lord, a royal messenger should come with them and bring them here from where they are staying before they hear and go elsewhere. I have arrested the eunuch about whom the king, my lord, wrote to me. At the moment I am at the disposal of Mar-Issar, but as soon as we have finished our work, I shall take him with me.

The letter does not reveal anything about the reasons why the eunuchs have escaped from Assyria but their crime cannot be a minor one since the king himself is chasing them. Since Mar-Issar, too, refers to Assyrians who have fled to Babylonia and who should be returned by right of the treaty concluded with the king (SAA 10 354:19ff),[496] there is little doubt that the eunuchs mentioned by Šumu-iddina belong to these runaways. Considering the date of both letters, it is reasonable to assume that the flight of the eunuchs and other people wanted by the king is connected with the quelling of the attempted coup d'état. Evidently some of the conspirators survived the punitive measures of the king, whose closest men seemed at this time to have been accompanied by bodyguards.[497]

It is necessary to take the letter of Šumu-iddina into consideration in this connection because it gives background to the mentioning of the eunuchs in the letters of Nabû-rehtu-uṣur (ABL 1217 r.13; CT 53 17 r.9, s.3) and makes

---

[496] SAA 10 354:19-26, r.2-3: "The king, my lord, has now, [with the...] of the heavens which is not altered, concluded a treaty [with] you before the sanctuary, [in front of] the gods and has adjured you: 'You shall not change [...] my words; [You shall retu]rn to me the [...]s and captives who [...] and [the Assyr]ians who have fled the country... [Now the]n each of them [has gone] to his country; [the king], my lord, should know (this)." The treaty stipulation quoted by Mar-Issar is not included in the treaties of Esarhaddon known to us, but cf. SAA 2 1:12-14; Borger 1956 (§ 68) 106 iii 32-34 and also KAI 224:19-20.

[497] Thus in the letter of the chief chanter Urad-Ea on the occasion of an Akitu procession of Sin (SAA 10 338 r.3-7): *ša-qurbūti* [*is*]*sīa* [*liš*]*purū* [*issu*] *pān parriṣūti* "A bodyguard [should be] sent with me because of [the tr]aitors." Note that the festival may have taken place in Harran which was the center of Sin worship in the Neo-Assyrian period (cf. above nn. 458 and 460).

the connection of these letters with the conspiracy of 671/670 all the more probable. These two independent sources alone warrant the conclusion that some of the eunuchs of the court were involved in the plot, or at least had come under enough serious suspicion that they were forced to flee the country. But the role played by the chief eunuch becomes crystal clear when we take into consideration yet another document.

6) The role played by the eunuchs in the above-mentioned documents calls our attention finally to SAA 10 179, a letter of Kudurru, a Babylonian scholar who has been deported and placed in confinement by the king (lines 3-4). The content of the letter makes a probable identification of him as the Kudurru from Bit Dakuri who according to the chronicles[498] was deported to Assyria together with Šumu-iddina, the *šandabakku* of Nippur,[499] in an unknown month of Esarhaddon's sixth year (675/4). In ABL 756 Kudurru, son of Šamaš-ibni, beseeches the king not to let him die from hunger "like a dog."[500] This makes it feasible that the writer of SAA 10 179 actually was the son of Šamaš-ibni, the powerful ruler of the Bit-Dakuri tribe who was deported to Assyria and executed three years earlier.[501]

A person with the name Kudurru is also mentioned in a list of hostages in which he is said to do scholarly work under the supervision of Sasî (SAA 11 156:14; cf ABL 1257:7) as well as among the twenty scholars recommended by Marduk-šapik-zeri (SAA 10 160:13).[502] Whether or not these Kudurru's should be identified with the author of SAA 10 179 will be discussed below (pp. 136-137).

According to the letter, Kudurru was fetched from his place of confinement by the cohort commander (*rab kiṣri*?)[503] by the command of Nabû-killanni the *rab šāqê* who needed Kudurru's expertise in scribal lore (lines 3-12). This happened in the month of Marchesvan (VIII) of an unknown year. Kudurru states that he was taken to the temple of Bel Harran (i. e. Sin), the upper room of which turned out to be the scene of a secret meeting in the presence of Nabû-killani. Besides him, only the cohort commander, the major-domo (*rab bēti*) and the chamberlain (*ša-muhhi-bētāni*) took part; also "the overseer of the city (*ša-muhhi-āli*) kept entering and leaving his presence" (lines 12-17). Kudurru spent the rest of the day drinking wine with these people until the sun set. Then, finally, the reason for his sudden release was disclosed. Moving

---

498 Grayson 1975a, 84:14-15; 126:19.

499 With regard to this Šumu-iddina who cannot be identical with the above mentioned *šatammu* of Babylon, see SAA 10 112:28ff and cf. below p. 138.

500 ABL 756 r.3-5.

501 Grayson 1975a, 83:2; 126:10-11. This chronicle entry is related to the inscription according to which Esarhaddon subdued Šamaš-ibni (who is called the "king" of Bit-Dakuri), returned to the citizens of Babylon and Borsippa the fields appropriated by Šamaš-ibni by force – probably during the years Babylon lay abandoned – and replaced him with Nabû-ušallim (Borger 1956 [§ 27] 52:62-70; cf. 33:22:23 and 32:2-14).

502 For these texts cf. below, pp. 135-138.

503 Thus provided that LÚ.GAL–*kaṣir* is a slip for LÚ.GAL–*kiṣir* and does not mean the "chief tailor"; cf. the note in SAA 10.

closer to Kudurru, Nabû-killanni started speaking to Kudurru with a scholarly series of the temple of Nusku in his hand and insisted that Kudurru, as an expert on scribal lore and divination, should perform the following divination before Šamaš: "Will the chief eunuch (LÚ.GAL–SAG) take over the kingship?" (lines 18-r.5) Kudurru could do nothing but set about it and perform the divination, the result of which was: "He will take over the kingship!" (*šarrūtu inašši*) (lines r.6-11) The following day the intriguers made merry until the sun was low and from that day on they kept promising that Kudurru would be taken back to his father's [house] and "the kingship of all [Babylon]ia" will be given to him[504] (lines r.12-18). This, together with the Babylonian language and handwriting of the letter, confirms that Kudurru derived from Babylonian aristocracy and makes his identification with the son of Šamaš-ibni probable indeed.

In brief, Kudurru gives an eyewitness account of a conspiracy of high officials, the aim of which was that the chief eunuch would take over the kingship. The poor scholar fears for his life and tries his hardest to convince the king that he did what he did at "gunpoint" and that the extispicy he performed was "but a colossal fraud" (*alla šāru mehû*, lit. "nothing but wind and storm") (lines r.9ff). "In Marchesvan" indicates that at least a couple of months have passed between the events described and the writing of the letter. Since Kudurru is obviously writing to the king on his own initiative, "lest [the king, my lord] hear about it and kill me" (lines r.22-23), it seems that the conspirators – who certainly would not have hushed up the role of Kudurru in the affair! – have not yet been exposed.

It goes without saying that the information provided by SAA 10 179 is of great importance for us since it matches the letters of Nabû-rehtu-uṣur in many details. First, it throws new light on the part of the eunuchs in the conspiracy – and that of the chief eunuch in particular (CT 53 17 r.9). Secondly, it tells about a conspiracy under the aegis of Harranean gods: the secret meeting took place in the temple of Sin – presumably in Nineveh[505] – and the divination was obviously performed with the series of the temple of Nusku in hand. Thirdly, one of those present in this meeting who also appears in ABL 1217 r.12 was "the city overseer" (*ša-muhhi-āli*), which was possibly, though not certainly, Sasî's title. Fourthly, the meeting took place in the month of Marchesvan (VIII) as did the "vision" of Nabû-rehtu-uṣur. All this constitutes a link between the meeting reported by Kudurru and the events known to Nabû-rehtu-uṣur. Even if there is also an interesting disagreement between the texts (according to the Nusku oracle in ABL 1217 r.3-5 it was Sasî and not the chief eunuch who was to be proclaimed king!), these pieces of information altogether provide us with a fairly uniform picture of events

---

504 [*ina* É]–AD-*ka ú-še-ri-ib-ka* [...] LUGAL-*ú-tu* [*ša* KUR–*ak-ka-di*]-*i gab-bu i-nam-dak-da*. In spite of the fact that the name of the country is almost totally broken away, Babylonia provides itself as the only serious alternative; the words *šarrūtu* and *gabbu* would hardly appear together with regard to a smaller entity such as a single tribe.

505 Nineveh was most probably the place of Kudurru's confinement and nothing in the letter indicates his being moved to another city.

that very probably are connected with those behind the letters of Nabû-rehtu-uṣur and also behind the chronicle entry concerning the events of Esarhaddon's eleventh year. The date of the events reported by Kudurru would thus be Marchesvan (VIII), 671, i.e., the same month in which Nabû-rehtu-uṣur claims to have become aware of the circumstances that compelled him to write his letters.

All in all, it may be stated that the information given by Nabû-rehtu-uṣur in his letters fits well with other sources that most likely deal with the conspiracy quelled in the month of Nisan (I), 670. There are good reasons to assume that the pieces of evidence presented above belong to the same puzzle.

The Trouble with Sasî

Since only the letters of Nabû-rehtu-uṣur and Kudurru include names of individuals involved in the conspiracy, it is very difficult to connect these persons with the information given by other sources, save general designations like "magnates" or "eunuchs." A true riddle is constituted by the name Sasî (Bab. Sasiya)[506] which occurs in numerous Neo-Assyrian or Neo-Babylonian sources of different kinds and from different times, certainly not referring to one single person. The sources can be grouped as follows:

1) The letters of Nabû-rehtu-uṣur ABL 1217+ and CT 53 17+. Even if Sasî is mentioned frequently in these letters, we do not gain much detailed data about him. The writer clearly considers him to be the leader of the plot. This opinion is based on the oracle delivered by the "slave girl" as well as on other second-hand information. Nabû-rehtu-uṣur's sources seem to be well informed but the possibility of intentional misleading cannot be ruled out. It is by no means certain that his idea about what is going on is correct.

The city of Harran plays a central role in the letters, but it is not explicitly stated that Sasî resided there. This could be concluded indirectly from the fact that the "slave girl," who belonged to the household of Bel-ahu-uṣur from Harran and proclaimed her prophecy against Esarhaddon "on the outskirts of Harran," found herself in the house of Sasî at some stage of the events. But the headquarters of Sasî could be sought in Nineveh as well, 1) if the discussions between Sasî and his allies (ABL 1217 r.11ff) were held in Nineveh instead of Harran, which is quite possible, and 2) if the title *ša-muhhi-āli* (LÚ.*ša*–UGU–URU) is applicable to the same person (whether to Sasî or another person) both in ABL 1217 and in SAA 10 179. Nevertheless, it is difficult to deny that the activities of Sasî had a connection with Harran without having been restricted to that city.

2) A group of documents refers to Sasî, a high official in Nineveh responsible for the supervision of scholars (SAA 10 176; SAA 11 156; ABL 1257):

---

[506] As to the name *Sāsî/Sāsīya/Šāšî*, corresponding to West Semitic *Šāšay*, cf. Tallqvist 1914, 193, 219 and Lipiński 1994, 57-58, 227.

SAA 10 176, a letter from three haruspices, Marduk-šumu-uṣur, Naṣiru and Aqaraya,[507] presents Sasî as a supervisor of scholars who obviously may act only by his permission (lines 8-r.5):

> *dullīni ina libbi qirsi ibašši šarru bēlīni ana Sāsî ṭēmu liškun lūšēṣûnāši memmēni lā urammannāši lā nūṣa*
>
> We have rites to perform in the *qirsu*. Let the king, our lord, give an order to Sasî that they should let us go. Nobody will release us, and we cannot go out.

SAA 11 156[508] is a memorandum on scribal work in the palace libraries of Nineveh. It presents a long lists of scholars working there, among them Kudurru and Kunaya who are under the supervision of Sasî, obviously as hostages (lines 14-19):[509]

> *Kudurru Kunāja utukkī lemnūti ugdammerū ṭēnšunu ina pān Sāsî*
>
> Kudurru and Kunaya have completed "Evil Demons." They are at the command of Sasî.

The same partners are concerned also in ABL 1257, a letter from the crown prince Assurbanipal to Esarhaddon (lines 6-12):[510]

> *ina* UGU ᵐ*ku-na-a-a* ᵐ*ku-dúr-ru šá* MAN EN *iq-bu-u-ni ma-a šu-pur liš-ú-lu a-na* ᵐ*sa-si-i ma-a šu-tú* [*ṭè*]*-en-šú-*[*nu*] *ú-da k*[*i-i*] *an-ni-i is-sap-*[*ra ma-a* ...]
>
> As to Kunaya and Kudurru, concerning whom the king, my lord, wrote as follows: "Send word that they question Sasî, he knows about them," he has written [to me as follows...]...

At this point it is worthwhile noting other sources also mentioning a scholar called Kudurru, two of which (SAA 10 179 and ABL 756) have already been discussed above. SAA 10 160 is a letter of Marduk-šapik-zeri, a scholar who has been kept in confinement for two years and is anticipating a death sentence.[511] He is recommending twenty proficient scholars, apprentices of

---

[507] These persons appear frequently, often together, in extispicy queries from the time of Esarhaddon: SAA 4 18 s.1; 49 r.9; 94 s.2; 129 s.1-2; 139 s.1-2; 142 r.15; 155 s.3; 157 s.1; 162:7; 185 s.2; 226 e.5; 236:3; cf. also SAA 10 173-177.

[508] See Parpola 1983, 458-459.

[509] Note that Ninurta-gimilli the son of the *šandabakku* (cf. below n. 520) who is mentioned right before Kudurru and Kunaya (lines 8-13) is said to have been put in fetters, and Sulaya (line r.2) probably is identical with the one who is "kept in the *Mašartu* Palace of Nineveh by order of the king," (BM 135586:37ff; see Parpola 1972) that is, in a kind of pretrial custody.

[510] Collation in Parpola 1983, 99, 459.

[511] For this letter, consisting of the fragments K 3034 (= CT 54 57) + K 7655 + K 5440 (= ABL 1321) + 82-5-22,123 (= CT 54 106) see Hunger 1987 who wrote his article before the pieces were joined together and, thus, examines CT 54 57 and 106 as separate letters.

his own, for the royal service. Among these we find "Kudurru, a refugee in[512] Ass[yria] (ᵐNÍG.GUB *hal-qu šá* KUR–*aš*-[*šur*.KI]); he is a competent [haruspex] and has studied exorcism and scribal lore; he is use[ful to the king], my lord" (lines r.13f). Furthermore, Kudurru appears among the subscribers of an extispicy query together with the above-mentioned Marduk-šumu-uṣur and Naṣiru who also were under the supervision of Sasî (SAA 4 18 s.3).[513]

Whether or not the Kudurru of SAA 11 156 and ABL 1257 is identical with the one recommended to the king by Marduk-šapik-zeri in SAA 10 160 r.13-14. or with the writer of SAA 10 179 cannot be concluded with certainty, of course. Kudurru was a common name at this time,[514] and even Marduk-šapik-zeri mentions two persons with this name in his letter.[515] Nevertheless, there are enough common features speaking in favor of the possibility that all these four texts would refer to one and same person. All the letters most probably date from the last years of Esarhaddon[516] and all of them present Kudurru as a proficient scholar belonging to the well-educated hostages in Assyria. This is well in line with his Babylonian origin, since it seems to have been customary at that time to hold young Babylonians from wealthy families as hostages in Assyria where they were indoctrinated into loyalty to Assyria in order to give them high positions in Babylonia later.[517]

If all the Kudurru's are one and the same person and if Sasî really is the "city overseer" (*ša-muhhi-āli*) not only in ABL 1217 r.12 but also in SAA 10 179:17, then we arrive at the exciting assumption that Sasî, the supervisor of the confined scholars, who was involved in the conspiracy reported by

---

[512] The SAA edition has "a refugee from Assyria" but this translation has been corrected in Mattila (ed.) 1995, 139 since Kudurru was a Babylonian hostage in Assyria, not an Assyrian refugee.

[513] This query asks whether Ursâ, king of Urartu, will invade Šubria, a country southwest of Lake Van conquered by Esarhaddon in Tebet (X) 673 (cf. Grayson 1975a, 84:19-20; 127:24-25); the query must postdate this event.

[514] Cf. the list of Dietrich 1970, 30 n.1.

[515] In the group of twenty scholars there is also another one called Kudurru who is "proficient in extispicy and has read Enuma Anu Enlil" (lines r.31-32). Since Marduk-šapik-zeri enumerates exactly "twenty able scholars" (20 UM.ME.A.MEŠ *le-ʾu-ú-tu* line r.35) including both Kudurru's, this other Kudurru must be a different person – unless the scholar has been forgetful enough to list the same person twice!

[516] ABL 1257, with which SAA 11 156 must be more or less contemporaneous, can date only from the years between 672 and 669; for the dating of SAA 10 179 cf. above. The date of SAA 10 160 is more difficult to define. Hunger 1987, 162 gives the possible dates when Jupiter stands in Pisces (cf. MUL.SAG.ME.GAR *ina* KUN.MEŠ line 14) which are the 15th of June, 672; the 20th of June, 660 and the 25th of June, 648. Of these three dates he cautiously argues for the year 660 as the date of the letter, because personal names similar to those in this letter are to be found in texts from Ur from the time of Šamaš-šumu-ukin (cf. Moren 1980, 190-191). It is rather improbable, however, that this particular celestial phenomenon would warrant the exact dating of the letter. Marduk-šapik-zeri lists in this letter a whole chain of observations made by him, as it seems, during the two years of his confinement (cf. lines 6-10). In fact, the 15th of June, 672, fits well in this period of time if the letter was written in 670.

[517] Cf. Parpola 1972, 33-34; Frame 1992, 240-241.

Nabû-rehtu-uṣur, also had a finger in the pie when Kudurru was released in order to perform a divination concerning the kingship of the chief eunuch in the month of Marchesvan (VIII), 671. This alone makes the figure of Sasî appear in a very bad light indeed, and there are some additional documents that throw suspicion on Sasî – without, however, revealing much about his actual activities.

3) A group of letters referring to the Babylonian affairs of Sasiya (SAA 10 112; CT 54 462; CT 54 37 and CT 54 493).

SAA 10 112 has been already referred to in connection with other correspondence of the well-known Babylonian scholar Bel-ušezib. In this letter, in addition to Esarhaddon's Mannean campaign, he talks in a critical tone about Šumu-iddina, the *šandabakku*[518] of Nippur, who has arbitrarily removed the dais of Nippur[519] and who is giving "four minas of gold and all kinds of Babylonian luxuries," smuggled to him by his son, to Sasiya, *x*-ahu and Ṣillaya (lines 28-r.6). The son of Šumu-iddina seems to have been placed under arrest.[520] Bel-ušezib is convinced that a conspiracy is being plotted against Esarhaddon and that Šumu-iddina is involved in it (lines r.6-9). He also suspects the Egyptian Šarru-lu-dari, a friend of Sasiya and Bel-eṭir, the governor of HAR,[521] of being an ally of Šumu-iddina and warns the king about all these people (lines r.11-13). The historical and astronomical details of the letter point to the year 675,[522] and the mentioning of Ṣillaya connects it with the anti-Assyrian actions performed by this person in the early and mid-670's.[523] Sasiya is associated with Ṣillaya in this text only.

---

[518] It seems probable that, at least in this case, both the syllabic LÚ.*šá-an-da-bak-ka* (line r.1) and the logographic LÚ.GÚ.EN.NA (line r.3.10.26) refer to Šumu-iddina and may represent one and the same title of the governor of Nippur, *šandabakku*. On the pronunciation of LÚ.GÚ.EN.NA as *šandabakku*, cf. Landsberger 1965, 75-77; Cole 1986, 129-131; Frame 1992, 225 n. 77. On the history of the office of *šandabakku* of Nippur, see Cole 1996, 45-55.

[519] That he and not his brother (Dietrich 1970, 47, 158; cf. CT 54 plate 10) is in question is suggested by the collations of Brinkman (1977, 318, 324) as well as of I. L. Finkel and M. J. Geller (SAA 10) (line r.1: ⸢LÚ.*šá*⸣*-an-da-bak-ka* instead of ⸢ŠEŠ.*šá*⸣*-an-da-bak-ka*).

[520] Line r.2f: [...] ⸢DUMU LÚ.GÚ.EN⸣.NA *šá a-kan-nu ka-lu-ú ina* GÌR.2 *šá* [...]... "[NN], the governor's son who is being held (as hostage) here at the feet of [...]..." Possibly identical with Ninurta-gimilli, son of the *šandabakku* who had taken part in the work in the palace libraries of Nineveh as a hostage but had subsequently been put in fetters and held in the Palace of Succession (SAA 11 156:8-13; cf. Parpola 1983, 458-459). This identification is, however, far from certain since SAA 11 156, probably dating from the year 670, is written much later. Furthermore, the governors of Nippur changed at a brisk pace, at least around the year 675 when there were three governors within one year (SAA 10 112 r. 10: *ina* MU.AN.NA 3 LÚ.GÚ.EN.NA.ME).

[521] The reading ⸢mdEN–SUR-*ir*⸣ LÚ.EN.NAM *šá* URU.HAR.KI, doubted by Brinkman 1977, 313, is now confirmed by the collation of Finkel and Geller in SAA 10. Whether or not URU.HAR.KI means Harran (Dietrich 1970, 32 n. 1, 48, 52 etc.), remains uncertain.

[522] I.e., the capture of Sidon in 677/676 (lines 13-15; cf. Grayson 1975a, 83:3; 126:12, 14) and the partial eclipse of the moon (lines 3-6); see Dietrich 1968, 234-235; 1970, 47.

[523] The information about Ṣillaya and his actions is put together and interpreted by Dietrich 1970, 39-50; see also Frame 1992, 84-88. The activities of Ṣillaya probably came

CT 54 462[524] is a letter of Marduk-naṣir who informs the king about the activities of Sasiya son of *x* (DUMU.*ni*-[*x x*]), Ereši, Remanni-Adad the chariot driver (^{m}*rém-a-ni*–^{d}IM LÚ.*mu-kil*–KUŠ.PA.MEŠ line 7), Nabû-uhašu and Bel-eṭir, the governor (? $^{md+}$EN–KAR-*ir* EN ⸢*x*⸣[525] [...] line 14). What exactly these people are doing remains obscure. They are said to have taken a rapid chariot (GIŠ.GIGIR *šá hum-mu*-[*ṭa*]) to somewhere, and even though the king, apparently, has asked them to return it, Sasiya and Bel-eṭir have held it back until this has come to the notice of the officials of the king (lines 9-19). If this interpretation of the badly broken text is correct, Sasiya seems to be involved in affairs that, without being exactly criminal, are somewhat suspicious and deserve the attention of the king. The dating of the letter as such is not possible, nor are we able to trace its geographical setting.[526]

CT 54 37[527] deals with the ousting of Ašaredu from the governorship of Cutha because of a denunciation against him by some persons mentioned in the letter. According to the writer, who may be the Cuthaean astrologer Nabû-iqbi ([^{md}PA–*i*]*q-bi*),[528] the king has removed Ašaredu from his office (*i-tab-kaš-šu* line 9), but no one has testified for him. The writer names three persons that might be able to pick out witnesses for Ašaredu: the "horse-driver" (LÚ.KA.DIB.ANŠE = *kartap sīsê* line 13), the governor of HAR (LÚ.⸢EN⸣.NAM *šá* URU.⸢HAR⸣ line 14) and Sasiya the mayor (LÚ.*ha-za-an-nu* lines 15-16). According to the writer, these three persons are loyal to the king (*šu-nu it-t*[*i*] LUGAL *be-lí-ia ki-i-nu* lines 16-17), and they should be asked before being bribed (*a-di la ṭa-a'-ti u šu*[*l-ma-nu a*]*-na muh-hi-šu-nu* [*i-nam-di-nu*] lines 18-19), and before the potential witnesses are killed (ERIM.MEŠ *i-mut*-[*tu*] line 20). There are no particulars in the letter that would support any specific dating, but if the writer is Nabû-iqbi, it may be noted that the earliest documents of his extant correspondence date from the last years of Esarhaddon.[529]

---

to an end in 674/3, provided that he was the head of Bit-Amukani, since the chronicles record that the Assyrian army invaded Šamele, a fortified town in that area, on the 8th of Adar of the seventh year of Esarhaddon (Grayson 1975a, 126:20; cf. Dietrich 1970, 56; Parpola 1983, 36-37).

[524] For transcription and translation of the readable lines, see Dietrich 1970, 162f no. 62; for interpretation, cf. ibid. pp. 51-52.

[525] According to Dietrich's copy in CT 54, the remnants of this sign could be interpreted as NAM, whereas the collation of C. B. F. Walker *apud* Brinkman 1977, 313 n. 54 gives it as URU.

[526] The assumption of Dietrich that the activities described in this letter would have taken place in Babylon or in its suburbs is based solely on the greeting of the letter that mentions Nabû and Marduk.

[527] For transcription and translation, see Dietrich 1970, 162-163 no. 63; for interpretation, see ibid. pp. 52-54 and cf. Brinkman 1977, 314.

[528] Cf. also the complaints of Nabû-iqbi about Ašaredu in SAA 10 163:8-12 and 164:7-11 (cf. Dietrich 1970, 162-165 nos. 64 and 65).

[529] See Parpola 1983, Appendix J. Dietrich 1970, 54 suggests that the letter could have been written before SAA 10 112, i.e., in early 675 at the latest, as it gives no hint of the conspiracy alleged in the latter.

Finally, CT 54 493, a letter from a Babylonian writer who introduces himself by the pseudonym Naram-Sin to an unknown king who may be Esarhaddon,[530] reports on Sasiya the governor of *x* (m*sa-si-ia* LÚ.EN.NAM [*x*] lines 6f) and Aššur-bahiani the governor of (the capital of) Bit-Zammanu ([LÚ.EN].NAM *ša* URU.É.*za-am-ma-nu* line 9). Badly broken as the letter is, we learn nothing about the activities of these people, and its relationship with the other letters of this group remains unclear.[531]

The letters of this group (CT 54 493 excluded) have certain connections with each other. They all deal with the Babylonian affairs of Sasiya. Bel-eṭir, the governor of HAR, cooperates with Sasiya in SAA 10 112, CT 54 462 and certainly also in CT 54 37. On the other hand, cavalry officers are mentioned repeatedly: Remanni-Adad the chariot driver (*mukīl appāti*) in CT 54 462, who may be identical with the Remanni-Adad who later on held a high appointment as Assurbanipal's charioteer,[532] and the *kartap sīsê* of CT 54 37.[533]

Only one of the letters can be firmly dated, i.e. SAA 10 112 to the year 675. This letter is also the only one of them that refers to a conspiracy (not to the one crushed in 670 but to the earlier intrigues around Ṣillaya in the mid-670's), whereas the others do not presuppose rebellious activities. Some of Sasiya's Babylonian affairs seem to have been, though not overtly conspiratorial, somewhat doubtful in the eyes of certain of his contemporaries. The rest of the letters may date from approximately the same time as SAA 10 112 but it is not excluded that they derive from later years. The central role played by the cavalry officers constitutes a link between the various officers mentioned in CT 53 249, ABL 1364 and CT 53 46 (cf. above), as well as with the *mukīl appāti* in ABL 445 (cf. below), a letter belonging to the next group of sources in which Sasî is also connected with shady transactions.

4) There are four letters throwing suspicion on Sasî: CT 53 44; ABL 445, 1245(?), 1308 – and one without a shade of suspicion: SAA 10 377.

CT 53 44 is a letter from an unknown writer (the name has not been preserved) who has fallen into disgrace and is apparently trying to clear his reputation (lines 3-r.6):[534]

---

[530] For this letter, see Dietrich 1968, 223-224 who proposes a dating in the early years of Esarhaddon. The pseudonym Naram-Sin could be an expression of Babylonian national spirit against the centralizing tendencies of Esarhaddon who ousted two tribal leaders, Nabû-zer-kitti-lišir of Bit-Yakin and Ṣillaya of Bit-Amukani, from their posts. Dietrich does not exclude the possibility that the letter was written by Ṣillaya himself.

[531] In the judgment of Dietrich 1968, 224 n. 82, the person called Sasiya in this letter is "certainly not" identical with the Sasiya active in the other letters of this group.

[532] No less than 55 transactions of his are published in SAA 6; cf. Kwasman & Parpola 1991, XXI.

[533] According to Dietrich 1970, 51ff, Remanni-Adad is meant here. This, of course, cannot be proven with absolute certainty since CT 54 37 does not mention the name of the person concerned. Still, the texts give a more uniform picture of the companions of Sasî than Brinkman 1977, 318-319 is willing to admit.

[534] Transliteration by S. Parpola; cf. the slightly different transliteration of Fales 1980, 142-143 n. 7.

> LÚ.EN.NAM *ša* KUR.*qu-*⸢*e*⸣ *i-zi-ir-ra-an-ni ma-a* LUGAL *a-na* ^{m}*sa-si-i liš-al ki-i ša* LUGAL *a-na* URU.KASKAL [*i*]*š-pur-an-na-ši-ni* [*ma*]*-a* LUGAL *ina* UGU-*hi-ia* [*ir-t*]*u-ú-bu* [*ma-a*] ⸢*a–dan*⸣*-niš* ⸢*ap*⸣*-ta-lah* (one unreadable line) ⸢*ú*⸣*-bi-lu-ú-*⸢*ni i*⸣*-qab-bi* [*m*]*a*$^{?}$-⸢*a*$^{?}$⸣ LÚ.ARAD *ša* LUGAL *a-na-ku* [*ma-a* A]D-*šú ina* ŠÀ-*bi a-de-e* [*us-s*]*e-ri-ba-an-*⸢*ni*⸣ [*ma-a mi*]*-i-nu ša ina* KUR.*gi-*[*x x x x x áš*]*-mu-ú-ni* ...
>
> The governor of Que[535] hates me; let the king ask Sasî like the king wrote to us in Harran. The king was furious with me and I got extremely frightened[...] they brought [...] and he spoke: "I am a servant of the king, his [fat]her [made] me enter the treaty. [W]hatever I [... he]ard in the land of Gi[...]..."

The following information may be extracted from these few preserved lines: The writer is or has been in Harran where he, together with some other people, has received an infuriated letter from the king. It seems the fact that the governor of Que hates the writer for some reason has also reached the ears of the king. Something scandalous has happened in Harran for which the writer has been blamed. Now he is frightened out of his wits and is trying to shift the responsibility onto Sasî who thus once more becomes associated with suspicious actions connected with Harran. The following protestations of loyalty remain anonymous indicating that intrigues against the king have been scented and people have been questioned about the matter.

The anonymous letter ABL 445 is addressed to the crown prince: ^{d}PA ^{d}AMAR.UTU *a-na* DUMU.MAN EN-*ia lik-ru-bu* "May Nabû and Marduk bless the crown prince, my lord!" (lines 1-2) This not only indicates that it postdates the year 672 but possibly also that the crown prince is regarded as a co-regent. Thus, the letter may be written in late 671/early 670 when Esarhaddon was sick and, perhaps, temporarily incapable of ruling (cf. SAA 10 316 r.9ff and see above, p. 129). The writer reports very briefly that he received a message from Nabû-naṣir the staff-bearer that Sin-balassu-iqbi, son of Nikkal-iddina (and governor of Ur) has sent with the "chariot driver" (*mukīl appāti*) one mina of gold to Sasî the mayor of *x* (1 MA.NA KUG.GI ^{md}30–TI-*su–iq-bi* DUMU ^{md}NIN.GAL–SUM-*na ina* ŠU.2 LÚ.*mu-kil*–KUŠ.PA.MEŠ *a-na* ^{m}*sa-s*[*i*]*-i* LÚ*.*ha-za-nu* [*ša*] ⸢URU.*x*⸣[536] *ú-še-bi-la* lines 4-r.2).

This text is followed by the common question: "What is it that the king, my lord, orders?" (*ma-a mi-i-nu šá* LUGAL *be-lí i-qab-bu-ú-ni* lines r.3-4). In letters addressed to the king this is a normal ending expressing that the writer is waiting for instructions of the king concerning the matter described in the letter.[537] In the present case, however, it looks like the question has been put

---

535 Cf. SAA 5 68:5; SAA 11 1 r.i 16; 15 ii 12; 34:3, 5; 59:1; 80 r.9; 136 i 6.

536 The reading of Harper LÚ.*ha-za-nu* [*ša*] DUMU.MAN, followed by Waterman 1930, 310 and Dietrich 1970, 51, 160-161, is corrected by Parpola in his collation *apud* Frame 1992, 99 n. 174, according to which the sign after URU could be either NINA or KASKAL; this would mean that only the beginning of two horizontal wedges are visible.

537 Cf. SAA 10 3 r.13; 21 r.12-13; 24 r.17-18; 38 r.2-3; 10 r.6; 181 r.6-7; 193 r.4-5; 272 r.3-4; 335 r.1-2; 375 r.3-4.

in the mouth of Sin-balassu-iqbi who, then, is calling Sasî his "king." If this is true, it would mean that in certain circles Sasî was already acknowledged as the king according to the oracle of Nusku in ABL 1217 r.3-5, or at least that Nabû-naṣir wants to give an impression to that effect.[538] However, in the light of the fact that Sin-balassu-iqbi, well known for his Assyrian sympathies,[539] held his position as the governor of Ur from the mid-670's until at least 658[540] – a career hardly possible for anyone guilty of a lèse-majesté – this turns out to be improbable. Unless Nabû-naṣir is intentionally misleading the crown prince, it seems reasonable enough to assume that the question has here its normal meaning and the "king my lord" refers to the king of Assyria – or, in this particular case, to the crown prince as the co-regent. The particle *mā*, rather than introducing a direct speech, replaces the more common *ūmâ* in this phrase. At any rate, the writer, who prefers to remain anonymous, holds the delivering of a substantial amount of gold to Sasî to be something that the king ought to know.

ABL 1245 mentions the crown prince (line 4) and thus dates from the years 672-669. Since the name Sasî appears in an entirely broken context (^{m}*sa-si-i* line r.2) it is very difficult to deduce what is said about him. It is noteworthy, in any case, that this writer[541] also is ready to denounce evildoers (lines r.11-14):

> *ša* LUGAL *be-lí a-na* ARAD-*šú iš-pur-an-ni ma-a man-nu la-ma-a-nu ma-a ú-kal-lam-ka le-ma-gúr a-na* MAN EN-*iá la áš-par*
>
> As to what the king, my lord, wrote to me: "Who displays much evil to you (and) is not agreeable?" – shall I not write to the king, my lord?

Whether or not Sasî has anything to do with the things the writer is willing to reveal, remains uncertain.

In ABL 1308 an anonymous writer reminds the king of a matter concerning a person called Nabû-kabti-ahhešu. He has obviously written about it earlier but failed to arouse the king's interest. Now he is urging that the king take the matter seriously (lines 1-9):

---

538 Thus Dietrich 1970, 51 with n. 1.

539 For example, according to Mar-Issar (SAA 10 354 r.14-18) he was willing to block the canal of Merodach-Baladan and thus leave many Babylonians without water.

540 As to Sin-balassu-iqbi, son of Nikkal-iddina, see Brinkman 1965, 248-253; Dietrich 1970, 38-39; Frame 1992, 99, 278.

541 If Paruṭu, the goldsmith of the palace of the queen, is not the writer of the letter but, as it seems, the letter is about him, then the letter is anonymous: ^{m}*pa-ru-ṭu* LÚ*.SIMUG.KUG.GI *ša* É MÍ.É.GAL *ki-i* LUGAL DUMU–LUGAL DUMU–KÁ.DINGIR.KI *ina* ŠÀ-*bi* KUG.UD *i-si-qi ina* É *ra-mi-ni-šú ú-se-ši-ib-šu* IM.GÍD.DA *ina* ŠÀ-*bi* LÚ*.*a-ši-pu-te a-na* DUMU-*šú iq-ṭi-bi* "(As to) Paruṭu, the goldsmith of the palace of the queen: like the king and the crown prince he has bought a Babylonian, settled him in his own house, and taught exorcistic literature to his son" (lines 2-8). Cf. the translation of Parpola 1997b, 321 n. 18 with the comment: "the man was not accused for teaching his son to read but for acquiring knowledge in magic, extispicy and astrology – subjects potentially highly dangerous to the monarchy (...) – without the king's permission."

> [*ina* UGU *a-bi-ti ša*] ^md^PA–IDIM–PAB.MEŠ-*šú* [*ša ina pa-ni-ti*] *a-na* LUGAL EN-*iá* [*áš-pur*]-*ú-ni a-ta-a* LUGAL *be-lí a-da-ka-an-ni* [*l*]*a iš-al la ú-ṣi-ṣi a-bu-tu-u qàl-li-su ši-i* LUGAL *be-lí a-na a-bi-it an-ni-te* LUGAL *be-lí lu la i-ši-a-ṭa bi-is* LUGAL *be-lí dul-la-ni-šú le-pu-uš an-nu-rig* ITI.ZÍZ ITI.ŠE *e-tar-bu-u-ni* ITI.MEŠ DÙG.GA.MEŠ *šú-nu a-na dul-la-a-ni e-pa-ši ṭa-a-ba*
>
> [Concerning the case of] Nabû-kabti-ahhešu [about which I wr]ote to the king, my lord, [before]: Why has the king, my lord, neither asked nor inquired about it until now? Is it an insignificant matter? O king, my lord! Let the king, my lord, not disregard this matter but let the king, my lord, perform his rites now as the months of Shebat (XI) and Adar (XII) are at hand. They are (both) favorable months. It is appropriate to perform the rites.

The rites that the letter is concerned with appear to be necessary for "averting of evil things [...], sins and misdeeds" (*a-na šu-te-tu-qe-e ša lum-*[*n*]*a-a-ni* [*x x*]*x-a-te šá hi-ṭa-a-te ša la ṭa-ba-te ep-šat* lines 10-11).

On the reverse the writer keeps urging the king to clear up the matter (lines r.3-7):

> [LUGAL *b*]*e-lí li-šá-al da-ba-bu šá-ni-iu-um-*[*ma i–da*]*-te a-na* LUGAL EN-*iá a-qa-bi an-nu-rig* ^m^*ha-am-na-a-nu* LÚ.SANGA *ša* ^m^*sa-si-i ina qa-an-ni-ma ú-ra-mu-šá-nu-u-ni i-si-ni ina* IGI LÚ.GAL.MEŠ *la i-zi-su-u-ni*
>
> Let the [king], my lord, inquire into the case, I shall [th]en tell the king, my lord another thing. Now Hamnanu and the priest[542] whom Sasî released instead (?) did not stand with us before the magnates.

Sasî is thus made responsible for "releasing" persons[543] whose behavior arouses suspicions about covert activities. The writer recommends that the king should indeed inquire into the matter and find out what is going on. He himself is ready to take prompt measures (lines r.7ff):

> *an-nu-te-am-ma* LUGAL *be-lí li-šá-al ma-a a-ke-e ra-mu-u-a-ku-nu* 2 3 *ṭè-ma-ni ina* ŠU.2-*iá liš-li-mu bi-is* [*ina* I]GI-*ia i-har-ri-di* TA *re-hu-u-te a-da-bu-bu*
>
> Let the king, my lord, ask about these (people): How were you released? May two or three commands be fulfilled by my hand, so that he (Sasî?) will stay[544] before my face and I can speak with the rest of them.

Once more Sasî is, at least indirectly, blamed for misusing his office. In the light of the evidence presented above, it seems quite probable that ABL

---

542 Or: "the scribe" (LÚ.UMBISAG) which would sound more appropriate; the fact is, however, that in the Neo-Assyrian period *ṭupšarru* is always written LÚ.A.BA or, less frequently, LÚ.DUB.SAR.

543 Cf. SAA 10 176:11-r.5: "Let the king, our lord, give an order to Sasî that they should let us go. Nobody will release us (*urammanāši*) and we cannot go out."

544 Literally: "watch" (*iharridi*).

1308 belongs to the same historical context as the letters of Nabû-rehtu-uṣur and other related documents. Obviously the king has become aware of the intrigues against him on the information of several informers without, however, adopting rigorous measures against them. According to the letter, the months of Shebat and Adar are at hand (*ētarbū*), thus it must have been written at the beginning of Shebat (XI) at the earliest, presumably in the year 671/670. The letters of Nabû-rehtu-uṣur and Kudurru talk about events which happened "in Marchesvan" (VIII) (671) which implies that the letters cannot have been written in this month – and not in the following month either as this would probably have been referred to as "the last month." Thus, we arrive at the month of Tebet (X) 671/670 as the earliest possible date of the letters of Nabû-rehtu-uṣur and Kudurru which would mean that these letters could have already reached the king before he received ABL 1308. But why has the king not gone properly into the matter? Why did Nabû-rehtu-uṣur and the writer of ABL 1308 have to write to the king repeatedly without their letters leading to the hoped-for actions?

Considering all the denigration of Sasî, it is very surprising indeed to find a letter (SAA 10 377) written in late Tebet (X), 671/670, that is, just a couple of months before the execution of the magnates recorded in the chronicles, with the following message concerning the substitute king familiar to us from previously discussed documents (lines 8-r.4):[545]

> UD-14-KÁM *ana Nīnu*[*a*] *Adad-šumu-uṣur ēt*[*arab*] *issi Aššūr-nāṣir rab* [*x*] *Sāsî Urad-E*[*a iddubub*] *mā adu lā attal*[*û iškunūni*] *lūšib*
>
> On the 14th Adad-šumu-uṣur enter[ed] Nineveh and [spoke] with Aššur-naṣir, the chief [*eunuch*],[546] Sasî and Urad-E[a]: "Let him sit (on the throne) before the eclip[se occurs]."

How can it be possible that Sasî, in spite of all the warnings, still appears in the king's entourage together with scholars of the highest rank belonging to the king's intimate circle such as the exorcist Adad-šumu-uṣur and the lamentation priest Urad-Ea? In my judgment, there are three possible ways to solve this riddle:

a) The Sasî in SAA 10 377 is a different person from the one mentioned in the other letters. This, however, seems like an emergency solution that shows the way out by the back door without really solving the problem. As matters stand, this alternative cannot be categorically rejected on the basis of the existing evidence, but it does not free us from examining carefully the other possible explanations.

---

545 For the date, see Parpola 1983, 222. The letter thus deals with the same substitute king ritual as the above-discussed letter of Mar-Issar SAA 10 352; cf. above pp. 68-77.

546 The title of Aššur-naṣir is given as "the chief [*eunuch*] in SAA (cf. Parpola 1983, 221) on the basis of ABL 965:14 in which a person with the same name appears as the chief eunuch; the letter is dated to 680 by Dietrich 1970, 28-29. For this problem, see below pp. 147-148.

b) The plot of which Sasî is accused has not yet been disclosed. This is not impossible because the letters of Nabû-rehtu-uṣur and Kudurru, written in Tebet (X), 671/670 as well, may slightly postdate SAA 10 377.

c) Sasî is indeed the same person as the one mentioned in the letters, but he is, in reality, not guilty of traitorous activities and the king is aware of this.

We shall return to this question after examining yet another group of texts.

5) A person called Sasî is mentioned in a collection of legal and administrative records and transactions. While most of these documents have no bearing in this connection (SAA 6 90; 160; SAA 11 27; 163; 207; As 13846aa; ND 2336; VAT 9862, CTN 3 5; 51; 54; 99; ADD 582; TIM 11 19; 2 R 64; SAAB 4, 74 r.6),[547] the remaining few are all the more important (SAA 6 251; 296; 314; 338; ADD 204; 398; 540).

SAA 6 251, a purchase document from the time of Esarhaddon, lists Sasî and Ubru-*x* among the witnesses. SAA 6 296, a contract concluded on the 1st of Nisan (I), 671, also has Sasî as a witness. This document is the earliest one in the series of contracts made by Remanni-Adad, the charioteer of Assurbanipal. It names a person called Ubru-Nabû as one of the holders of Remanni-Adad's animals. He may be identical with the above mentioned Ubru-*x* as well as with the Ubru-Nabû mentioned by Nabû-rehtu-uṣur in CT 53 118:8.

The name Sasî also appears in a few other documents from Assurbanipal's first years. SAA 6 314 and 338 are likewise purchase documents of Remanni-Adad but they derive from the time of Assurbanipal. Both mention Sasî the mayor (*hazannu*) as a witness, as does also the undatable ADD 540 r.3. The contract SAA 6 314, dated to 11th of Shebat (XI), 666, even names the city of which Sasî was the mayor but, unfortunately, the name of the city is broken away. This document of Remanni-Adad deals with an estate in the town Ispallurê in the region of Izalla, that is, in the northern part of the valley of

---

[547] The following attestations of the name Sasî are either too early (**A**) or too late (**B**) to be of relevance here, if not undatable (**C**):

A:
- CTN 3 99 r.ii 2: Sasî among the *mušarkisu* officers in a list of the officers of Sargon II from ca. 710-708 (date according to Dalley & Postgate 1984, 176);
- SAA 11 207 r.ii 2: Sasî, the farmer (?) in a text belonging to the so called Harran Census dating from the late reign of Sargon II (cf. Fales & Postgate 1995, XXXIII);
- SAA 6 160:11: Sasî as a witness of a purchase document from the year 687;
- SAA 6 90:6: Sasî as a witness of a purchase document from the year 683.

B:
- ND 2336:10: Sasî as a witness of a legal transaction from the year 658;
- TIM 11 19 r.5: Sasî as a witness of a court order from the year 656;
- CTN 3 54 r.12: Sasî as a witness of a purchase document from the year 647;
- As 13846aa s.3: Sasî as a witness of a legal transaction from the year 646;
- CTN 3 51 r.10: Sasî as a witness of a purchase document from the year 644 or 629 (both eponym years of Nabû-šarru-uṣur);
- SAAB 4, 74 r.6: Sasî as a witness of a judicial decision from Guzana from the year 630 (post-canonical eponym of Adad-remanni); see Fales 1990;
- CTN 3 5 r.7: Sasî as a consignee of goat-hair textiles in a document probably from the year 623 (eponym of Aššur-matu-taqqin; cf. CTN 3 6 which dates to 623-ii-16).

C:
- SAA 11 27:1-3 a note of royal accoutrements mentioning Sasî as the holder of "22 bows for the king's own use" and the "sinews for the bowstrings";
- SAA 11 163 ii 8: Sasî among 140 fugitives in the province of Šimu;
- ADD 582 r.1: Sasî as a witness of a legal document;
- VAT 9862 r. 2: Sasî as a witness of a legal document;
- 2 R 64 r.iv 8: Sasî mentioned in a very long name list with an unknown purpose.

the Habur River.[548] Finally, a man with this name has sealed a transaction concerning his slave in the year 668 (ADD 204:1) and witnesses a purchase document probably from the year 664 (ADD 398 r.1).[549]

Especially noteworthy in SAA 6 314 is the list of witnesses that includes not only Sasî but also persons called Adad-šumu-uṣur the chief [exorcist], Issar-nadin-apli [the scribe][550] and [Nabû-r]ehtu-uṣur! Considering the indisputable date of the document this list of witnesses is more than confusing. On the basis of all the evidence presented above one would assume that Sasî and Issar-nadin-apli would have been among the first to be executed in the month of Nisan (I), 670, but, as it seems, their names are four years later listed together with people that once charged them with high treason, as if nothing happened – and all this concerning affairs not so far away from Harran!

The alternative explanations of the role of Sasî in the 671/670 conspiracy can now be reconsidered with the above documentation at hand. Again, it can be claimed as an emergency solution that the witnesses listed in these various documents are different persons from the aforementioned ones, but this is a flimsy conclusion which requires another possible explanation to be examined, namely that we are dealing with the same Sasî who, innocent or not, survived the execution of Nisan (I), 670. If this is true, there still remain two ways to explain the role of Sasî: either he was indeed involved in the conspiracy but somehow managed to convince the king of his loyalty – or his involvement in the plans of the insurrectionists was nothing but a cover-up! In reality, Sasî was there as a fink, keeping the king informed about their actions. According to this scenario, he would have been a talented lobbyist who had good contacts with the military high command, and this quality made him a useful tool in the king's hands as an infiltrator. If his reputation already was somewhat dubious (cf., e.g., SAA 10 112; CT 54 462; ABL 445), then he could play the role of an accomplice with all the more credibility.

This explanation, startling as it may be, suggests itself not only because Sasî finally seems to have saved his life in spite of all the severe charges against him, but also with regard 1) to the fact that the repeated warnings of Nabû-rehtu-uṣur and the writer of ABL 1308 met with little response from the king, and 2) to the fact that it was the chief eunuch and not Sasî for whom Kudurru was forced to predict the kingship (SAA 10 179 r.4-11). It should also be noted that Remanni-Adad who was associated with Sasî, subsequently held a prominent position as the charioteer of Assurbanipal.

If the role of Sasî in the conspiracy, then, was nothing but that of an infiltrator, who were the actual insurrectionists who were killed in the executions of 670? The episode witnessed by Kudurru names Nabû-killanni, the

---

548 As to Ispallurê and Izalla, cf. SAA 12 50 and see Parpola 1970b, 40, 177; Postgate 1976/80a/b.

549 This date is based on the restoration of the Neo-Assyrian Text Corpus project (lines r.12-13): [ITI.*x* UD-*x*]-KÁM *lim-m*[*u* ^{m}MAN–*lu–dà*]-*ri* LÚ*.GAR.KUR URU.BÀ[D–^{m}MAN–GIN] "[Month *x*, *x*th] day, eponym [year of Šarru-lu-da]ri, governor of Du[r-Šarruken].

550 For the title, cf. SAA 6 311 r.7; 315 r.7; 316 r.14.

chief cupbearer (*rab šāqê*) as its principal architect (SAA 10 179:6, 11, 16), and if the letters CT 53 249 and ABL 1364, as well as CT 53 46, are affiliated with this event, it is conceivable that high cavalry officers like "charioteers" (*mukīl appāti*) and "third men" (*tašlīšu*) were involved. This is probable in any case, since it is difficult to imagine an attempted coup d'état in Assyria without military participation. Moreover, there is no doubt about the involvement of the eunuchs (*ša-rēši*) in the plot. The letters of Mar-Issar (SAA 10 354) and Šumu-iddina (TKSM 21/676) show that there were eunuchs who had enough reason to escape the sword of the king in the year 670. In particular, the chief eunuch (*rab ša-rēši*) – who was a military officer of the highest rank (cf. SAA 4 78-80, 88, 95-99 etc.) – had been suspected by Nabû-rehtu-uṣur (CT 53 17) and exposed as the candidate for kingship by Kudurru (SAA 10 179).

Even though the execution of the chief eunuch in 670, thus, is more than probable, there are no records that explicitly mention it and the identity of the chief eunuch in the crucial years 671-670 is, unfortunately, extremely difficult to figure out. During Esarhaddon's time, two persons are attested in this office: Aššur-naṣir in a letter from the very beginning of his reign (ABL 965)[551] and Ša-Nabû-šû in several documents from his last years which, however are difficult to date precisely.[552] If the oracle queries SAA 4 9, 63 and 88 are concerned with events of the mid and late 670's, then Ša-Nabû-šû would be the chief eunuch who probably lost his head in 670, but this dating of the queries is not irrefutable.[553] An alternative solution, i.e., that Ša-Nabû-

[551] This letter, dated to the year 680 by Dietrich 1970, 28-29, mentions "Aššur-naṣir the chief eunuch" ([m]*aš-šur*–ŠEŠ-*ir* LÚ.GAL–SAG.MEŠ line 14). The name appears without a title in CT 53 170 r.7-8, a letter dated by Parpola 1983, 129 to ca. 670, together with Danî (a scribe? cf. ADD 857 ii 40), as well as in SAA 8 164 as the signer of the report.

[552] In addition to SAA 11 37:5, Ša-Nabû-šû is attested as the chief eunuch in many oracle queries from the time of Esarhaddon (SAA 4 9:2, 12, r.3; 63:2, [13], r.9; 78 r.3; [79:3, 7, r.6]; 80:[1], r.6; 88:2, 4, 15, r.6; 96:3; 97 r.1; 98 r.5; 99 r.6). SAA 4 96-99 cannot be dated precisely; for the rest of the queries, cf. the next footnote.

In SAA 7 4, a list of court personnel, Ša-Nabû-šû appears without any professional designation (line i 5) while a person with the title 'chief eunuch' appears on the *preceding* line: [...]-*a-a* LÚ.GAL–⸢SAG⸣ (line i 4). The list includes also "Šamaš-šarru-uṣur, chief eunuch of the crown prince" (LÚ.⸢GAL–SAG DUMU–LUGAL⸣ line i 16). This document cannot be firmly dated. Fales & Postgate 1992, XVII-XIX hold it possible that the whole group of lists of persons now published as SAA 7 1-12 may refer to the same occasion; if this is the case, the year 673 provides itself as terminus post quem because the provinces Upumu (SAA 7 3:8) and Kulimmeri (SAA 7 3:9) existed only from that year on. The suggestion that the treaty ceremonies of early 672 might be that occasion is, of course, only tentative.

[553] SAA 4 9 mentions the Tabalean kings Mugallu and Iškallû. Esarhaddon indeed undertook a campaign against Mugallu in Elul (VI), 675 (Grayson 1975a, 83:10; 126:15), but Iškallû is not mentioned in this chronicle entry and the query, thus, may refer to a later event as well. SAA 4 63 deals with Median problems that may or may not be datable between the years 674-672 (cf. Starr 1990, LX-LXI). SAA 4 78-80 are concerned with the expedition to Ellipi initiated by the crown prince Assurbanipal (SAA 4 79 r.5 etc.) and thus postdating 672; a more precise dating is not possible.

SAA 4 88 queries whether the mission of Ša-Nabû-šû to Egypt will be attacked by Necho and Šarru-lu-dari, "Egyptian kings." This query is to be connected either with the

šû was appointed to the office of chief eunuch only *after* the executions of 670, is suggested by the fact that Aššur-naṣir still appears in the letter SAA 10 377, written in Tebet (X) 671/670. Even if his title is partly broken away (LÚ*.GAL–[*x*]), it has every chance to be the chief eunuch; Aššur-naṣir is not a common name and persons with a title beginning LÚ.GAL are not too numerous either. Furthermore, the year 658 is the eponym of Ša-Nabû-šû, a name rarer still. Hence, the chief eunuch executed in Nisan (I), 670, could be Aššur-naṣir as well. The sources, even if they are many, do not yield an unambiguous solution to this problem.

Assurbanipal queried the god Šamaš whether he should appoint Nabû-šarru-uṣur – who may have been his *rab mūgi* or *rab kiṣri*[554] – to the office of the chief eunuch (SAA 4 299). The answer of the god is likely to have been a firm positive one since this person appears as the chief eunuch of Assurbanipal in many documents around the years 658/657.[555] Whether or not

---

ill-fated campaign to Egypt in the month of Adar (XII), 674/673, recorded somewhat inconsistently in the chronicles (Grayson 1975a, 84:16; 126:20; cf. Spalinger 1974, 300-302; Onasch 1994, 23), or with the successful invasion of the year 671. The earlier dating would suggest itself because Ša-Nabû-šû has been sent to Egypt while the king himself does not seem to take part in the mission – as he certainly did in 671 but not demonstrably in 674. On the other hand, Necho I, the first king of the 26th (Saite) Dynasty, held this position only from the year 672 on and became a vassal ruler of Esarhaddon and Assurbanipal after the invasion of 671. If the later date is correct, then it can assumed that the chief eunuch was sent to Egypt after the conquest of 671 and the query is concerned with the loyalty of the newly vassaled Necho. Should this be true, then the Egyptian mission of the chief eunuch could be connected with the dubious events in Harran – which is on the way to Egypt, cf. SAA 10 174! – in the year 671 subsequent to the conquest. However, it cannot be ruled out that Ša-Nabû-šû was sent to Egypt later still.

There is no need to assume, as Onasch 1994, 153, 160 does, that Ša-Nabû-šû is one of the eunuchs mentioned by Assurbanipal in his account of the revolt of Necho and Šarru-lu-dari a few years later. This is not impossible as such, but SAA 4 88 apparently derives from the time of Esarhaddon (line 10!), so Šarru-lu-dari seems to have been allied with Necho years before the conspiracy. Šarru-lu-dari is already mentioned as a potential conspirator in the letter of Bel-ušezib from the year 675 (SAA 10 112 r.11); however, according to Onasch 1994, 41, "scheint es zumindest zweifelhaft, ob der dort genannte *Šarru-lū-dāri* noch einmal mit einem verantwortungsvollen Posten betraut worden ist und daher mit dem gesuchten Herrscher von Pelusium identisch sein kann."

554 See Fales 1988, 117-118. Nabû-šarru-uṣur appears as the *rab mūgi* of the crown prince Assurbanipal in SAA 4 89:2, 4, r.5 and 90:3, r.6, both queries from the 4th of Nisan (I) of an unknown year. Since they are concerned with an attempted mission of the *rab mūgi* to Arwad and Egypt, they must be connected with the conquest of Egypt in 671. A person with the same name but with the title *rab kiṣri* [*ša marʾi šarri*] is attested as a witness in two purchase documents of Remanni-Adad from the years 671-669 (SAA 6 299 r.5 and 325 r.20) and most probably also in three further documents from 671/670 in which the title is broken away (297 r.3; 298 r.9 and 300 r.8), as well as in SAA 7 5 r.ii 9; 9 r.i 21 and, perhaps, 6 ii 5. A concordance of the attestations of this name can be found in Fales 1988, 120-124.

555 Nabû-šarru-uṣur is called the chief eunuch of Assurbanipal in SAA 12 26:11,28, r.19 and, possibly, in 27:31, both documents dating from the year 657. The oracle queries in which he bears this title deal with Assurbanipal's wars against Mannea and Gambulu (SAA 4 267:2, r.7; 270 [r.7]; 271:[2,]10, r.7; 272:[3, r.6]). Two of these are firmly dated,

Nabû-šarru-uṣur was already appointed to this office in the beginning of Assurbanipal's reign is not certain; however, the "report" format of the query suggests a date not too early in Assurbanipal's reign.[556] If Ša-Nabû-šû was the chief eunuch only since 670, he may have held this office until about 658 – his own eponym year – when he was replaced by Nabû-šarru-uṣur.

Two final questions remain: who, after all, was Sasî, and what had the city of Harran to do with the events that led to the executions of 670?

It may seem like an over-optimistic and maximalist assessment to suggest that almost all of the above-discussed documents that mention the name Sasî refer to one and the same person. However, the dense web of factors linking together these documents, which probably all derive from a period of time of less than a decade with a clear emphasis on the years 671-670, points strongly towards the conclusion that the pieces indeed are from the same puzzle.

Provided that there is only one Sasî referred to in most of these texts, it is certain that he was an official of a high rank. His official title, however, constitutes a problem, since the designations *hazannu* (ABL 445 r.1; CT 54 37:15-16; SAA 6 314 r.10; 338 r.10; ADD 540 r.3) and *ša-muhhi-āli* (ABL 1217 r.11-12; SAA 10 179:17) are not interchangeable.[557] If both of them are applied to Sasî, then we either have to reckon with inaccuracies of persons not quite familiar with the city bureaucracy, or to conclude that Sasî had been promoted (or demoted?[558]) from *hazannu* to *ša-muhhi-āli* between the sending of the letters ABL 445 and 1217 – but we do not know for sure which one of the letters was written first! During the reign of Assurbanipal he would, then, have returned to the office of *hazannu*. If this is considered too enigmatic to be probable, then the conclusion must be drawn that the title *ša-muhhi-āli* is not the title of Sasî but refers to another person in ABL 1217, and Kudurru is not talking about him when he mentions the *ša-muhhi-āli*

SAA 4 271 to the year 658 and 272 to 657. SAA 4 267 and 270 may also derive from these years but, since the conflict which they reflect is rooted in the year 664 at the latest (Starr 1990, LXIV; cf. above, p. 48), an earlier date is not excluded. Nabû-šarru-uṣur appears as the chief eunuch once more in SAA 4 292 r.8. That this document belongs to the group of queries referring to the Šamaš-šumu-ukin war of 652-650 is conceivable from its "report" format (see Starr 1990, LXIV).

[556] See Aro 1966, 109-111; Starr 1990, XIV.

[557] For these offices, see Klengel-Brandt & Radner 1997, 152-155. The office of *hazannu*, which does not necessarily require a geographical unit (cf. CAD H 165 and Brinkman 1977, 313, n. 52), and that of the modern "mayor" do not quite converge. SAA 6 86 r.5-7 lists Nabû-belu-uṣur, *hazannu* of Nineveh, Nabû-rim-ilani, *hazannu* of Nineveh and Nabû-šarrani, *ša-muhhi-āli* of Nineveh as witnesses of a purchase document. This implies not only that there could have been several *hazannu*s simultaneously in one and the same city but also that *ša-muhhi-āli* denotes a different office in that particular city.

[558] This question arises from the fact that in older documents, the last one being from the year 676, *ša-muhhi-āli* appears before *hazannu* which indicates that the former, at least in the city of Assur, was a superior position. This order of rank, however, turns upside down somewhere in the middle of the 7th century. See the documetation of Klengel-Brandt & Radner 1997, 153 with the statement: "Ob diese Umstrukturierung nur in der Verwaltung von Assur vorgenommen wurde oder auch in den anderen assyrischen Städten stattfand, sollte untersucht werden."

"entering and leaving their presence" (SAA 10 179:17). On the basis of these two letters, the participation in the conspiracy of *ša-muhhi-āli*, whatever his name was, is probable in any case.

Both attestations of the city in which Sasî was *hazannu* are, to our misfortune, broken away. If Nineveh and Harran provide themselves as alternatives,[559] then the former is more likely, since Sasî was responsible for the supervision of scholars who doubtless worked in Nineveh, and it was within his power to "release" people for different assignments.

As to the second question, the sources (ABL 1217, CT 53 107, CT 53 44) make it plain that Sasî had connections with Harran. On the other hand, the Nusku oracle of the "slave girl" in a suburb of Harran and the false extispicy of Kudurru in the temple of Bel Harran, albeit in Nineveh, leave little doubt that the conspiracy had at least an important outpost there.

In conclusion, the theory of Dietrich of a conspiracy led by Sasî, mayor of Harran, around the year 675[560] should be modified to the effect that the conspiracy more probably took place four years later and was led by the chief eunuch in Nineveh rather than by Sasî who participated in the conspiracy only as the undercover agent of the king and likewise more probably resided in Nineveh. Nevertheless, I hope to have produced some additional evidence, required by Brinkman,[561] for the conviction that there indeed was a conspiracy in which both Sasî and Harran had a role to play. This does not mean, however, that a definitive solution can (or ever could) be reached. The "Swiss cheese"[562] constituted by the complex and uneven, though abundant set of sources is full of holes that can be filled only with circumstantial reasoning. Therefore, the door certainly remains open for alternative interpretations.

Prophecy

The long roundabout way through the historical puzzle around the enigmatic person of Sasî and his alleged involvement in the turbulence of the years 671/670 has now brought us back to our main theme, prophecy and its use in the letters of Nabû-rehtu-uṣur. The extensive historical detour has been necessary for the proper understanding of the Nusku oracle quoted by Nabû-rehtu-uṣur as well as his own reactions.

For Nabû-rehtu-uṣur, the alleged activities of Sasî represented an outrageous transgression of the king's treaty which should have been confronted accordingly. This is why the oracle of Nusku that promised the kingship for Sasî, proclaimed by the "slave girl" on the "outskirts of Harran" was taken very seriously by him. He himself responded to this prophecy with another

---

559 Cf. above, n. 536.

560 Dietrich 1970, 50-55.

561 Brinkman 1977, 314-315.

562 Prof. Jack M. Sasson used this fitting metaphor of ABL 1217 in an oral discussion in Philadelphia, 19th of November, 1995.

prophecy by placing the words of Nikkal, the Harranean goddess, against the (so-called) words of Nusku, the Harranean god. Even if he probably regarded the Nusku oracle as a pseudoprophecy, he fully recognized that the words of the "slave girl" were no harmless nonsense of some soothsayer but were presented with a claim to be real divine words (*abat Nusku šī* "This is the word of Nusku") and were likely to be believed as such by many. The proclamation of this oracle confirmed what he had already been informed of, namely that there were schemes afoot against the king, the principal architect of which – according to his conviction – was Sasî.

That the oracle promising the kingship to Sasî, according to my interpretation, was nothing but a political bluff does not diminish the tremendous impact it had on Nabû-rehtu-uṣur and, presumably, on many others. The probable location of its proclamation (the cedar temple of Sin and Nusku erected for Esarhaddon on his way to Egypt) was well chosen to guarantee its publicity and symbolic weight. The purpose of a sham manoeuvre is to produce the effect of a real one and turn attention away from the actual operations, and this was undoubtedly attempted by the people who were behind the Nusku oracle. The reaction of Nabû-rehtu-uṣur proves that the purpose was achieved.

But who was misleading whom? This is very difficult to conclude from letters written by a person who has swallowed the story whole. Two alternative solutions suggest themselves. 1) The conspirators tried to bluff the king and veil their activities by turning the public attention to one of their accomplices, maybe because his double role was uncovered, or 2) the king himself, fully aware of the schemes against him, arranged this fake in order to confuse the plans of his adversaries. In both cases the king was better informed of the actual events than Nabû-rehtu-uṣur whose letters in all their severity probably made him laugh up his sleeve.

Whoever was behind the Nusku oracle in the neighbourhood of Harran, it provides another example of the use – or abuse – of prophecy for political purposes. A comparable case is the letter of Nabû-nadin-šumi who suggests the banishment of a person on grounds of a prophecy concerning anyone who is disloyal to the king (SAA 10 284), but there the reference is made to an actual prophecy of Ištar, whereas we here have to do with a purposely-made, *ad hoc* engineered oracle.

As such, the letter offers another example of the problem of pseudoprophecy that we know so well from the Hebrew Bible (Deut 13:2-6; 18:15-22; Jer 6:13-15; 23:13-32; 27:14-17; 28; 29:8-9, 15, 21-23; Ez 13; Micah 3:5-12 etc.).[563] Nabû-rehtu-uṣur certainly doubts the truthfulness of the Nusku oracle of the "slave girl." But how could he possibly be positive about that? His writings indicate that he knew about the oracle only by hearsay without being aware of its shady background in concrete terms, but even if it had been proclaimed in due order in his presence he would have had the same difficulty. The ultimate difference between a true and a false prophecy can only

[563] See further Nissinen 1996, 172-175, 193-195.

be that a true prophecy really originates from a deity and a false one does not – but this is a matter of belief that cannot be verified by any controllable means. In the absence of explicit criteria for the distinction between true and false prophecy there were two possibilities: to suggest an extispicy ritual on the account of the "slave girl," and to counter the prophecy with another prophecy which he certainly believes to be a true one: the "word of Nikkal," the source of which he does not indicate perhaps because he regards it as common knowledge. What made him sure of the true origin of the word of Nikkal could only be its contents. It reassured the rule of Esarhaddon like the prophecies usually did, while the oracle of the "slave girl" was directed against the ruling king and, for that reason only, could only be a pseudo-prophecy.

Nabû-rehtu-uṣur shows in his letters that he was actually well aware of prophecies and their contents. According to his own account, he himself had been initially convinced of the existence of the conspiracy on the basis of a vision (*diglu*) contemplated by him a few months before he wrote his letters (CT 53 17:10 and 938:10). This does not mean that he should be regarded as a prophet – visions could be seen by other people as well[564] – but he obviously had a strong predilection for prophecy. This becomes evident not only from the second-hand citation of the Nusku oracle but also from his use of prophetic phraseology, even to the point of a paraphrase or a quotation. CT 53 107:12ff apparently quotes the words of Ištar which, however, are almost totally destroyed. It has also been observed that the warnings against neglecting the "word" (*dabābu*) of Nikkal/Mullissu (ABL 1217:8, CT 53 17:8-9 and 938:8-9) imply that a prophecy has just been quoted or paraphrased; to be sure, CT 53 17:8 and 938:8 state this plainly: "This word is (a word) of Mullissu" (*dabābu anniu ša Mullissi šū*).[565] What precedes is fully comparable with the existing prophetic oracles both as regards destroying (*karāru*[566]) the enemies and protecting the life and rule of the king.[567]

Moreover, Nabû-rehtu-uṣur not only paraphrased prophetic oracles but was generally inclined to use their language, as becomes obvious from the following affirmation: *lā tapallah Bēl Nabû Mullissu* [*issīka*] *izzazzū* "Have no fear; Bel, Nabû and Mullissu are standing [with you]" (CT 53 17 r.14-15).[568] This could be borrowed from any prophetic oracle – including Second Isaiah!

---

564 See above, pp. 55-56.

565 Cf. SAA 9 1.10 vi 7-8: *dabābu pāniu ša aqabakanni* "the previous utterance which I spoke to you"; 9 1.1 i 15-16 *ajjūte dibbīja ša aqabakanni* "What words have I spoken to you?"

566 Cf. SAA 9 1.1 i 12-14: *anāku Issār ša Arbail ša nakarūtēka ina pān šēpēka akkarrūni* "I am Ištar of Arbela, who cast your enemies before your feet."

567 Cf. SAA 9 2.3 ii 1-5: *nakarūtēka mar* [*šunūni x x x*] *ina libbi ekallīka lū* [*kammusāka*] *māt Aššūr issīka u*[*sallam*] *ša kal ūme kallamār*[*i maṣṣartaka*] *anaṣṣar agûka u*[*kanna*] "[*I will annihilate*] whatever enemies you [have]. *As for* [*you, stay*] in your palace; I will [reconcile] Assyria with you. I will protect [you] by day and by dawn and [consolidate] your crown."

568 Fales 1980, 138 has also recognized here the use of a "'prophetic' language."

(*ʾal-tîrāʾ kî ʿimmĕkā ʾānî* Is 41:10; cf. 43:5) – since "fear not" is well known as a prophetic formula[569] and the standing of the gods with the king is the primary concern of virtually every Neo-Assyrian prophecy known to us. If this kind of affirmation were to stand isolated in a text without further allusions to prophetic expressions, it would be difficult to conclude anything about its possible origins. In the context created by our writer, however, its use points strongly in the direction of prophecy.

The wish of Nabû-rehtu-uṣur that the king stay in safety in his palace ([*...atta*] *tuqūnu ina ekallīka šībi* ABL 1217 s.3, cf. CT 53 17 s.2) shows his predilection for prophetic expressions. In prophetic speech the verb *tuqqunu* (D 'to put in order') and its derivates commonly signify the stability of the kingdom of Assyria and the safety of its king or crown prince, guaranteed by the goddess Ištar against all fomenters of disorder (SAA 9 1.2 i 30-35, SAA 9 1.10 vi 22-26 and SAA 9 2.5 iii 19-20):[570]

> *šar māt Aššūr lā tapallah nakru ša šar māt Aššūr ana ṭabahhi addana* [*ina*] *bēt rēdūtēka* [*utaqq*]*anka* [*urabba*]*kka*
>
> King of Assyria, have no fear! I will deliver up the enemy of the king of Assyria for slaughter. [I will] keep you safe and [*make*] you [*great* in] your Palace of Succession.
>
> *aklu taqnu takkal mê taqnūti tašatti ina libbi ekallīka tataqqun*
>
> You shall eat safe food and drink safe water, and you shall be safe in your palace
>
> *Aššūr-ahu-iddina lā tapallah māt Aššūr utaqqan ilāni zēnûti issi māt Aššūr usal*[*l*]*am*
>
> Esarhaddon, have no fear! I will put Assyria in order and reconcile the angry gods with Assyria.

The last quotation shows that the semantic field of *tuqqunu* includes more than just physical security: it stands for the equilibrium of heaven and earth represented by the stable rule of the king. The repeated urging of Nabû-rehtu-uṣur concerning the king's safety implies not only his worry about the king's personal well-being but a concern for the constancy of the divine order by which the kingdom stands or falls.

---

569 SAA 9 1.1 i 5; 1.2 i 30; 1.4 ii 16; 1.8 v 21; 2.1 i 13; 2.2 i 15; 2.3 i 38(?); 2.4 iii 17; 2.5 iii 19, 29; 2.6 iv 20(?), 30; 4:5; 7:2, r.6, 11; SAA 3 13:24; ABL 1249:5.

570 Cf. SAA 9 2.1 i 6; 2.3 ii 11; 2.6 iv 27; 5:9; 6:2-3; 11:5; SAA 3 13:17.

CHAPTER SEVEN

PROPHETS IN THE SUCCESSION TREATY OF ESARHADDON

Text

SAA 2 6 § 10

[108]*š[u]m-ma a-bu-tú la* DÙG.GA-*tú la de-iq-tú* [109]*la ba-ni-tú ina* UGU ^{m}*aš-šur*–DÙ–A DUMU–MAN GAL *ša* É–UŠ-*ti* [110]DUMU ^{m}*aš-šur*–PAB–AŠ MAN KUR–*aš-šur* EN-*ku-nu la tar-ṣa-at-u-ni* [111]*la ṭa-bat-u-ni lu-u ina pi-i* LÚ.KÚR-*šú* [112]*lu-u ina pi-i sal-me-šú* [113]*lu ina pi-i* ŠEŠ.MEŠ-*šú* [114]ŠEŠ.MEŠ–AD.MEŠ-*šú* DUMU–ŠEŠ.MEŠ–AD.MEŠ-*šú* [115]*qin-ni-šu* NUMUN É–AD-*šu lu-u ina pi-i* ŠEŠ.MEŠ-*ku-nu* [116]DUMU.MEŠ-*ku-nu* DUMU.MÍ.MEŠ-*ku-nu lu ina pi-i* LÚ.*ra-gi-me* [117]LÚ.*mah-he-e* DUMU *šá-ʾi-li a-mat* DINGIR [118]*lu-u ina pi-i nap-har ṣal-mat*–SAG.DU *mal ba-šú-u* [119]*ta-šam-ma-a-ni tu-pa-za-ra-a-ni* [120]*la ta-lak-a-ni-ni a-na* ^{m}*aš-šur*–DÙ–A DUMU–MAN GAL-*u* [121]*ša* É–UŠ-*te* DUMU ^{m}*aš-šur*–PAB–AŠ MAN KUR–*aš-šur* [122]*la ta-qab-ba-a-ni*

> If you hear any evil, improper, ugly word which is not seemly nor good to Assurbanipal, the great crown prince designate, son of Esarhaddon, king of Assyria, our lord, either from the mouth of his enemy or from the mouth of his ally, or from the mouth of his brothers or from the mouth of his uncles, his cousins, his family, members of his father's line, or from the mouth of your brothers, your sons, your daughters, or from the mouth of a prophet, an ecstatic, an inquirer of oracles, or from the mouth of any human being at all, you shall not conceal it but come and report it to Assurbanipal, the great crown prince designate, son of Esarhaddon, king of Assyria.

Background

From the time of Sargon II at the latest, the Assyrian throne was handed down from father to son in a dynastic manner. In the Sargonid period it was the standard procedure to choose one of the king's sons as the crown prince long before the succession became an issue. It is difficult to know whether it was the birthright of the eldest of the king's sons to be designated as crown prince or the one who was considered the most qualified to become the king's successor was chosen. Choosing the eldest son may have been held to be the normal procedure, but, on the other hand, the king was free to choose his successor.[571] To justify the choice, the investiture of the crown prince was

[571] Cf. Ben-Barak 1986, 96. According to Lewy 1952, 271, the eldest son of the king was by his birthright the successor to the throne. Only when the first-born son died before the king was a choice made among the remaining sons, none of whom, then, enjoyed a privileged position. It might indeed have been the usual practice that the eldest of the king's sons became his successor, and contradictory practices needed a special justification. This does not, however, prove that the position of crown prince was his absolute birthright. If this would have been the case, the practise of extispicy would not have been necessary. Cf. Pečírková 1993, 247.

preceded by extispicy in order to get a firm answer from the god Šamaš on the matter; e.g., SAA 4 149 r.7-9:

> *ašâlka Šamaš bēlu rabû kī Aššūr-ahu-iddina šar māt Aššūr māršu ša šumšu ina niāru annâ šaṭru ana bēt rēdūti ušērebūma*
>
> I ask you, Šamaš, great lord, whether Esarhaddon, king of Assyria, should enter his son, whose name (Sin-nadin-apli) is written in this papyrus, into the Succession Palace.[572]

In the case of a favorable response, the crown prince entered into the Palace of Succession (*bēt rēdūti*). From then on he was officially called *mār šarri (rabiu) ša bēt rēdūti* "the crown prince of the Palace of Succession" or, elliptically, just *mār šarri*, properly translated as "the crown prince."[573]

In the *bēt rēdūti* the crown prince was prepared for his future career by schooling in the skills necessary for exercising kingship over the empire. Nevertheless, the crown prince had clearly a much higher status than that of a mere apprentice. The sources from the Sargonid period present the designation of the crown prince as a political event of the highest prominence. On this occasion, all the officials and even the vassal kings were obliged to conclude a treaty or swear a loyalty oath in which they agreed to the designation of the crown prince and bound themselves to his authority.[574] This was necessary because the crown prince could be delegated to take over administrative duties in the court during the absence of the king, e.g., during the time of long campaigns. Should the king die in battle, the crown prince could immediately take over.[575]

All this underpinning of the status of *mār šarri* did not prevent the royal succession from being one of the major problems of the Assyrian court in the Sargonid period. Even though the succession was arranged to be as indisputable as possible by designating the crown prince as the legitimate heir in good

---

[572] Starr 1990, 160; cf. Borger 1956 (§ 27) 40:13-14 for the case of Esarhaddon.

[573] See Parpola 1983, 166-167; Kwasman & Parpola 1991, XXVII-XXIX. It should be noted that *mār šarri*, then, did not refer to the rest of the king's sons who were called by their names only. If there were crown princes for Assyria and Babylonia simultaneously, as was the case of Assurbanipal and Šamaš-šumu-ukin, this could in the case of need be specified in their respective titles. In ABL 113:6, 6-7, for example, the former is called *mār ša[rri rabi]u* and the latter *mār šarri ša Bābili*. For the desigation *mār šarri ašarēdu* see Lewy 1952, 280 n. 85.

[574] The best known example of this is, of course, the great vassal treaty of Esarhaddon (SAA 2 6), but there are other treaties (SAA 2 3 and 8) and references to the investitures of crown princes in other sources; cf. Parpola 1987b, 184-186. Even if Tadmor (1982b, 147) is right in his assertion that, *according to the available evidence*, the investiture of Esarhaddon was "the first time in the history of Assyria that the court and citizenry were obliged to take a loyalty oath to the heir apparent" in order to prevent potential usurpations, it cannot be excluded that a similar oath could have been sworn in earlier instances. Against the common view that Sargon II would have been an usurper cf. below n. 577.

[575] Cf. Mayer 1993, 172-173 for the position of the crown prince Sennacherib during the Cimmerian campaigns of Sargon in 710-708.

time, this system seldom worked without serious troubles. The very name of Sargon himself has been interpreted as implying controversies in his succession (*Šarru-kēn* 'the Legitimate King'),[576] and we know that he consciously avoided mentioning his predecessors so that we do not even know for sure who his father was.[577] Sennacherib was also consistent in leaving his father's name unmentioned in his written records.[578]

The text under scrutiny is the tenth paragraph of the so-called Succession Treaty of Esarhaddon concerning the succession of his son Assurbanipal and concluded on the 12th of Iyyar (II), 672 in the presence of "all Assyria" and the vassal rulers.[579] The motivation for the succession arrangements may have arisen, not only from the political difficulties of that time including the failed attempt to conquer Egypt, but also from the death of Esarhaddon's wife.[580] The investiture of Assurbanipal was a major event in the Assyrian Empire, a grandiose occasion that may have been the greatest one ever arranged for the designation of a crown prince.[581] Thus, the king's exorcist Adad-šumu-uṣur (SAA 10 185:5-13):

---

[576] Cf, however, Chamaza 1992, 31-32 who explains the name as a contracted pronuciation of *Šarru-ukīn* "the king has obtained/established order."

[577] Thomas 1993 has recently called attention to two pieces of evidence which suggest that Sargon II was the son of Tiglath-Pileser III – just like his predecessor Shalmaneser V. The first document, published before by E. Unger, is an enamelled tile with the inscription *ekal Šarru-ukīn šarri rabî šarri danni šar kiššati šar māt Aššūr mār Tukulti-apil-Ešarra šar māt Aššūrma* "Palace of Sargon, the great king, the mighty king, king of the universe, king of Assyria, son of Tiglath-Pileser, king of Assyria." The second one is a letter addressed to Sargon and referring to Tiglath-Pileser as his father (CT 54 109 r.10-11; see Dietrich 1967, 82). Cf. also Chamaza 1992, 31-32.

[578] Tadmor 1981, 26: "This exceptional silence can only be explained as an extreme expression of Sennacherib's antagonism towards his father's political and religious policies." There is, however, an important exception to this rule, namely SAA 3 33, in which Sennacherib tells about his investigating by means of extispicy, what the "Sin of Sargon" was; for this text, see Tadmor & Landsberger & Parpola 1989.

[579] Borger 1996, 15-16 A i 8-22: "Esarhaddon, king of Assyria, my father and begetter, heeded the command of Aššur and Mullissu, the gods in whom he trusted, who told him that I was to exercise the kingship. On the 12th of Iyyar (II), at the noble command of Aššur, Mullissu, Sin, Šamaš, Adad, Bel, Nabû, Ištar of Nineveh, Ištar of Arbela, Ninurta, Nergal and Nusku, he convened the people of Assyria, great and small, from coast to coast, made them swear a treaty oath (*adê*) by the gods and established a binding agreement to protect my crownprinceship and future kingship over Assyria." As to the occasion, see further Tadmor 1983, 38, 43-45; Watanabe 1987, 2-5.

[580] See Tadmor 1983, 41-43. Both events are recorded in the chronicles; the unsuccessful invasion of Egypt in Grayson 1975a, 84:16 and the death of Esarhaddon's wife in Grayson 1975a, 85:22; 127:23.

[581] Cf. Tadmor 1983, 38, according to whom this ceremony was unprecented in Assyria. However, this was probably not the first case when the investiture of the crown prince was accompanied by a treaty, since the Nin. A (§ 27) inscription refers to a treaty on the occasion of the investiture of Esarhaddon (Borger 1956 [§ 27] 40:15-19), and SAA 2 3, referred to by Tadmor 1983, 38 n. 9, most probably is a copy of that treaty (see Parpola 1987b, 163-164 and Parpola & Watanabe 1988, XXVIII).

> *ša ina šamê lā epišūni šarru bēlī ina kaqqiri ētapaš uktallimannāši mara'ka pitūtu tartakas šarrūtu ša māt Aššūr ina pānīšu tussadgil mara'ka rabiu ana šarrūti ina Bābili tassakan issēn ina imittīka šaniu ina šumēlīka tussāziz*
>
> What has not been done in heaven, the king, my lord, has done upon earth and shown us: you have girded a son of yours with headband and entrusted to him the kingship of Assyria; your eldest son you have set to the kingship in Babylon. You have placed the first on your right, the second on your left side!

The vast dimensions of the celebration can be accounted for by the fact that Esarhaddon wanted to make sure that history this time would not repeat itself; Esarhaddon, as we know, replaced his elder brother with serious consequences. Therefore, the preparations of the investiture of Assurbanipal included also scribal work – not only the great succession treaty (SAA 2 6) but also the inscription in which Esarhaddon gives an account of his own rise to the status of crown prince and the subsequent war of succession which led to his enthronement (Nin. A = Borger 1956 § 27), and, possibly, the collection of prophecies which attached to the same events (SAA 9 1).[582] All this was presented as evidence of irrevocable divine will concerning the kingship of Esarhaddon. At the same time, any potential antagonists were reminded of the will of the gods and of the fate of those who try to resist its coming true.[583]

Esarhaddon had every reason to bring strong evidence in support of his succession arrangement which was hardly less controversial than that of his father. The decision to appoint his younger son Assurbanipal as crown prince of Assyria and give the politically less weighty crownprinceship of Babylonia to his elder son Šamaš-šumu-ukin was also something that "has not been done in heaven" but what Esarhaddon has now "done upon earth." It did not meet with undivided approval, and the subordinate role of Šamaš-šumu-ukin as a dependent monarch of Babylonia created growing discontent.[584] The bad blood cropped up violently when a civil war between these brothers broke out two decades later (652-648).[585]

Thus, the great emphasis laid by Esarhaddon on the legitimacy of the succession arrangement as well as on his servants' loyalty to the crown prince is not to be wondered at. While the Assyrian treaties in general imposed sanctions against potential rebels, Esarhaddon's own experience certainly strengthened his sensitivity to the threat of a rebellion.[586]

---

582 Cf. above, p. 31.

583 Cf. Parpola 1997c, LXIX-LXX.

584 See Brinkman 1984, 85-92; Frame 1992, 102-130 and cf. the comment of Mayer 1995, 395: "Mag Assurbanipal von Asarhaddons Söhnen der fähigste gewesen sein und mag er auch bei der Bevölkerung und den ohne Zweifel vorhandenen nationalistischen Gruppen eine große Popularität genossen haben, so war doch allen Vereidigungen und vertraglichen Absicherungen zum Trost der Konflikt auf längere Sicht hinaus vorprogrammiert."

585 For this war, see Dietrich 1970, 78-125; Brinkman 1984, 93-104; Frame 1992, 131-190.

586 Thus Tadmor 1983, 44.

Prophecy

Paragraph 10 represents the type of treaty stipulation that contains the obligation to report to the king any sign of disloyalty among his subjects. A stipulation of this kind is included in most of the well-preserved Neo-Assyrian treaties[587] and is likely to have constituted a standard part of the treaties between the king and his allies or his subjects. Its wording and extent differs from treaty to treaty, the basic structure being the following: "If you should hear an improper word (*abutu lā deqtu* etc.) from the mouth of... you shall report it to the king."[588] While some of the treaties do not specify the people from the mouth of whom the "improper word" might be heard,[589] others make more or less comprehensive lists on which usually the members of the royal family,[590] the high officials of the court,[591] others belonging to the royal entourage or just "any human being at all" (*naphar ṣalmat qaqqadi mal bašû*)[592] appear as the potential evilspeakers.

Being by far the largest of the extant treaties, the Succession Treaty of Esarhaddon also includes the most elaborate lists of people that may be suspected of intrigues against the king. Two paragraphs contain obligations to report these people to the king (§§ 6 and 10) while others are concerned with other kinds of actions against suspected persons (§§ 12, 14, 20, 22, 27, 29). From our point of view it is important that this treaty also mentions professional diviners in this context. Not only the scholars (*ummânī*) are pointed out (§ 6:79)[593] but also people called *raggimu, mahhû* and *šā'ilu*. The three titles may imply three different kinds of diviners with respectively characteristic roles and techniques, but a clear distinction between them is difficult to draw and a certain overlapping of their roles should be reckoned with.[594] To date, this is the only occurrence of *raggimu* and *mahhû* appearing

---

587 SAA 2 3:2-4; 4:4-7; 6:§§ 6, 10-13, 57; 8 r.2-27; 9:6-9, 12-16; 13 iii 10-17; cf. SAA 2 2 iii 23ff.

588 Cf. SAA 2 3:2-4; 4:4-7; 8 r.2-27 etc.

589 SAA 2 3:2 does not specify any potential group of persons behind the "improper things" that could be heard, whereas SAA 2 13 iii 11 mentions only a (foreign) king, and SAA 2 9:12-13 talks about a "detestable person" and a "conspirator."

590 E.g., "his (the king's) progeny" (SAA 2 4:4); "his brothers, his uncles, his cousins, his family, members of his father's line" (SAA 2 6 §§ 6, 20 cf. §§ 27, 29); "his brothers or of royal line" (SAA 2 8:21-22).

591 I.e., magnates (LÚ.GAL.MEŠ), governors (LÚ.NAM.MEŠ), "bearded" (LÚ.*šá–ziq-ni*) and eunuchs (LÚ.SAG.MEŠ); cf. the passages mentioned in the previous footnote.

592 SAA 2 6 § 6:79-80; § 10:118; § 20:223; § 29:339-340; cf. "a citizen of Assyria or a citizen of any other country" (*lū mar māt Aššūr lū mar māt šanītimma*) SAA 2 6 § 14: 163-164; § 20:222-223; § 27:321-322; § 29:338-339.

593 This solves the problem of Cryer 1994, 215: "It is interesting that Esarhaddon makes no such demand of his vassal's extispicy priests or astrologers; did he assume that they would remain loyal to their sovereign in any case, or did he simply assume that his own court diviners would keep him informed on that level of divination?"

594 Cf. the respective terminology in Hebrew where a difference between *nābî', ḥōzæ,*

together; it seems like a word-pair combining the colloquial and literary equivalents for "prophet." On the other hand, *šā'il(t)u*, a rare word in Neo-Assyrian,[595] is usually – though not exclusively – connected with dream interpretation and thus comes near to the designation *šabrû*.[596] As a compound, the three designations are grouped together in a way that virtually unites them into one association of specialists in non-inductive divinatory methods.

The unparalleled appearence of scholars and prophets as potential intriguers in the Succession Treaty of Esarhaddon could be said to be due to Esarhaddon's special appreciation of them: being particularly receptive to scholarly advice and prophetic words he could also recognize the danger they might constitute when used against him by his adversaries. This might be quite true but the same may apply to other kings, too. That the case of Esarhaddon is better documented than the others does not make him any more helpless or "superstitious" than the other kings were. Since only a few treaties have been preserved, the lack of mention of diviners and prophets in them may be purely coincidential.

The appearance of prophets as potential betrayers is somewhat surprising. The entire corpus of surviving prophecies is favorable to the king and every oracle is uttered in order to support his rule. The references to prophecy discussed thus far in this study imply a close and confidential relationship between the prophets and the king, presenting the prophets as staunch supporters and propagandists of the royal ideology. All this notwithstanding, SAA 2 6 § 10 takes it for granted that prophecy could also be used against the king. The paragraph implies that every single prophet was not under the immediate control of the king, so that he needed to be informed by others about their sayings in order to uproot any sign of disloyalty among his subjects. The prophets' loyalty to the king may in general have been substantially higher than that of many others, but even prophets were human beings. If a prophet swerved from the straight path, he or she was at least potentially in a good position to foment opposition against the king under the divine authority. The possibility that someone might fraudulently pose as a prophet may also have been reckoned with. For this reason it is quite consistent that the prophets are mentioned in the treaty stipulations concerning the obligation to inform the king about evil words against him. The letter of Nabû-rehtu-uṣur (ABL 1217) shows that the warning was well-grounded indeed: in the very next year the king receives a report of a (pseudo)prophecy proclaimed against him.

Paragraph 10 has a biblical parallel in Deuteronomy 13, a passage that is paralleled by the Succession Treaty of Esarhaddon in many respects. In this

---

rō'œ, ḥōlem, qōsem, 'ōnen and *kaššāp* is often unclear even if the designations are not synonymous; cf. Kaiser 1993, 213-219; Blenkinsopp 1995, 123-129.

[595] To my knowledge, the Neo-Assyrian occurrences of *šā'ilu*, in addition to SAA 2 6 § 10:117, include only the entry in the lexical text MSL 12 233:33.

[596] For *šā'il(t)u*, see Oppenheim 1956, 221; Cryer 1994, 158; AHw 1133-1134; CAD Š/1 110-112; for *šabrû*, CAD Š/1 15 and above, p. 56.

multi-layered deuteronomistic text[597] the Israelites are ordered by Yahweh not to listen to the "prophet or dreamer" (*nābî' 'ô ḥōlem ḥălôm*) that may appear among them and entice them into the worship of other gods. Instead, he should be put to death because of the "disloyal talk" (*dibbær sārâ*) against Yahweh with which he has led the people astray (Deut 13:2-6).[598] Members of the family and closest friends ("your brother, your father's son or your mother's son, or your son or daughter, or the wife of your bosom or your dearest friend" vv. 7ff) as well as miscreants in other cities (vv. 13ff) are to be treated accordingly when found out to have misled the Israelites into apostasy. All this reads like a theological application of the Succession Treaty of Esarhaddon. The king of Assyria and the God of Israel hold similar positions over the people with whom the treaty (*adê*) or covenant (*bĕrît*) is being made.[599] Deut 13 shows a remarkable similarity to the (Neo-)Assyrian treaty phraseology in general,[600] providing itself as an illustrative example of the deuteronomistic continuation of ideas inspired by the Neo-Assyrian treaty ideology. That the false prophets are regarded as a serious risk factor in Deut 13 may, in addition to the domestic experiences, also have roots in a similar concern of the neighboring superpower.

The problem of pseudoprophecy shows itself once more, this time in a framework more ideological than in ABL 1217 which was related to a specific case. In the Succession Treaty of Esarhaddon, like in Deut 13, the threat constituted by false prophets concerned the religious, ideological and political fundamentals of the society which, in practice, constituted the decisive criterion of which kind of prophecy could be regarded as legitimate.[601] A true prophecy against the rule of Esarhaddon or Assurbanipal in Assyria was as unimaginable as one in favor of the worship of other gods than Yahweh in post-exilic Israel.

---

[597] According to Veijola 1995, 309, the basic layer of Dtn 13, which already is deuteronomistic and dates from the early post-exilic period, consists of vv. 2, 3*, 4-7, 9, 10aa, 11b-14, 16a, 17aa^2, 18b, 19. Cf. the analysis of Dion, according to which the basic layer (vv. 2a, 3b, 4a*, 6a*, b, 7*, 9-18) derives from the time of Josiah (1991, 204-205). This date is to be considered far too early, however, since the language of Deut 13 is fully deuteronomistic and the warning about the prophets presupposes not only the Assyrian treaty phraseology but also the polemics of the Book of Jeremiah against the pseudoprophets (see Veijola 1995, 297-301; 1996, 246).

[598] Cf. SAA 2 6 § 57:502-503 and see Jenni 1981.

[599] Even if the word *bĕrît* is not mentioned in Deut 13 the text is deeply rooted in the covenant theology. According to Veijola, the oldest stratum of Deut 13 belongs to the covenantal redaction of Deuteronomy (DtrB) identified by him; see Veijola 1996, 245-247.

[600] See, e.g., Dion 1991, 198-199; Veijola 1995, 287-314; Levinson 1995; Nissinen 1996, 179-180.

[601] On the distinguishing between true and false prophecy on confessional or ideological grounds, see, e.g., Huffmon 1976a, 184; Coggins 1993, 93; Nissinen 1996, 194-195.

CHAPTER EIGHT

CONCLUSION

Prophecy, Politics and Ideology

The sources discussed in this study leave no room for doubt that prophecy was an established institution in the Neo-Assyrian Empire. Form the point of view of the Assyrian imperial ideology, prophets formed a part of the human apparatus needed by the gods to reveal their will and make the people – first and foremost the king – act accordingly. From a political and sociological point of view, again, prophets belonged to the machinery of imperial propaganda, the purpose of which was to substantiate the necessity of the existence and growth of the imperium. This is at least the impression given by the preserved prophecies and quotations of prophecies in other sources, which are almost without exception addressed to the king of Assyria or to the members of the royal family. To what extent prophetical services were available to private persons outside the court is still unclear, though the account of Urad-Gula of his turning to a prophet (SAA 10 294) indisputably proves that this was within the bounds of possibility.

In general, the prophets appear as staunch supporters of the king and his regime; the two exceptions (ABL 1217 and SAA 2 6 § 10) only prove the rule. The prophets were there to proclaim divine support for the newly enthroned king – even for the substitute king, as evidenced in our sources (SAA 10 352; LAS 317). In times of crisis the prophets encouraged the king with their words, proclaiming the love of the gods, particularly that of Ištar, for the divinely chosen king, and their support for his rightful undertakings, especially the military ones. But their words were not repeated only when the king's life or rule was in danger, they could be referred to in peaceful times as well, if a political decision required a divine authorization.

The available documentation shows that prophetic words were used in internal and external politics alike. An example of the significance of prophecy in the internal decision-making is provided by Nabû-nadin-šumi who suggests the banishment of a person from Assyria by virtue of a prophetic word (SAA 10 284). Prophecy also played a prominent role in the attempted coup in the years 671/670, when the audience was confused by a pseudo-prophecy of Nusku, according to which the ruling dynasty was doomed to destruction (ABL 1217; CT 53 17 and 938).

In the realm of external politics, habitually practiced by means of military campaigns, the prophetic involvement is even better documented, not only in the extant prophecies concerned with foreign matters[602] but also in the sources of this study, the inscriptions in particular. In their campaigns, the kings were followed by diviners and prophets who, like the one called Quqî (SAA 7 9 r.i 23), seemed to have been members of the military body.

From the modern historian's standpoint, wars were necessary for the Assyrian empire to maintain its political and economic power,[603] whereas

---

[602] E.g. SAA 9 2.4 iii 12-15; SAA 9 7:8-r.5.

[603] Van der Spek 1993, 269: "If imperialism is successful, the state cannot do without it anymore."

from the point of view of the Assyrian imperial ideology, all wars were divine wars initiated by the great gods rather than the king of Assyria. According to our sources, notably the inscriptions, war was a religious duty and the king, being the paragon of piety, was duty-bound to wage war against the barbarous and insolent enemy. The king could act only upon the command of the gods which was the only and sufficient justification for war.[604] This was also the reason for which prophets, like all diviners, were needed in the course of the campaigns. As is abundantly demonstrated by the countless queries preceding the wars, the king had to ask the gods' permission for his campaigns by extispicy. Prayers, fictitious as their wording in the inscriptional accounts doubtless is, have certainly been uttered, both when the campaigns were in preparation and during them. In the dynamics of the divine-human communication, human prayers and divine messages transmitted by prophets and diviners responded to each other. Hence, as a response to his prayers, the king obtained messages of divine encouragement in the form of dreams and prophecies which "made his heart confident." This did not mean, however, that the king would not have lent an ear to his scholarly advisers who also were diviners.[605]

In addition to warfare, the king's religious duties also included building and restoring temples for the gods and supplying them with worthy offerings and unceasing worship. This is why prophets, like other diviners, also exhort the king in his temple restoration work, assuring him of their necessity.

The question about the religious and political function of prophecy is ultimately hermeneutical and dependent on the standpoint from which it is examined. For the modern reader who does not share the ideology and religion of the sources but examines them as documents of power and propaganda, the function of prophecy appears to be the legitimation of the Assyrian royal ideology and imperialistic policy. For the contemporary Assyrian, again, prophecy was honored as the direct speech of the gods, providing the necessary evidence of the divine will that was to be executed on earth. In other words, while the modern outsider regards the prophets as instruments of the imperial ideology, the ancient insider who had internalized this ideology would have seen the king as a mere tool in the hands of the gods, the messengers of whom the prophets were. From the insider's point of view, the rule of the divinely chosen king was not in need of any further legitimation. According to this line of thought, the prophetic encouragement was a manifestation of divine support for the king who was fulfilling tasks commanded by the gods, rather than excuses that would sanction the king's political and military maneuvers.[606] Prophecies were regarded as signs of a special and intimate relationship between the gods and the king; a written prophecy could

---

[604] See, e.g., Weippert 1972; van der Spek 1993, 264-267.

[605] Cf. Bel-ušezib's advice concerning Esarhaddon's Mannean war in SAA 10 111, 112 and 113.

[606] On this ideology, see Parpola 1997c, XXXVI-XLIV.

even serve as a *ṭuppi adê* , an actual document of this divine-royal "covenant" (SAA 9 3.3 ii 27).

A special issue in Assyrian imperial politics – whether internal or external is and was a problem! – was constituted by Babylonia. This becomes evident more than once in the sources examined in this study. For Esarhaddon, the reconstructing of Babylon, violently destroyed by his father in 689, was a moral obligation of which he was reminded by the prophets. At the same time Babylonia was regarded as a potential hotbed of insurrection which had to be kept under control, not only by military discipline but also by peaceful means, e.g., educating sons of Babylonian noble families in Assyria. One of them was Kudurru who was forced to perform a divination concerning the kingship of the chief eunuch and, having accomplished this task, was promised the kingship of Babylonia (SAA 10 179).

The attitude towards Babylonia and the Babylonians depends on the writer. Mar-Issar, Esarhaddon's agent in Babylonia, views them from the standpoint of the imperial authority; for him, the fate of Damqî, the son of a Babylonian official who died as the substitute king, constituted a clever political move which kept the Babylonians in wholesome fear (SAA 10 352). He also chased fugitives, probably the eunuchs involved in the recently crushed conspiracy, who had fled to Babylonia in the year 670 (SAA 10 354). On the other hand, Bel-ušezib who is a Babylonian himself, discreetly but repeatedly reminds Esarhaddon of his duties towards Babylonia, referring to celestial omens (SAA 10 109) and prophecy (SAA 10 111). It may be that respect for these divine messages partially accounts for the fact that the Babylonian policy of Esarhaddon was more lenient than that of his father.

True and False Prophecy

As effective a political weapon as prophecy was, the possibility that it could be used for purposes not consistent with the official ideology could not be ignored altogether. This is why the potential disloyalty of the prophets is acknowledged in the Succession Treaty of Esarhaddon (SAA 2 6 § 10). Whether or not the warning expressed in this treaty article was already based on concrete experiences is unknown, but the letters of Nabû-rehtu-uṣur written in the very next year show that messages against the king claiming to be of prophetic origin could actually be proclaimed in public.

The Nusku oracle quoted in ABL 1217 r.4-5 proves undisputedly that words presented as divine messages could be used against the king. It is no wonder that extant prophecies of this kind are no longer available to us: any such oracle, if written down, would certainly have been destroyed by the king or by his officials at the first opportunity (cf. Jer 36:11-26!). This may be the reason why we have to content ourselves with such enigmatic sources as the letters of Nabû-rehtu-uṣur unfortunately are.

To all appearances, the oracle of Nusku which proclaimed the destruction of the ruling dynasty and promised the kingship to Sasî was a "false" prophecy, that is, not transmitted in due order but fabricated for political purposes using the proclaimer of the message, the "slave girl," as a decoy. A related case is constituted by the false extispicy which Kudurru was forced to perform, according to which the chief eunuch would take over the kingship (SAA 10 179 r.11). Both were intended to give the impression of a true divine message among the implied audience.

The problem of true and false prophecy emerges from the very nature of prophecy: there is no way of verifying the existence of the most fundamental component in the communication process, the divine sender of the message – it can only be believed. Since it is imperative for any society receptive to prophetic messages to be able to evaluate which words should be regarded as genuine divine messages and which not, there must be some kind of common notion about how a divine message can or may sound to be acceptable. That Nabû-rehtu-uṣur calls the proclaimer of the Nusku oracle a "slave girl" instead of prophetess may indicate that he was reluctant to acknowledge the divine authority behind her words, the message of which was diametrically opposed to what he regarded as a true prophecy. The Succession Treaty of Esarhaddon also implies that words against the king and the crown prince, even if spoken by a prophet, were regarded as doubtful. In the final analysis, then, the criteria for distinguising between true and false prophecy could be only ideological: a prophecy against the ruling king is false, no matter who the proclaimer is and what powers he or she claims to be vested with.[607]

Prophecy and Divination

In the light of the Neo-Assyrian sources discussed in this study, the tendency to consider prophecy an integral part of divination rather than in contrast with it[608] turns out to be justified. The inscriptions in particular make it evident that prophecy constituted an essential part of the divinatory apparatus in the service of the king of Assyria. On the other hand, the inscriptions do make a distinction between prophets (*raggimu* or *mahhû*) and other practitioners of divination whose professional lore is of a different kind. Prophets are never mixed up with haruspices or astrologers, but there are borderline cases, notably dreams and visions,[609] in which the distinction is less clear. However, if dreams and visions are experienced by people other than prophets – by a *šabrû*,[610] a foreign king (Gyges of Lydia),[611] or the entire army[612] – this is usually indicated.

---

[607] On this problem, see Huffmon 1976a, 184; Coggins 1993, 93; Nissinen 1996, 193-195.

[608] See above, p. 6.

[609] On the distinction or, preferably, similarity of these two categories, see Grabbe 1995, 145-148.

[610] Borger 1996, 40-41 A iii 118-127; 100-101 B v 49-76.

[611] Cogan & Tadmor 1977, 75-76; Borger 1996, 30-31 A ii 95-110; 182-183 E 16-17.

[612] Borger 1996, 50 A v 95-103.

The contents of dreams and visions often show a great resemblance to prophecies, and prophetic oracles are indeed called "visions" (*diglu*) a couple of times (SAA 9 11 r.6; SAA 10 294 r.32). However, visions are by no means the monopoly of the prophets but can be seen by others as well; for example, the suspicions of Nabû-rehtu-uṣur about the undertakings of Sasî were initially based on a *diglu* he had had in the month of Marchesvan (VIII), 671 (CT 53 17:10 and 938:10). Hence, it is not so much the contents of the message or even the means of communication but rather the social role and identity that made prophets differ from other mediators of the divine will.

As a form of what is believed to be a divine-human communication, prophecy is presented in line with astrology, extispicy and visionary activity, that is, as one form of divination. In the eyes of the contemporaries, the political and ideological function of the prophetic activity may not have been decidedly different from other kinds of divination. However, the designations *raggimu* and *mahhû* are not interchangeable with designations of other diviners. Evidently the prophets constituted a divinatory category separate from others in terms of professional occupation, divinatory technique and way of life. Thus, both the similarity and dissimilarity of prophecy and divination can be observed; which one is emphasized depends on the observer.[613] Speaking of prophecy as a category separable from (other) diviners does not need to imply the traditional notion of prophecy as "'higher up' on the evolutionary ladder"[614] of divine-human communication; what matters is the identity of the prophets in contrast to related divinatory identities. This identity includes both divinatory techniques and social roles, and the Neo-Assyrian prophets evidently represent a class of their own in both respects.

The view of a modern scholar is, of course, that of a total outsider who does not participate in the social structures of which the observed phenomena are part. Therefore, the modern distinctions may or may not conform with the conceptions represented by the sources. However, when we take the views concerning prophecy and divination in contemporary sources under scrutiny, we do not find a synchronic agreement about their sameness or differences either. While in the eyes of the draftsmen of the inscriptions, prophecy, astrology, extispicy and other kinds of divination were by and large equal in religious function and political significance, the prophets and diviners themselves, from the point of view of their own identities and idiosyncrasies, would not necessarily have subscribed to this view.

There are no records of major clashes between prophets, scholars and other diviners; nevertheless, a few traces of competition between prophets and scholars are observable. At least some scholars seem to have been somewhat dismissive of the expertise of the prophets: the exorcist Urad-Gula was

[613] Cf. Overholt 1989, 141: "To speak of divination and prophecy as in some respects 'different' implies an emphasis on the observable activities of the bearers of these roles (physical techniques over against 'direct' inspiration, waiting to be consulted over against taking the initiative, etc.). To speak of them as the 'same' assumes that the most relevant point of comparison is the social function of intermediation/communication."

[614] Barstad 1993, 47.

disappointed with the services of a prophet whom he consulted only after having tried everything else (SAA 10 294), whereas the astrologer Bel-ušezib feels his professional skills and identity underestimated in comparison with nameless "prophets and prophetesses" (SAA 10 109). This may correspond with the differences in their art of divination and social roles. The prophets were not educated in the canonical scriptural tradition and they did not draw their messages from interpretation of observable omens. Instead, they were trained to transmit the direct speech of the gods, presumably in a state of trance. They were not obliged to produce any kind of rational evidence for the divine word. This might have led to a certain degree of disparagement on the part of the scholars who had enough trouble with various dilettantes who provided the king with unreliable information.[615]

As far as can be concluded from the available tiny pieces of evidence, the eventual discordance between prophets and diviners had to do with institutional prestige rather than with religious or ideological matters. When it comes to the application of royal ideology to concrete actions, the scholars seem to have had no difficulty in relying on prophetic words (Bel-ušezib: SAA 10 111; Nabû-nadin-šumi: SAA 10 284). Hence, while the social role of the prophets differed from other diviners, the social function of prophecy was essentially the same as that of divination in general. In addition, the prophecies that were written down and even compiled in larger collections, possibly by the same scholars that authored the royal insciptions, could be equalled with the scholarly tradition in general.

Prophets and Prophecy in Non-Prophetical Sources

The references to prophecy in non-prophetical Neo-Assyrian sources are few and sporadic. Still, they are indispensable sources that illustrate many important aspects of the role of prophecy in Neo-Assyrian society that are not visible in the oracles which were considered to be worth preserving and deposited in the archives. In the texts examined in this study, the prophets are viewed from the outsider's standpoint and their utterances are utilized by people who found them useful for different purposes.

The identity of the prophets seems to be of very limited importance for those who refer to their activities or quote their words. Outside the 13 names included in the Neo-Assyrian prophetic corpus,[616] only two additional names can be found in non-prophetical sources: the prophetess Mullissu-abu-uṣri (LAS 317) and the prophet Quqî (SAA 7 9). In the latter case, the name is

---

615 Cf. Starr 1990, XXXI-XXXII.

616 Ahat-abiša (SAA 9 1.8), Bayâ (SAA 9 1.4, [2.2]), Dunnaša-amur (SAA 9 9 and 10; = Sinqiša-amur?), Ilussa-amur (SAA 9 1.5), Issar-beli-da''ini (SAA 9 1.7), Issar-la-tašiyaṭ (SAA 9 1.1), La-dagil-ili (SAA 9 1.10, 2.3 and 3), Mullissu-kabtat (SAA 9 7), [Nabû]-hussanni (SAA 9 2.1), Remutti-Allati (SAA 9 1.3), Sinqiša-amur (SAA 9 1.2, [2.5]), Tašmetu-ereš (SAA 9 6) and Urkittu-šarrat (SAA 9 2.4). See Parpola 1997c, XLVIII-LII.

required by the genre of SAA 7 9 as a name list, while in LAS 317 the name of the prophetess is needed because the writer of the letter, Adad-ahu-iddina, does not use her words in a general way for the purpose of encouraging the king or justifying his own suggestions but specifically calls for the king's opinion of her words that he himself is reluctant to accept. In the remaining cases, there seems to have been no specific reason to mention names. In the case of Bel-ušezib (SAA 10 109), though, the general reference to "prophets and prophetesses" may indicate his intentional indifference to the prophets as persons, but otherwise it is the activity of the prophets or the words transmitted by them that matters in the first place, not their personalities.

No writer refers to prophecy without good cause. The motives are manifold, ranging from personal matters like jealousy (Bel-ušezib: SAA 10 109) or despair (Urad-Gula: SAA 10 294) to political counselling (Nabû-nadin-šumi: SAA 10 284). A pseudoprophecy against Esarhaddon is denounced on the basis of a treaty article (SAA 2 6 § 10) in which such an obligation is imposed (Nabû-rehtu-uṣur: ABL 1217). One writer quotes a prophetic oracle to convince the king about the justification of a procedure that had caused astonishment and fear (Mar-Issar: SAA 10 352), another repeats the words of a prophetess in a letter to the king because he himself is not convinced that he should take heed of them (Adad-ahu-iddina: LAS 317).

If we did not have our handful of extant prophetic oracles at our disposal, it could be claimed in the light of the above-presented material that in the Neo-Assyrian Empire prophetic oracles were hardly written down at all. It is usually the spoken word of a prophet(ess), viz. a god(dess), that is referred to without even alluding to any kind of scribal activity as a vehicle for the divine message. This explains the random character of the preserved documents of prophecy and also gives cause for suspicions that what we see is nothing more than the tip of the iceberg. Our knowledge of the role of the prophets and the contents of the messages transmitted by them is more due to coincidences than to a careful and systematic *Überlieferung* of prophetic oracles. Fortunately for us, Esarhaddon and Assurbanipal seem to have been exceptions in this respect as they, unlike their predecessors, let a number of oracles be collected, copied and preserved in their files. Thanks to them we know that prophecies *could* be written down and even deposited on special occasions, even if this was not the standard procedure. These copies could also be utilized and reinterpreted by the scholars who compiled other works, notably the inscriptions.

In the case of Esarhaddon it can be plausibly argued that the scholars who authored his inscriptions actually made use of the prophetic oracles addressed to Esarhaddon, and the possibility cannot be ruled out that the same hands were responsible for the compilation of the collections of prophecies. The same cannot be said of the inscriptions of Assurbanipal in which prophecy is referred to but the surviving oracles show no direct influence on these references. Since, however, the extant five tablets (SAA 9 7-11) in all likelihood do not represent the whole corpus of prophecy written down during his reign, the question of whether or not the scholars who wrote the inscriptions of Assurbanipal actually utilized written prophecy must be left in abeyance until further documents, hopefully, come to light.

In the letters, the recognizing of a prophetic quotation is usually not difficult. In some cases, the words are said to have been delivered by a *raggimu* (SAA 10 352; LAS 317), and even in the remaining ones the contents of the quotation leave little doubt about its prophetic – or pseudoprophetic – origin (SAA 10 111 and 284; ABL 1217). The inscriptions, particularly those of Assurbanipal, are more problematic because prophetic words cannot always be distinguished from divine messages of another kind. If divine orders are obtained by means of extispicy, this is usually recognizable by terminology, but, as already stated, the borderline between prophecy and visions experienced by people other than prophets is sometimes difficult to draw. For the inscriptionists who embedded the divine messages in their accounts, it does not seem to have been imperative to specify every time their actual transmitters. This does not mean, however, that prophecy was not regarded as a divinatory category in its own right. The *ummânu* of Assurbanipal who knows to itemize "good omens, dreams, speech omens and prophetic messages" (B v 95) shows that the distinction between different methods of divination is not unfamiliar to him.

Esarhaddon and Assurbanipal are the only Assyrian kings whose inscriptions include references to prophecy. Again, recognizing this should not lead to the conclusion that the prophetic activity would have been restricted to the time of these kings only. Instead, the fact that Esarhaddon and Assurbanipal – unlike their predecessors, as it seems[617] – deposited prophetic oracles as well as referred to them in their inscriptions, emphasizes the special appreciation of prophecy by these two kings – and not only of prophecy itself but of the divinatory tradition as a whole, of which prophecy formed a part. The same kings who let the prophecies be written down also gave the imprimatur for the inscriptions which had to accord with the views and preferences of the king even if their literary form was shaped by the scholars.[618] The draftsmen who produced the inscriptions of Esarhaddon and Assurbanipal did not just record events in a chronological order, and their technique of composition differed from that of those who composed the annals of the previous Neo-Assyrian kings. In contrast to their predecessors, they are profoundly concerned with hemerology, celestial and other omens, extispicy and prophecy.[619]

The references to the prophetic messages in the inscriptions of Esarhaddon and Assurbanipal, thus, cannot be sufficiently explained by the simple fact that these kings actually received them. The question remains why the previous kings of Assyria failed to mention prophecy in their inscriptions. Rather

---

[617] Note, however, that no archives of the Assyrian kings before Esarhaddon have been found so far (Weippert 1981, 99).

[618] Tadmor 1981, 32.

[619] See Weippert 1981, 99; Brinkman 1983, 36-37. The only exception to this rule is apparently the scribe who composed the recension E of Esarhaddon's Bab. A (Borger 1956 § 11) inscription omitting all references to divination; see Cogan 1983, 78-84.

than assuming that they did not receive prophetic messages at all, this may be accounted for the fact that, according to the available documentation, Esarhaddon was the first and Assurbanipal the last Assyrian king who let the prophecies be written down and, above all, filed them in their archives and even had individual oracles compiled in larger collections. This gave the writers of the inscriptions something to rely on, and more: the prophecies were no longer disposable *ad hoc* utterances concerning a specific case but became part of the written tradition, a reference record that could be used and interpreted by succeeding generations.[620] Given the limited set of sources, it is impossible to be certain whether or not this development in Assyria is historically limited to the time of Esarhaddon and Assurbanipal only; if this is the case, then the phenomenon of collecting and reusing prophecy was rather short-lived in Assyria when compared with the huge process of reinterpretation of prophecy in the Hebrew Bible. Be that as it may, the Assyrian sources make it possible to observe the beginnings of a development similar to that, which in the case of the Hebrew Bible, has generated the biblical prophetic literature.

---

[620] Cf. Ellis 1989, 143.

BIBLIOGRAPHY

Albright, W. F.

1958 "An Ostracon from Calah and the North-Israelite Diaspora." *BASOR* 149, 33-36.

Aro, Jussi

1966 "Remarks on the Practice of Extispicy in the Time of Esarhaddon and Assurbanipal." In *La divination en Mésopotamie ancienne et dans les régions voisines.* CRRAI 14. Paris, pp. 109-117.

Auld, A. Graeme

1983 "Prophets through the Looking Glass: Between Writings and Moses." *JSOT* 27, 3-23.

1984 "Prophets and Prophecy in Jeremiah and Kings." *ZAW* 96, 66-82.

Aynard, J.-M.

1957 *Le Prisme du Louvre AO 19.939*. Bibliothèque de l'École des Hautes Études 309. Paris.

Barstad, Hans M.

1993 "No Prophets? Recent Developments in Biblical Prophetic Research and Ancient Near Eastern Prophecy." *JSOT* 57, 39-60.

Bauer, Theo

1933 *Das Inschriftenwerk Assurbanipals, I–II.* Assyriologische Bibliothek, Neue Folge 1–2. Leipzig. (Repr. 1972.)

Beaulieu, Paul-Alain

1993 "The Historical Background of the Uruk Prophecy." In Cohen & Snell & Weisberg (eds.) 1993, 41-52.

Becking, Bob

1992 *The Fall of Samaria: An Historical and Archaeological Study*. Studies in the History of the Ancient Near East 2. Leiden etc.

Ben-Barak, Zafrira

1986 "Succession to the Throne in Israel and in Assyria." *OLP* 17, 85-100.

Blenkinsopp, Joseph

1995 *Sage, Priest, Prophet: Religious and Intellectual Leadership in Ancient Israel.* Louisville, Kentucky.

Borger, Rykle

1956 *Die Inschriften Asarhaddons, Königs von Assyrien.* AfO.B9. Graz.

1971 "Gott Marduk und Gott-König Šulgi als Propheten: Zwei prophetische Texte." *BiOr* 38, 3-24.

1988 "König Sanheribs Eheglück." *ARRIM* 6, 5-11.

1996 *Beiträge zum Inschriftenwerk Assurbanipals: Die Prismenklassen A, B, C = K, D, E, F, G, H, J und T sowie andere Inschriften*. Wiesbaden.

Bottéro, Jean

1992 *Mesopotamia: Writing, Reasoning, and the Gods*. Trans. Z. Bahrani and M. Van De Mieroop. Chicago/London.

Brinkman, J. A.

1965 "Ur: 721-605 B.C." *Or* NS 34, 241-258.

1968 *A Political History of Post-Kassite Babylonia, 1158-722 B.C.* AnOr 43. Roma.

1973 "Sennacherib's Babylonian Problem: An Interpretation." *JCS* 25, 89-95.

1977 "Notes on Arameans and Chaldeans in Southern Mesopotamiain the Early Seventh Century B.C." *Or* NS 46, 304-325.

1983 "Through a Glass Darkly: Esarhaddon's Retrospects on the Downfall of Babylon." *JAOS* 103, 35-42.

1984 *Prelude to Empire: Babylonian Society and Politics, 747-626 B.C.* Occasional Publications of the Babylonian Fund 7. Philadelphia.

1987/90 "Marduk-šapik-zēri." *RLA* 7, 378.

Carroll, Robert P.

1983 "Poets not Prophets: A Response to 'Prophets through the Looking Glass.'" *JSOT* 27, 25-31.

1989 "Prophecy and Society." In R. E. Clements (ed.), *The World of Ancient Israel: Sociological, Anthropological and Political Perspectives*. Cambridge, pp. 203-225.

1990 "Whose Prophet? Whose History? Whose Social Reality? Troubling the Interpretative Community again. Notes towards a Response to T. W. Overholt's Critique." *JSOT* 48, 33-49.

Carter, Elizabeth & Stolper, Matthew W.

1984 *Elam: Surveys of Political History and Archaeology*. University of California Publications: Near Eastern Studies 25. Berkeley etc.

Chamaza, G. W. Vera

1992 "Sargon II's Ascent to the Throne: The Political Situation." *SAAB* 6, 21-33.

Cogan, Mordechai (Morton)

1974 *Imperialism and Religion: Assyria, Judah and Israel in the Eighth and Seventh Centuries B.C.E.* SBL.MS 19. Missoula, Montana.

1983 "Omens and Ideology in the Babylon Inscription of Esarhaddon." In Tadmor & Weinfeld (eds.) 1983, 76-87.

Cogan, Mordechai & Tadmor, Hayim

1977 "Gyges and Ashurbanipal: A Study in Literary Transmission." *Or* NS 46, 65-85.

Coggins, Richard J.

1993 "Prophecy – True and False." In H. A. McKay & D. J. A. Clines (eds.), *Of Prophet's Visions and the Wisdom of Sages: Essays in Honor of R. Norman Whybray on his Seventieth Birthday*. JSOTS 162. Sheffield, pp. 80-94.

Cohen, Mark E. & Snell, Daniel C. & Weisberg, David B.

1993 *The Tablet and the Scroll: Near Eastern Studies in Honor of William W. Hallo*. Bethesda, Maryland.

Cole, Steven W.

1986 "Four Early Neo-Babylonian Lists of Officials and Professionals from Nippur." *JAC* 1, 127-143.

1996 *Nippur in Late Assyrian Times c. 755-612 BC*. SAAS 4. Helsinki.

Cryer, Frederick H.

1991 "Der Prophet und der Magier. Bemerkungen anhand einer überholten Diskussion." In R. Liwak & S. Wagner (eds.), *Prophetie und geschichtliche Wirklichkeit im alten Israel: Festschrift für Siegfried Herrmann*. Stuttgart etc., pp. 79-88.
1994 *Divination in Ancient Israel and its Near Eastern Environment: A Socio-Historical Investigation*. JSOTS 142. Sheffield.

Dalley, Stephanie & Postgate, J. N.

1984 *The Tablets from Fort Shalmaneser*. CTN 3. London.

Dalman, Gustaf H.

1938 Aramäisch-neuhebräisches Handwörterbuch zu Targum, Talmud und Midrasch. Hildesheim (repr. 1967).

Delattre, A.

1889 "The Oracles Given in Favour of Esarhaddon." *The Babylonian and Oriental Record* 3, 25-31.

Deller, Karlheinz

1965 (Review of CAD A/1.) *Or* NS 34, 259-274.

Dietrich, Manfried

1967 "Neue Quellen zur Geschichte Babyloniens, I." *WO* 4, 61-103.
1968 "Neue Quellen zur Geschichte Babyloniens, II." *WO* 4, 183-251.
1970 *Die Aramäer Südbabyloniens in der Sargonidenzeit (700-648)*. AOAT 7. Kevelaer/Neukirchen-Vluyn.
1973 "Prophetie in den Keilschrifttexten." *JARG* 1, 15-44.
1979 *Neo-Babylonian Letters fron the Kuyunjik Collection*. CT 54. London.

Dietrich, Manfried & Loretz, Oswald (eds.)

1993 *Mesopotamica – Ugaritica – Biblica. Festschrift für Kurt Bergerhof zur Vollendung seines 70. Lebensjahres am 7. Mai 1992*. AOAT 232. Kevelaer/Neukirchen-Vluyn.

Dijkstra, Meindert

1980 *Gods voorstelling: Predikatieve expressie van zelfopenbaring in oudoosterse teksten en Deutero-Jesaja*. Dissertationes Neerlandicae, Series Theologica 2. Kampen.
1995 "Is Balaam Also among the Prophets?" *JBL* 114, 43-64.

Dion, Paul E.

1991 "Deuteronomy 13: The Suppression of Alien Religious Propaganda in Israel during the Late Monarchical Era." In B. Halpern & D. W. Hobson (eds.), *Law and Ideology in Monarchic Israel*. JSOTS 124. Sheffield, pp. 147-216.

Donner, H. & Röllig, W.

1979^4/ 73^3/76^3 *Kanaanäische und aramäische Inschriften I–III*. Wiesbaden.

Drijvers, H.J.W.

1980 *Cults and Beliefs at Edessa*. Études préliminaires aux religions orientales dans l'empire Romain 82. Leiden.

Durand, Jean-Marie

1988 *Archives épistolaires de Mari I/1*. ARM 26. Paris.
1997 "Les prophéties des textes de Mari." In Heintz (ed.) 1997, 115-134.

Ebeling, Erich

1953 *Literarische Keilschrifttexte aus Assur*. Berlin.

Ellis, Maria deJong

1987 "The Goddess Kititum Speaks to King Ibalpiel: Oracle Texts from Ishchali." *MARI* 5, 235-266.

1989 "Observations on Mesopotamian Oracles and Prophetic Texts: Literary and Historiographic Considerations." *JCS* 41, 127-186.

Fales, Frederick Mario

1980 "New Assyrian Letters from the Kuyunjik Collection." *AfO* 27, 136-153.

1982 "The Enemy in Assyrian Royal Inscriptions: 'The Moral Judgement.'" In Nissen & Renger (eds.) 1982, 425-435.

1988 "Prosopography of the Neo-Assyrian Empire, 2: The Many Faces of Nabû-šarru-uṣur." *SAAB* 2, 105-124.

1990 "A Payment in Reeds." *SAAB* 4, 73-75.

Fales, F.M. (ed.)

1981 *Assyrian Royal Inscriptions: New Horizons in Literary, Ideological and Historical Analysis*. OAC 17. Roma.

Fales, F.M. & Lanfranchi, G.B.

1981 "ABL 1237: The Role of the Cimmerians in a Letter to Esarhaddon." *East and West* 31, 9-33.

1997 "The Impact of Oracular Material on the Political Utterances and Political Action of the Sargonid Dynasty." In Heintz (ed.) 1997, 99-114.

Fales, F.M. & Postgate, J.N.

1992 *Imperial Administrative Records, Part I: Palace and Temple Administration*. SAA 7. Helsinki.

1994 *Imperial Administrative Records, Part II: Provincial and Military Administration*. SAA 11. Helsinki.

Fox, Michael V.

1973 "*Ṭôb* as a Covenant Terminology." *BASOR* 209, 41-42.

Frame, Grant

1992 *Babylonia 689-627 B.C.: A Political History*. Uitgaven van het Nederlands Historisch-Archaeologisch Instituut te Istanbul. Istanbul.

1995 *Rulers of Babylonia from the Second Dynasty of Isin to the End of Assyrian Domination (1157–612 BC)*. RIMB 2. Toronto etc.

Gadd, C. J.

1958 "The Harran Inscription of Nabonidus." *Anatolian Studies* 8, 35-92.

Gallery, Maureen

1980 "The Office of the *šatammu* in the Old Babylonian Period." *AfO* 27, 1-36.

Gerardi, Pamela DeHart

1987 *Assurbanipal's Elamite Campaigns: A Literary and Political Study*. Diss. University of Pennsylvania.

Grabbe, Lester L.

1995 *Priests, Prophets, Diviners, Sages: A Socio-Historical Study of Religious Specialists in Ancient Israel*. Valley Forge, Pennsylvania.

Grayson, A. Kirk

1975a *Assyrian and Babylonian Chronicles.* TCS 5. Locust Valley, New York.

1975b *Babylonian Historical-Literary Texts.* Toronto Semitic Texts and Studies 3. Toronto/Buffalo.

1980 "The Chronology of the Reign of Ashurbanipal." *ZA* 70, 227-245.

1980/83 "Königslisten und Chroniken. B. Akkadisch." *RLA* 6, 86-135.

1991 "Assyria: Sennacherib and Esarhaddon (704-669 B.C.). Assyria 668-635 B.C.: The Reign of Ashurbanipal." In *The Cambridge Ancient History.* Second Edition, Volume III, Part 2. Cambridge etc., pp. 103-161.

Grayson, A. K. & Lambert, W. G.

1964 "Akkadian Prophecies." *JCS* 18, 7-30.

Green, Tamara

1992 *The City of the Moon God: Religious Traditions of Harran.* Religions in the Graeco-Roman World 114. Leiden etc.

1996 "The Presence of the Goddess in Harran." In E. N. Lane (ed.), *Cybele, Attis and Related Cults. Essays in Memory of M. J. Vermaseren.* Religions in the Graeco-Roman World 131. Leiden etc.

Haldar, Alfred

1945 *Associations of Cult Prophets among the Semites.* Uppsala.

Heintz, Jean-Georges

1997 "La 'fin' des prophètes bibliques? Nouvelles théories et documents sémitiques anciens." In Heintz (ed.) 1997, 195-214.

Heintz, Jean-Georges (ed.)

1997 *Oracles et prophéties dans l'antiquité: Actes du colloque de Strasbourg 15-17 juin 1995.* Université des Sciences Humaines de Strasbourg, Travaux du Centre de Recherche sur le Proche-Orient et la Grèce Antiques 15. Paris.

Hoftijzer, J. & van der Kooij, G.

1991 *The Balaam Text from Deir Alla Re-evaluated: Proceedings of the International Symposium held at Leiden, 21–24 August 1989.* Leiden.

Holloway, S.W.

1995 "Harran: Cultic Geography in the Neo-Assyrian Empire and its Implications for Sennacherib's 'Letter to Hezekiah' in 2 Kings." In S. W. Holloway & L. K. Handy (eds.), *The Pitcher is Broken. Memorial Essays for G. W. Ahlström.* JSOTS 190. Sheffield, pp. 276-314.

Hölscher, Gustav

1914 *Die Propheten: Untersuchungen zur Religionsgeschichte Israels.* Leipzig.

Huffmon, Herbert B.

1976a "The Origins of Prophecy." In F. M. Cross, W. E. Lemke & P. D. Miller (eds.), *Magnalia Dei. The Mighty Acts of God: Essays on the Bible and Archaeology in Memory of G. Ernest Wright.* Garden City, New York, pp. 171-186.

1976b "Prophecy in the Ancient Near East." *The Interpreter's Dictionary of the Bible, Supplementary Volume, pp. 697-700.*

1992 "Ancient Near Eastern Prophecy." *Anchor Bible Dictionary* 5, 477-482.

Hunger, Hermann

1968 *Babylonische und assyrische Kolophone.* AOAT 2. Kevelaer/Neukirchen-Vluyn.

1987 "Empfehlungen an den König." In Rochberg-Halton (ed.) 1987, 157-166.

Hunger, Hermann & Kaufman, Stephen A.

1975 "A New Akkadian Prophecy Text." *JAOS* 95, 371-375.

Hurowitz, Victor Avigdor

1993 "ABL 1285 and the Hebrew Bible: Literary Topoi in Urad Gula's Letter of Petition to Assurbanipal." *SAAB* 7, 9-17.

Ishida, Tomoo

1977 *The Royal Dynasties in Ancient Israel: A Study on the Formation and Development of Royal-Dynastic Ideology*. BZAW 142. Berlin/New York.

Jacobsen, Thorkild

1943 "Primitive Democracy in Ancient Mesopotamia." *JNES* 2, 159-172.

1957 "Early Political Development in Mesopotamia." *ZA* 52, 91-140.

1959 "An Ancient Mesopotamian Trial for Homicide." In *Studia Biblica et Orientalia 3: Oriens Antiquus*. AnBib 12. Rome, pp. 130-150.

1978/79 "Iphur-Kishi and His Times." *AfO* 26, 1-14.

Jacoby, Felix

1958 *Die Fragmente der griechischen Historiker*. III C/1. Leiden.

Jenni, Ernst

1981 "Dtn 19,16: *sarā* 'Falschheit.'" In A. Caquot & M. Delcor (eds.), *Mélanges bibliques et orientaux en l'honneur de M. Henri Cazelles*. AOAT 212. Kevelaer/Neukirchen-Vluyn, pp. 201-211.

Jepsen, Alfred

1934 *Nabi: Soziologische Studien zur alttestamentlichen Literatur und Religionsgeschichte*. München.

Johag, I.

1977 "*ṭwb* – Terminus Technicus in Vertrags- und Bündnisformularen des Alten Orients und des Alten Testaments." In H.-J. Fabry (ed.), *Bausteine biblischer Theologie: FS G. Johannes Botterweck*. BBB 50. Köln/Bonn, pp. 3-23.

Kaiser, Otto

1993 *Der Gott des Alten Testaments. Theologie des Alten Testaments 1*. UTB.W 1747. Göttingen.

Klengel-Brandt, Evelyn & Radner, Karen

1997 "Die Stadtbeamten von Assur und ihre Siegel." In Parpola & Whiting (eds.) 1997, 137-159.

Kwasman, Theodore & Parpola, Simo

1991 *Legal Transactions of the Royal Court of Nineveh, Part I: Tiglath-Pileser III through Esarhaddon*. SAA 6. Helsinki.

Laato, Antti

1996 *History and Ideology in the Old Testament Prophetic Literature: A Semiotic Approach to the Reconstruction of the Proclamation of the Historical Prophets*. CB.OT 41. Stockholm.

Labat, René

1959 "Asarhaddon et la ville de Zaqqap." *RA* 53, 113-118.

Lambert, W. G.

1960 *Babylonian Wisdom Literature*. Oxford.

1978 *The Background of Jewish Apocalyptic*. The Ethel M. Wood Lecture delivered before the University of London on 22 February 1977. London.

Landsberger, Benno

1965 *Brief des Bischofs von Esagila an König Asarhaddon*. Mededelingen der Koninklijke Nederlandse Akademie van Wetenschappen, afd. Letterkunde. Nieuwe Reeks 28/6. Amsterdam.

Landsberger, Benno & Bauer, Theo

1927 "Zu neuveröffentlichten Geschichtsquellen der Zeit von Asarhaddon bis Nabonid." *ZA* 37, 61-98.

Lanfranchi, Giovanni B.

1989 "Scholars and Scholarly Tradition in Neo-Assyrian Times: A Case Study." *SAAB* 3, 99-114.

Langdon, Stephen

1912 *Die Neubabylonischen Königsinschriften*. VAB 4. Leipzig.

Larsen, Mogens Trolle

1974 "Unusual Eponymy-Datings from Mari and Assyria." *RA* 68, 14-24.

Lemaire, André

1997 "Oracles, politique et littérature dans les royaumes Araméens et Transjordaniens (IXe-VIIIe s. av. n.è.)." In Heintz (ed.) 1997, 171-193.

Levinson, B. M.

1995 "'But You Shall Surely Kill Him.' The Text-Critical and Neo-Assyrian Evidence for MT Deut 13:20." In Georg Braulik (ed.), *Bundesdokument und Gesetz. Studien zum Deuteronomium*. HBS 4. Freiburg, pp. 37-63.

Lewis, Theodore J.

1996 "The Identity and Function of El/Baal Berith." *JBL* 115, 401-423.

Lewy, Hildegard

1952 "Nitokris-Naqî'a." *JNES* 11, 264-286.

Lewy, Hildegard & Lewy, Julius

1948 "The God Nusku." *Or* NS 17, 146-159.

Lindblom, Johannes

1934 *Profetismen i Israel*. Stockholm.
1962 *Prophecy in Ancient Israel*. Philadelphia.

Lipiński, Edward

1994 *Studies in Aramaic Inscriptions and Onomastics, II*. OLA 57. Leuven.

Longman, Tremper, III

1991 *Fictional Akkadian Autobiography: A Generic and Comparative Study*. Winona Lake, Indiana.

Loretz, Oswald

1985 "Die 'Hörner' der Neumondsichel – Eine Keilschriftparallele (Ee V 13-18) zu KTU 1.18 IV 9-11." In A. Caquot, S. Légasse & M. Tardieu (eds.), *Mélanges bibliques et orientaux en l'honneur de M. Mathias Delcor*. AOAT 215. Kevelaer/Neukirchen-Vluyn, pp. 113-116.

Luckenbill, D. D.

1924 *The Annals of Sennacherib*. The University of Chicago Oriental Institute Publications 2. Chicago.

Machinist, Peter

1976 "Literature as Politics: The Tukulti-ninurta Epic and the Bible." *CBQ* 38.

Malamat, Abraham

1987 "A Forerunner of Biblical Prophecy: The Mari Documents." In P. D. Miller, Jr. & P. D. Hanson & S. D. McBride (eds.), *Ancient Israelite Religion: Essays in Honor of Frank Moore Cross*. Philadelphia, pp. 68-82.

Mattila, Raija

1987 "The Political Status of Elam after 653 B.C. According to *ABL* 839." *SAAB* 1, 27-30.

1990 "Balancing the Accounts of the Royal New Year's Reception." *SAAB* 4, 7-22.

Mattila, Raija (ed.)

1995 *Nineveh, 612 BC: The Glory and Fall of the Assyrian Empire. Catalogue of the 10th Anniversary Exhibition of the Neo-Assyrian Text Corpus Project*. Helsinki.

Mayer, Walter

1988 "Der babylonische Feldzug Tukultī-Ninurtas I. von Assyrien." *Cananea selecta. Festschrift für Oswald Loretz zum 60. Geburtstag*. SEL 5, pp. 143-161.

1993 "Die chronologische Einordnung der Kimmerier-Briefe aus der Zeit Sargons II." In Dietrich & Loretz (eds.) 1993, 145-176.

1995 *Politik und Kriegskunst der Assyrer*. ALASPM 9. Münster.

McEwan, G. J. P.

1982 "Agade after the Gutian Destruction: The Afterlife of a Mesopotamian City." *AfO.B* 19, 8-15.

Menzel, Brigitte

1981 *Assyrische Tempel. Band I: Untersuchungen zu Kult, Administration und Personal. Band II: Anmerkungen, Textbuch, Tabellen und Indices*. Studia Pohl, Series Maior 10/I-II. Rome.

Mieroop, Marc Van De

1993 "An Inscribed Bead of Queen Zakûtu." In Cohen & Snell & Weisberg (eds.) 1993, 259-261.

Millard, Alan

1985 "La prophétie et l'écriture – Israël, Aram, Assyrie." *RHR* 202, 125-144.

1994 *The Eponyms of the Neo-Assyrian Empire 910–612 BC*. SAAS 2. Helsinki.

Moren, S. M.

1980 "Note brève." *RA* 74, 190-191.

Nassouhi, E.

1924/25 "Prisme d'Assurbânipal daté de sa trentième année, provenant du temple de Gula à Babylone." *AfK* 2, 97-106.

Nissen, Hans-Jörg & Renger, Johannes (eds.)

1982 *Mesopotamien und seine Nachbarn: Politische und kulturelle Wechselbeziehungen im Alten Vorderasien vom 4. bis 1. Jahrtausend v. Chr.* Berliner Beiträge zum vorderen Orient 1 [= CRRAI 25]. Berlin.

Nissinen, Martti

1991 *Prophetie, Redaktion und Fortschreibung im Hoseabuch: Studien zum Werdegang eines Prophetenbuches im Lichte von Hos 4 und 11.* AOAT 231. Kevelaer/Neukirchen-Vluyn.

1993 "Die Relevanz der neuassyrischen Prophetie für die alttestamentliche Forschung." In Dietrich & Loretz (eds.) 1993, 217-258.

1996 "Falsche Prophetie in neuassyrischer und deuteronomistischer Darstellung." In Veijola (ed.) 1996, 172-195.

Noort, Eduard

1977 *Untersuchungen zum Gottesbescheid in Mari: Die "Mariprophetie" in der alttestamentlichen Forschung.* AOAT 202. Kevelaer/Neukirchen-Vluyn.

Noth, Martin

1928 *Die israelitischen Personennamen im Rahmen der gemeinsemitischen Namengebung.* BWANT 3. Folge Heft 10. Stuttgart.

Onasch, Hans-Ulrich

1994 *Die assyrischen Eroberungen Ägyptens. Teil 1: Kommentare und Anmerkungen.* ÄAT 27/1. Wiesbaden.

Oppenheim, A. Leo

1954/56 "Sumerian: inim.gar, Akkadian: *egirrû*, Greek: *kledon*." *AfO* 17, 49-55.

1956 *The Interpretation of Dreams in the Ancient Near East.* Philadelphia.

1966 "Perspectives on Mesopotamian Divination." In *La divination en Mésopotamie ancienne et dans les régions voisines.* CRRAI 14. Paris, pp. 35-43.

Overholt, Thomas W.

1989 *Channels of Prophecy: The Social Dynamics of Prophetic Activity.* Minneapolis.

1990 "Prophecy in History: The Social Reality of Intermediation." *JSOT* 48, 3-29.

Parpola, Simo

1970a *Letters from Assyrian Scholars to the Kings Esarhaddon and Assurbanipal. Part I: Texts.* AOAT 5/1. Kevelaer/Neukirchen-Vluyn.

1970b *Neo-Assyrian Toponyms.* AOAT 6. Kevelaer/Neukirchen-Vluyn.

1972 "A Letter from Šamaš-šumu-ukīn to Esarhaddon." *Iraq* 34, 21-34.

1980 "The Murderer of Sennacherib." In Bendt Alster (ed.), *Death in Mesopotamia.* Mesopotamia 8 (= CRRAI 26). Copenhagen, pp. 171-182.

1983 *Letters from Assyrian Scholars to the Kings Esarhaddon and Assurbanipal. Part II: Commentary and Appendices.* AOAT 5/2. Kevelaer/Neukirchen-Vluyn.

1987a "The Forlorn Scholar." In Rochberg-Halton (ed.) 1987, 257-278.

1987b "Neo-Assyrian Treaties from the Royal Archives of Nineveh." *JCS* 39, 161-189.

1988 "The Neo-Assyrian Word for 'Queen.'" *SAAB* 2, 73-76.

1993a *Letters from Assyrian and Babylonian Scholars.* SAA 10. Helsinki.

1993b "Mesopotamian Astrology and Astronomy as Domains of the Mesopotamian 'Wisdom.'" In H. D. Galter (ed.), *Die Rolle der Astronomie in den Kulturen Mesopotamiens.* Grazer Morgenländische Studien 3. Graz, pp. 47-59.

1995 "The Assyrian Cabinet." In M. Dietrich & O. Loretz (eds.), *Vom Alten Orient zum Alten Testament. Festschrift für Wolfram Freiherrn von Soden zum 85. Geburtstag am 19. Juni 1993.* AOAT 240. Kevelaer/Neukirchen-Vluyn, pp. 379-401.

1997a *The Standard Babylonian Epic of Gilgamesh. Cuneiform Text, Transliteration, Glossary, Indices and Sign List.* State Archives of Assyria Cuneiform Texts 1. Helsinki.

1997b "The Man Without a Scribe and the Question of Literacy in the Assyrian Empire." In B. Pongratz-Leisten & H. Kühne & P. Xella (eds.), Ana šadî Labnāni lū allik. *Beiträge zu altorientalischen und mittelmeerischen Kulturen. Festschrift für Wolfgang Röllig*. Kevelaer/Neukirchen-Vluyn, pp. 315-324.

1997c *Assyrian Prophecies*. SAA 9. Helsinki.

Parpola, Simo & Watanabe, Kazuko

1988 *Neo-Assyrian Treaties and Loyalty Oaths*. SAA 2. Helsinki.

Parpola, Simo & Whiting, Robert (eds.)

1997 *ASSYRIA 1995: Proceedings of the 10th Anniversary Symposium of the Neo-Assyrian Text Corpus Project Helsinki, September 7-11, 1995*. Helsinki.

Payne Smith, R.

1902 *A Compendious Syriac Dictionary Founded upon the Thesaurus Syriacus of R. Payne Smith*. Oxford. (Repr. 1979.)

Pečírková, Jana

1985 "Divination and Politics in the Late Assyrian Empire." *ArOr* 53,155-168.

1993 "Politics and Tradition in the Assyrian Empire." In J. Zabłocka & S. Zawadzki (eds.), *Šulmu IV: Everyday Life in Ancient Near East. Papers Presented at the International Conference Poznań, 19–22 September, 1989*. Uniwersytet im. Adama Mickiewicza w Poznaniu. Seria Historia 149. Poznań, pp. 243-248.

Piepkorn, A. C.

1933 *Historical Prism Inscriptions of Ashurbanipal I: Editions E, B_{1-5}, D & K*. AS 5. Chicago.

Pinches, T. G.

1939/41 "Keilschrifttexte nach Kopien von T. G. Pinches. 12. Ein babylonischer Eponym." *AfO* 13, 51-54.

Pingree, David & Reiner, Erica

1974/77 "A Neo-Babylonian Report on Seasonal Hours." *AfO* 25, 50-55.

Pohlmann, Karl-Friedrich

1994 "Erwägungen zu Problemen alttestamentlicher Prophetenexegese." In I. Kottsieper et al. (eds.), *"Wer ist wie du, Herr, unter den Göttern?" Studien zur Theologie und Religionsgeschichte Israels für Otto Kaiser zum 70. Geburtstag*. Göttingen, pp. 325-341.

Pongratz-Leisten, Beate

1997 "The Interplay of Military Strategy and Cultic Practice in Assyrian Politics." In Parpola & Whiting (eds.) 1997, 245-252.

Postgate, J. N.

1969 *Neo-Assyrian Royal Grants and Decrees*. Studia Pohl: Series Maior 1. Rome.

1972/75 "Ḫarrān." *RLA* 4, 122-125.

1976/80a "Išpalluri." *RLA* 5, 198.

1976/80b "Izalla." *RLA* 5, 225-226.

1987/90 "Mannäer." *RLA* 7, 340-342.

1992 *Early Mesopotamia: Society and Economy at the Dawn of History*. London/New York.

Postgate, J. N. & Reade, J. E.

1976/80 "Kalḫu." *RLA* 5, 303-323.

Reade, Julian

1987 "Was Sennacherib a Feminist?" In J.-M. Durand (ed.), *La femme dans le Proche-Orient antique*. CRRAI 33. Paris, pp. 139-145.

Reade, J. E. & Walker, C. B. F.

1981/82 "Some Neo-Assyrian Royal Inscriptions." *AfO* 28, 113-122.

Redford, Donald B.

1992 *Egypt, Canaan, and Israel in Ancient Times*. Princeton, New Jersey.

Rochberg-Halton, Francesca (ed.)

1987 *Language, Literature and History: Philological and Historical Studies Presented to Erica Reiner*. AOS 67. New Haven.

Röllig, Wolfgang

1987/90 "Literatur. § 4. Überblick über die akkadische Literatur." *RLA* 7, 48-66.

1993/97 "Milqia." *RLA* 8, 207-208.

Saggs, H. W. F.

1968 "The Tell-el-Rimah Tablets, 1965." *Iraq* 30, 154-174.

Schmidtke, Friedrich

1916 *Asarhaddons Statthalterschaft in Babylonien und seine Thronbesteigung in Assyrien 681 v.Chr. AOTU* I,2. Leiden.

Schroeder, Otto

1920 "ummânu — Chef der Staatskanzlei?" *OLZ* 23, 204-207.

Seux, M.-J.

1967 *Épithètes Royales Akkadiennes et Sumériennes*. Paris.

1976 *Hymnes et prières aux dieux de Babylone et d'Assyrie*. Paris.

1980/83 "Königtum." *RLA* 6, 140-173.

Soden, Wolfram von

1969[2] *Grundriß der akkadischen Grammatik*. AnOr 33/47. Rome.

1956 "Beiträge zum Verständnis der neuassyrischen Briefe über die Ersatzkönigriten." In K. Schubert (ed.), *Vorderasiatische Studien: Festschrift für Prof. Dr. Viktor Christian, gewidmet von Kollegen und Schülern zum 70. Geburtstag*. Wien.

1977 "Aramäische Wörter in neuassyrischen und neu- und spätbabylonischen Texten. Ein Vorbericht. III." *Or* NS 46, 183-197.

Spalinger, Anthony

1974 "Esarhaddon and Egypt: An Analysis of the First Invasion of Egypt." *Or* NS 43, 295-326.

1976 "An Egyptian Motif in an Assyrian Text." *BASOR* 223, 64-67.

Spek, R. J. van der

1993 "Assyriology and History: A Comparative Study of War and Empire in Assyria, Athens, and Rome." In Cohen & Snell & Weisberg (eds.) 1993, 262-270.

Starr, Ivan

1990 *Queries to the Sungod: Divination and Politics in Sargonid Assyria*. SAA 4. Helsinki.

Streck, Maximilian

1916 *Assurbanipal und die letzten assyrischen Könige bis zum Untergange Niniveh's*. Vols. I–III. VAB 7. Leipzig.

Strong, S. Arthur

1893 "On Some Oracles to Esarhaddon and Ašurbanipal." *BA* 2, 627-645.

Tadmor, Hayim

1975 "Assyria and the West: The Ninth Century and its Aftermath." In H. Goedicke & J. J. M. Roberts (eds.), *Unity and Diversity: Essays in the History, Literature, and Religion of the Ancient Near East*. Baltimore/London, pp. 36-48.

1981 "History and Ideology in the Assyrian Royal Inscriptions." In Fales (ed.) 1981, 13-33.

1982a "The Aramaization of Assyria: Aspects of Western Impact." In Nissen & Renger (eds.) 1982, 449-470.

1982b "Treaty and Oath in the Ancient Near East: A Historian's Approach." In G. M. Tucker & D. A. Knight (eds.), *Humanizing America's Iconic Book: Society of Biblical Literature Centennial Addresses 1980*. Chico, California, pp. 127-152.

1983 "Autobiographical Apology in the Royal Assyrian Literature." In Tadmor & Weinfeld (eds.) 1983, 36-57.

1997 "Propaganda, Literature, Historiography: Cracking the Code of the Assyrian Royal Inscriptions." In Parpola & Whiting (eds.) 1997, 325-338.

Tadmor, Hayim & Landsberger, Benno & Parpola, Simo

1989 "The Sin of Sargon and Sennacherib's Last Will." *SAAB* 3, 3-51.

Tadmor, Hayim & Weinfeld, Moshe (eds.)

1983 *History, Historiography and Interpretation: Studies in Biblical and Cuneiform Literatures*. Jerusalem/Leiden.

Tallqvist, Knut

1914 *Assyrian Personal Names*. ASSF 43/1. Helsinki.

Thomas, Fredy

1993 "Sargon II., der Sohn Tiglat-Pilesers III." In Dietrich & Loretz (eds.) 1993, 465-470.

Thompson, R. C.

1931 *The Prisms of Esarhaddon and Ashurbanipal found at Nineveh, 1927-8*. London.

Thureau-Dangin, François

1912 *Une relation de la huitième campagne de Sargon (714 av. J.–C.)*. TCL 3. Paris.

Toorn, Karel van der

1987 "L'oracle de victoire comme expression prophétique au Proche-Orient ancien." *RB* 94, 63-97.

1997a "The Iconic Book: Analogies between the Babylonian Cult of Images and the Veneration of the Torah." In K. van der Toorn (ed.), *The Image and the Book: Iconic Cults, Aniconism, and the Rise of the Book Religion in Israel and the Ancient Near East*. Leuven, pp. 229-248.

1997b "In the Lion's Den: The Babylonian Background of a Biblical Motif." Paper read at the Annual Meeting of the Society of Biblical Literature in San Francisco, Nov. 24, 1997 (Forthcoming).

Uehlinger, Christoph

1997 "*Figurative Policy*, Propaganda und Prophetie." In J. A. Emerton (ed.), *Congress Volume Cambridge 1995*. Supplements to Vetus Testamentum 66. Leiden/New York/Köln, pp. 297-349.

Veijola, Timo

1995 "Wahrheit und Intoleranz nach Deuteronomium 13." *ZThK* 92, 287-314.

1996 "Bundestheologische Redaktion im Deuteronomium." In Veijola (ed.) 1996, 242-276.

Veijola, Timo (ed.)

1996 *Das Deuteronomium und seine Querbeziehungen*. SFES 62. Helsinki/Göttingen.

Wall-Romana, Christophe

1990 "An Areal Location of Agade." *JNES* 49, 205-245.

Watanabe, Kazuko

1987 *Die* adê-*Vereidigung anläßlich der Thronfolgeregelung Asarhaddons*. BaghM Beiheft 3. Berlin.

Waterman, Leroy

1930/36 *Royal Correspondence of the Assyrian Empire. Translated into English, With a Transliteration of the Text and a Commentary*. Vols. I–IV. University of Michigan, Humanistic Series 18. Ann Arbor.

Weidner, E. F.

1944/69 "Die astrologische Serie Enuma Anu Enlil." *AfO* 14, 172-195, 308-318; *AfO* 17, 71-89; *AfO* 22, 65-75.

Weinfeld, Moshe

1973 "Covenant Terminology in the Ancient Near East and its Influence on the West." *JAOS* 93, 190-199.

1977 "Ancient Near Eastern Patterns in Prophetic Literature." *VT* 27, 178-195.

Weippert, Manfred

1972 "'Heiliger Krieg' in Israel und Assyrien: Kritische Anmerkungen zu Gerhard von Rads Konzept des 'Heiligen Krieges im alten Israel.'" *ZAW* 84, 460-493.

1981 "Assyrische Prophetien der Zeit Asarhaddons und Assurbanipals." In Fales (ed.) 1981, 71-115.

1982 "De herkomst van het heilsorakel voor Israël bij Deutero-Jesaja." *NedThT* 36, 1-11.

1985 "Die Bildsprache der neuassyrischen Prophetie." In H. Weippert, K. Seybold & M. Weippert, *Beiträge zur prophetischen Bildsprache in Israel und Assyrien*. OBO 64 Freiburg Schweiz/Göttingen, pp. 55-93.

1988 "Aspekte israelitischer Prophetie im Lichte verwandter Erscheinungen des Alten Orients." In G. Mauer & U. Magen (eds.), Ad bene et fideliter seminandum. *Festgabe für Karlheinz Deller zum 21. Februar 1987*. AOAT 220. Kevelaer/Neukirchen-Vluyn, pp. 287-319.

1997a *Jahwe und die anderen Götter: Studien zur Religionsgeschichte des antiken Israel in ihrem syrisch-palästinischen Kontext*. FAT 18. Tübingen.

1997b "Prophetie im Alten Orient." In M. Görg & B. Lang (eds.), *Neues Bibel-Lexikon*. Lieferung 11. Zürich/Düsseldorf, pp. 196-200.

1997c "'Das Frühere, siehe, ist eingetroffen...': Über Selbstzitate im altorientalischen Prophetenspruch." In Heintz (ed.) 1997, 147-169.

Widengren, Geo

1948 *Literary and Psychological Aspects of the Hebrew Prophets*. Uppsala.

Wilson, Robert R.

1980 *Prophecy and Society in Ancient Israel*. Philadelphia.

Zawadzki, Stefan

1988 *The Fall of Assyria and Median-Babylonian Relations in Light of The Nabopolassar Chronicle.* Trans. U. Wolko & P. Lavelle. Uniwersytet im. Adama Mickiewicza w Poznaniu. Seria Historia 149. Poznań/Delft.

1990 "Oriental and Greek Traditions about the Death of Sennacherib." *SAAB* 4, 69-72.

Zenger, Erich

1995 "Eigenart und Bedeutung der Prophetie Israels." In E. Zenger et al. (eds.), *Einleitung in das Alte Testament.* Kohlhammer Studienbücher Theologie 1,1. Stuttgart etc., pp. 293-303.

Zimmerli, Walther

1980 "Das Phänomen der 'Fortschreibung' im Buche Ezechiel." In J. A. Emerton (ed.), *Prophecy: Essays presented to Georg Fohrer on his sixty-fifth Birthday 6 September 1980.* BZAW 150, Berlin/New York, pp. 174-191.

Zimmern, H.

1910 "Gilgameš-Omina und Gilgameš-Orakel." *ZA* 24, 166-171.

Zobel, Hans-Jürgen

1971 "Das Gebet um Abwendung der Not und seine Erhörung in den Klageliedern des Alten Testaments und in der Inschrift des Königs Zakir von Hamath." *VT* 21, 91-99.

INDEXES

Numbers in italics refer to footnotes, normal numbers to pages.

PERSONAL NAMES

(Esarhaddon and Assurbanipal excluded)

GEOGRAPHIC AND ETHNOGRAPHIC NAMES

(Assyria excluded)

GOD, STAR AND TEMPLE NAMES

AKKADIAN WORDS

TEXTUAL REFERENCES

Mesopotamian Texts

Bible

Aramaic Texts

State Archives of Assyria

VOLUME I
THE CORRESPONDENCE OF SARGON II, PART I
Letters from Assyria and the West
Edited by Simo Parpola
1987

VOLUME II
NEO-ASSYRIAN TREATIES AND LOYALTY OATHS
Edited by Simo Parpola and Kazuko Watanabe
1988

VOLUME III
COURT POETRY AND LITERARY MISCELLANEA
Edited by Alasdair Livingstone
1989

VOLUME IV
QUERIES TO THE SUNGOD
Divination and Politics in Sargonid Assyria
Edited by Ivan Starr
1990

VOLUME V
THE CORRESPONDENCE OF SARGON II, PART II
Letters from the Northern and Northeastern Provinces
Edited by Giovanni B. Lanfranchi and Simo Parpola
1990

VOLUME VI
LEGAL TRANSACTIONS OF THE ROYAL COURT OF NINEVEH, PART I
Tiglath-Pileser III through Esarhaddon
Edited by Theodore Kwasman and Simo Parpola
1991

VOLUME VII
IMPERIAL ADMINISTRATIVE RECORDS, PART I
Palace and Temple Administration
Edited by F. M. Fales and J. N. Postgate
1992

VOLUME VIII
ASTROLOGICAL REPORTS TO ASSYRIAN KINGS
Edited by Hermann Hunger
1992

VOLUME IX
ASSYRIAN PROPHECIES
Edited by Simo Parpola
1997

VOLUME X
LETTERS FROM ASSYRIAN AND BABYLONIAN SCHOLARS
Edited by Simo Parpola
1993

VOLUME XI
IMPERIAL ADMINISTRATIVE RECORDS, PART II
Provincial and Military Administration
Edited by F. M. Fales and J. N. Postgate
1995

VOLUME XII
GRANTS, DECREES AND GIFTS OF THE NEO-ASSYRIAN PERIOD
Edited by L. Kataja and R. Whiting
1995

State Archives of Assyria Studies

VOLUME I

Neuassyrische Glyptik des 8.-7. Jh. v. Chr.
unter besonderer Berücksichtigung der Siegelungen
auf Tafeln und Tonverschlüsse
by Suzanne Herbordt
1992

VOLUME II

The Eponyms of the Assyrian Empire 910–612 BC
by Alan Millard
1994

VOLUME III

The Use of Numbers and Quantifications
in the Assyrian Royal Inscriptions
by Marco De Odorico
1995

VOLUME IV

Nippur in Late Assyrian Times
c. 755–612 BC
by Steven W. Cole
1996

VOLUME V

Neo-Assyrian Judicial Procedures
by Remko Jas
1996

VOLUME VI

Die neuassyrischen Privatrechtsurkunden
als Quelle für Mensch und Umwelt
by Karen Radner
1997

VOLUME VII

References to Prophecy in Neo-Assyrian Sources
by Martti Nissinen
1998